ALFRED MARSHALL'S LECTURES TO WOMEN

Alfred Marshall's Lectures to Women

Some economic questions directly connected to the welfare of the laborer

Edited by

Tiziano Raffaelli
Eugenio Biagini
Rita McWilliams Tullberg

Foreword by Giacomo Becattini

Edward Elgar
Aldershot, UK – Brookfield, US

Published by
Edward Elgar Publishing Limited
Gower House
Croft Road
Aldershot
Hants GU11 3HR
UK

Edward Elgar Publishing Company
Old Post Road
Brookfield
Vermont 05036
US

British Library Cataloguing in Publication Data
Alfred Marshall's Lectures to Women: Some
Economic Questions Directly Connected to
the Welfare of the Laborer
I. Raffaelli, Tiziano
330.092

Library of Congress Cataloguing in Publication Data
Alfred Marshall's lectures to women : some economic questions directly
connected to the welfare of the laborer / edited and introduced by
Tiziano Raffaelli, Eugenio Biagini and Rita McWilliams Tullberg
224p. 23cm.
Includes index.
1. Marshall, Alfred, 1842–1924. 2. Economics. 3. Labor.
4. Working class. I. Raffaelli, Tiziano, 1950– . II. Biagini, Eugenio F.
III. Tullberg, Rita McWilliams, 1943– .
HB103.M3A68 1995 95–30785
331—dc20 CIP

ISBN 1 85898 310 X

Printed and bound in Great Britain by
Biddles Ltd, Guildford and King's Lynn

Contents

Contributors

Giacomo Becattini, *Trinity Hall, Cambridge, UK, and Dipartimento di Scienze Economiche, Università di Firenze, Italy*

Eugenio Biagini, *Department of History, Princeton University, US*

Rita McWilliams Tullberg, *Darwin College, Cambridge, UK, and Stockholm, Sweden*

Tiziano Raffaelli, *Dipartimento di Filosofia, Università di Pisa, Italy*

Editorial note

The *Lectures to Women* consist of two separate sets of notes, both covering the six lectures delivered by Marshall in the Easter Term of 1872–73. The main text is by Mary Paley Marshall, with a few corrections by Alfred Marshall. These notes were taken by Mary Paley while attending a series of six lectures given by Marshall, but were probably revised, as their neatness and fluency attest. The lecture notes are supplemented by Marshall's lecture outlines. In the main, these summarise and sometimes add to the contents of Mary Paley's notes.

At a later date, Marshall looked over Mary Paley's notes, made a few alterations and added some comments. These alterations and comments, together with editorial footnotes clarifying references and occasional inconsistencies in the text, are given in footnotes at the end of the Lecture 6. All the editorial additions to the texts are given in square brackets. A question mark inside square brackets means that the following word is dubious. Footnotes make it clear when square brackets are in the original. Familiar abbreviations (such as 'wh', 'wd', 'sd', 'gt' respectively for 'which', 'would', 'should', 'great') have been written out in full. The few mistakes in spelling and punctuation have been corrected and undue repetition of the same word removed.

The *Lectures* are known to scholars who have had the opportunity of examining them in Cambridge, but we believe they are of interest to a wider audience. We think it will be useful to have a critical edition of them.

The notice of lectures for the Easter Term to be given under the auspices of the Lectures for Women scheme had an appendix stating that 'Mr. Marshall will deliver some lectures at 3 o'clock on Friday in Room L, on "Some Economic Questions directly connected with the Welfare of Labor".' (Cambridge University *Reporter*, 22 April 1873) The notice continued:

> These Lectures will be introductory to a systematic course on Political Economy which will be commenced in October; but they will also be adapted to the wants of those who do not propose to make a special study of Political

> Economy. No papers will be set in connexion with this course: no fees will be charged to those who attend it.

The Lectures for the May Term 1873 are unique in their content and purpose. An idea of the ordinary courses on Political Economy can be had by looking at the notes of Ward's lectures of 1875, still preserved in the Marshall Library. Their content is a comment on Mill and covers the more general subjects of Political Economy as demanded by the Higher Local Examination syllabus. On the contrary, Marshall's 1873 *Lectures* have a definite and particular subject of their own.

We have also thought it useful to reprint some contemporary and related texts. 'The future of the working classes' was read at a conversazione of the Cambridge Reform Club on 25 November 1873, first published in the St John's College Magazine, *The Eagle*, and reprinted in *Memorials of Alfred Marshall*. The paper summarises the subject-matter of the *Lectures for Women*. Marshall's annotations in his copy of an off-print of the article are given in the footnotes, together with a few meaningful differences between this version and the one printed in the *Cambridge Independent Press* and reprinted for private circulation by Thomas Tofts.

The exchange with Holmes in the *Bee-Hive*, in 1874, is known through Harrison's article (*Economic Journal*, 1963, vol. 73, pp. 422–30), which contains the text of two articles by Marshall. These have been reprinted here together with Holmes's articles to illustrate how methodological and social issues, similar to those discussed in the *Lectures*, are dealt with when addressing a different public.

Foreword

Giacomo Becattini

In the summer of 1970, when Rita McWilliams and Piero Sraffa first acquainted me with Marshall's papers, my attention was immediately drawn to the *Lectures to Women* of 1873. This turned out to be a clearly-structured text, quite compact, and within certain limits – which the reader will discover for himself – a systematic essay, revealing glimpses of a hitherto unknown Marshall. For at that time, knowledge of Marshall's early life was still relatively poor; J. K. Whitaker had not yet published *The Early Economic Writings* and the new generation of research into his life and works had not yet commenced. Thus the portrait of Marshall as a young scholar rested essentially on the figure that emerged from the *Memorials* edited by Pigou.

One of the aspects that stood out most clearly in the *Memorials* was the liberal, indeed almost radical, position assumed by the young Marshall, who, together with Sidgwick, and following in the footsteps of J. S. Mill, had taken part in the first stirrings of the movement for women's emancipation. Also well-known were his relations with the trade union movement, as testified by his replies to the trade unionist Holmes on the *Bee-Hive*, published by R. Harrison. However this somewhat scanty documentation could do little to dispel the aura of historiographic haze that still enveloped the figure of the young Marshall, preventing the world of scholarship from gaining sufficient insight to set him in his true position within the cultural and political framework of the era. On first perusal, not even the *Lectures to Women* appeared to provide much assistance in clarifying the picture, written as they were in such a manner as to render an assessment of the level of discourse somewhat arduous; the extent to which the *Lectures* should be considered genuinely scientific, or merely moralistic, remained highly debatable. The frequently sermonizing tone, corresponding to an understandably paternalistic attitude on the part of an 'accomplished' scholar (aged 31) towards naive young girls, ensured a certain degree of restraint in interpreting potentially shocking statements such as

> I claim then to have shown ... why the developments of our arts of production has done so little to prevent the sacrifice of man to production. And it is not easy to say why things are as they are ... . Why every day is not a Sunday, devoted to culture, with just so much work perhaps, as is necessary for the health of the body, with time to learn and to think, to be educated to science and art. (See below, p. 96)

One of the striking elements in the *Lectures*, at least for a reader such as myself, was the fact that Marshall had no qualms about repeating in the quiet environment of Cambridge a number of assertions whose social implications could be classed as extremely revolutionary:

> It is a notorious truth that those countries which are richest have also the greatest amount of poverty; the reason of this is obvious – where competition is free, where the movement of every individual is completely unshackled, there wealth is accumulated rapidly, and there also by the same causes, misery, crime and all that is bad is accumulated too; (see below, p. 125)

declarations that sounded as though they had been penned by none other than Marx himself. Indeed it is no mystery that during this period Marshall was endeavouring to come to grips with German socialism. Lassalle and Marx were among his reading material. The subject formed a common discussion point with J. M. Ludlow and Sidgwick, and possibly with F. D. Maurice as well. Certainly the debate centring on these ideas was no easy rite of passage from the faith of his fathers to a new age persuasion, as shown, in one way or another, by Henry Sidgwick's renouncement of the fellowship and his decision to remove the clause in the marriage service whereby the wife declares her obedience to her husband. And, one may speculate, neither was his participation in assemblies organized by agricultural labourers on strike something that could be taken lightly at Cambridge. Fortunately, however, Marshall was shielded by the protective shoulders of a great College and of a radical who was highly regarded both by part of the establishment and by part of the trade unions such as Henry Fawcett.

I hardly need state that these lectures, together with the philosophical manuscripts, which were totally ignored at the time and to a large extent subsequently as well, made a great impression on me. I used the *Lectures* in the long introduction to the Italian translation of *The Economics of Industry*, which I titled 'Invito ad una rilettura di Marshall'. From the *Lectures* I drew, naturally enough, that which my cultural background and the interests I was cultivating at the time stirred me to cull, consisting essentially in Marshall's attention to the effects of working conditions on man's character and on his prospects.

As far as the philosophical manuscripts were concerned, my ignorance in matters philosophical prevented me from deriving any benefit from them. I did however encourage two young Italian philosophers (first Cristiano Camporesi from Florence, and later Tiziano Raffaelli from Pisa) to pore over these texts and endeavour to glean whatever pearls of wisdom they might contain. But twenty years were to pass before the task bore fruit (see bibliography), a clear demonstration that until questions are brought into sharp focus, the answers cannot be had. This process of honing the questions required that some rotation should be introduced into the reading of Marshall by his natural commentators – economists – in such a manner as to allow these epistemological and psychological problems to be set within their natural context.

In the twenty-year span between 1970 and today the *Lectures* have been used by several Marshallian scholars, each of whom has extracted some fragment to adduce in support of his or her own deeply-felt arguments.

Yet over the years one problem still remained to be dealt with: how to make available to the world of Marshallian scholars, and more generally to historians of economic thought, a text that is certainly inspiring, and which, I believe, constitutes an important work. There was also a need to render it accessible to those who lacked the opportunity to go and consult it at the Marshall Library in Cambridge.

It was for this reason that in 1983 I asked the Faculty of Economics of Cambridge to grant authorization to transcribe the text of the *Lectures*.

As time passed, however, my interests gradually shifted from study of the life of Marshall to other issues in applied economics, with the result that the task of an in-depth appraisal of the *Lectures* to which I had committed myself became far more burdensome. In the meantime the literature on the period has increased exponentially, so that a brief standstill, even if only for just a few years, has made it practically impossible for me adequately to frame this episode of Marshall's life against the background of his period as the latter is depicted in the present-day specialized literature.

Hence the alternative plan that I put forward, namely to invite a number of scholars actively working in this field to provide a contextualized commentary on this Marshallian text.

Three lines of enquiry have been adopted: the *Lectures* as part of the movement for higher education for women in the Victorian era; the *Lectures* as indicative of Marshall's stand *vis-à-vis* the political-ideological framework of his time; the *Lectures* as an indicator of Marshall's methodological tendencies concerning the study of social phenomena. For each of these three avenues of research, three recognized specialists have been invited to make a contribution: Rita McWilliams Tullberg, Ernesto Biagini and Tiziano Raffaelli. Their achievements are now unveiled to the reader. For my part, let me simply add that they have been given a completely free rein to respond to the text according to the lights of their own personal interpretation. May the hundred flowers bloom......

We unanimously decided to include within the packet of this revisitation of the early Marshall some further documents in addition to the *Lectures* themselves. In particular, it was felt that readers wishing to dip into this rich store would benefit greatly from the possibility of reading the talk given by Marshall in the same year, 1873, on 'The future of the working classes', since there is a clear affinity between this subject-matter and the central issues of the *Lectures*. We also include the complete text of the exchanges with the trade unionist Holmes, of which Harrison published only the Marshallian part. A simultaneous re-reading of these texts, together with the 'critiques' by Biagini, McWilliams and Raffaelli, could introduce a number of thought-provoking issues into the on-going debate. However this may be, I firmly believe that the task I set myself – that of breathing fresh life into the young Marshall – has now been accomplished.

Here my foreword has come to an end, and specialized readers are invited to skip the next two pages and immerse themselves directly in the author's own words, to be receptive to the echo of his phrases in the notes offered by his attentive pupil Mary Paley and in the papers by our three experts.

Let me conclude by saying that 'rusty' though I may be as a Marshallologist, I would not like to miss this opportunity to offer the willing reader a few considerations deriving from my long-standing acquaintance with this figure and his work. They may, to be sure, be reflections that appear to have made time stand still over the last few years as far as historiographic debate in this academic field is concerned, yet for this very reason my considerations enjoy the distinct advantage of representing the perspective of a partial outsider, the vision of one who is less caught up in the pet views (destined to be recognized as such only at a later date) of the moment.

There are a few points I would like to make. First and foremost, let me start by suggesting that readings of Marshall conducted with a 'progressive' slant, taking the Fabians and then the perspective adopted by Labour – if not by the Marxists – as the basic yardstick, with the result of consistently finding Marshall short on political ideology, should be revised in the light of events of the last few years. For what has collapsed is truly not merely the Berlin Wall, i.e. the attempt to build socialism, but also 'progressive' statalism itself. To those of his era who criticized him from the left, Marshall appeared as a masqued conservative, who played his cards very close to his chest and at the most crucial moments invariably found some subtle, incomprehensible objection by virtue of which he would oppose each and every progressive cause. So it was when it was a question of granting degrees to women and likewise as regards welfare for the poor.

It does not appear to strike anyone that history may have proved Marshall right. Consider one of the central and emblematic points of the argument: the tendency to capitalist concentration in the present-day world. Marshall writes:

> The creation of vast businesses involves great risks unless there be good reason to expect that men competent to manage them will be forthcoming. It is often assumed that they are sure to be forthcoming: but history gives little support to this belief (Marshall, 1919, p. 363). A new tradition is in danger of growing up, to the effect that a small business must be out of place in the new age: for that belongs to large businesses. This tradition in its exaggerated form is repeated parrotwise. (pp. 581–2)

It requires little effort to imagine the self-satisfied disdain sentences of this kind must have stirred in Fabian circles. One glance at the diaries of Beatrice Webb – an idol of the left – suffices to confirm this impression.

Nor is there ever a glimmer of awareness that behind his invariable resistance to proposals put forward by the English left of the time, there lay some deeper reason, pertaining either to principle or to method, something that was not cheaply reconstructed *a posteriori* on a flimsy framework of feelings and political resentment, or on the ancestral fears of the man-in-the-street, but rather had matured within him fairly early on in his intellectual development. Considering matters from this standpoint, the most prominent aspect of Raffaelli's re-reading of the philosophical manuscripts can be seen to lie in its endeavour to offer a few essential keys for a better understanding of the role of 'character' in the overall Marshallian thought system. And a 'system' it certainly was – not the medley of ideas on life and the world of a run-of-the-mill Victorian who was expected to be consistent (at least in so far as it was humanly possible in this type of affairs) only when he was playing at being an economist.

What is significant is that the re-reading of the philosophical manuscripts does indeed allow Marshallian scholars to make a number of steps forward in this direction. For here we learn that the process by which the mind is enriched with greater complexity and, along with the mind, society as well, has a fairly clear yardstick: prospectiveness, i.e. the capacity to be far-sighted, Pigou's telescopic ability. It is attractive to think that the personal starting point of this position can perhaps be traced back to Alfred's youthful passion for chess. Here in chess the problem is simple: it is a question of dominating an ever greater mass of possible developments, of imagining an ever greater number of possible futures. Imagination, logical strength, mental energy; such are the inputs of this process. And even the moral qualities of the imaginary machine Marshall described in his manuscript *Ye Machine*, which is destined, in my view, to become an influential text, can be traced back to the capacity for far-sightedness. Whoever knows what good is, a near contemporary of Marshall's – Benedetto Croce – would later say, cannot but be good. The progress of mankind lies in extending (spatially) and prolonging (over time) the mental horizon of a growing number of individuals.

Now, let us attempt to project this idea on the social conditions of Victorian England. What is the result that emerges? That any measure which allows the shrinking from responsibility is negative inasmuch as it induces a foreshortening of the temporal horizon, while any measure that contributes to overcoming bottlenecks in the shouldering of personal responsibility is positive. There is no suggestion here of *laissez-faire, laissez-passer*; on the contrary the aim is to do socially that which all caring parents do for their own children – namely, help them overcome hurdles they cannot surmount unaided, but not act as their surrogates in the attempt. The Victorian maxim 'helping people to help themselves', which, when re-used against Marshall by certain of his socialist critics, can sound crass and condescending, almost as if by these words Marshall had expressed a cowardly reluctance to become involved in the interplay of social interests, is in actual fact a condensed handbook of advanced pedagogy.

But the fragmentation of social thought leads to this and much more; may the economist never know what the pedagogist has discovered.

Bibliography

Camporesi C. (1980), *L'uno e i molti: l'idealismo britannico dal 1830 al 1920*, Firenze: La Nuova Italia.

Camporesi C. (1985), *Scepsi scientifica*, Roma: Ianua.

Harrison R. (1963), 'Two early articles by Alfred Marshall', *Economic Journal*, vol. 73, pp. 422–30.

Marshall A. (1919), *Industry and Trade*, London: Macmillan.

Marshall A. (1925), *Memorials of Alfred Marshall*, ed. by A. C. Pigou, London: Macmillan.

Marshall A. (1994), 'Early philosophical writings', ed. by T. Raffaelli, *Research in the History of Economic Thought and Methodology. Archival Supplement*, vol. 4, pp. 95–159.

Marshall A. and M. P. (1881), *The Economics of Industry*, London: Macmillan, 2nd edition; Italian translation: *Economia della produzione*, tradotto da C. e A. Zanni, a cura di G. Becattini, Milano: ISEDI.

Raffaelli T. (1990), 'Gli studi filosofici del giovane Marshall', *Atti Accademia Nazionale dei Lincei, Rendiconti Classe di Scienze Morali*, series 9, vol. 1, pp. 121–60.

Raffaelli T. (1991), 'The analysis of the human mind in the early Marshallian manuscripts', *Quaderni di Storia dell'Economia Politica*, vol. 9, pp. 29–58.

Raffaelli T. (1992), 'Editing economists' non-economic manuscripts: the case of Marshall's early philosophical papers', *Revue Européenne des Sciences Sociales*, vol. 30, pp. 81–92.

Raffaelli T. (1994), 'Marshall's analysis of the human mind', *Research in the History of Economic Thought and Methodology. Archival Supplement*, vol. 4, pp. 53–93.

Whitaker J. K. (ed.) (1975), *The Early Economic Writings of Alfred Marshall (1867–1890)*, London: Macmillan.

Part I

1. Of microscopes and telescopes; with directions for their combined uses in the social sciences, adapted to the elementary instruction of women

Tiziano Raffaelli[1]

> For all men are by nature provided of notable, multiplying glasses, that is their passions and self-love, through which every little payment appeareth a great grievance; but are destitute of those perspective glasses, namely moral and civil science, to see as far off the miseries that hang over them, and cannot without such payments be avoided. (*Leviathan*, II.xviii)

I. Introduction

The *Lectures to Women* is the first Marshallian text which deals extensively with the method of political economy.[2] Like in many of his other writings of this period, Marshall's aim is here to disentangle political economy from party politics and class issues.[3] Looked at from this point of view, the metaphorical title of this prefatory note, fully extended in an old-fashioned way, could symbolize their contents.

What follows tries to substantiate the metaphor, which highlights Marshall's emphasis on the need for both a broad outlook into the distant future and scrupulous knowledge of present conditions. While regretting the lack of perspective glasses, Marshall was not prepared to abandon the multiplying ones to the passions. Warnings about careful handling recall the limits of appropriate uses of scientific tools.

In Section 2, arguing the case for Marshall's lifelong continuity on methodological issues, I contend that different wordings of the relation between economics and politics are due to his consciousness of its various aspects more than to changes of opinion. In Section 3 Marshall's two natures of preacher and scientist are investigated and his proposed remedies for poverty and destitution analyzed.

Imaginative telescopic glances into the future and their independence from both experience and – partially – abstract science are the subjects of Section 4. This introduces a discussion of the practical meaning of the principle of continuity and of its indispensable service for achieving radical changes through a policy of microscopic self-growing steps. Section 5 comes more closely to describing the uses of the microscope in the investigation of complex systems, and should lead to a better grasp of Marshall's thought on the limited and combined uses of these scientific tools.

II. The Economist in the Social Theater

Delivered just a year before the publication in the *Bee-Hive* of his articles on 'The laws of political economy' and 'The province of political economy', the *Lectures* provide useful supplementary information about Marshall's early conceptions of the functions of political economy and its relation to ethics and politics. Harrison, comparing the articles with later texts, maintains that Marshall came later 'to resent the restraints' of science (Harrison, 1963, p. 430) and to fill the gap between matters of fact and reason, on the one hand, and moral judgments on the other, a gap which the articles were unreservedly meant to keep wide open.

These *Lectures*, on the contrary, suggest a very early beginning of Marshall's 'propensity to moralise' (Harrison, ibid.), disproving the break and revealing that the preacher was not a later addition due to advancing age. They help us to avoid stressing the contrast between two phases in Marshall's thought, a contrast which is more apparent than real. In fact, he never denied that '[political economy] does not possess the power of giving direct and complete answers on points involving questions of right and wrong' (below, p. 183), nor that a moral judgment 'involves one premise which, however true it may be, political economy is not competent to authorize' (below, p. 191).[4] The lesson on the autonomy of ethics, which he had learned from John Grote's and Sidgwick's critiques of Mill's naturalistic ethics, made him forever conscious that economics can only *help* to solve social problems (which is what he writes in the passage of the *Principles* referred to by Harrison as presumed proof of a change of opinion). He always insisted, as he had done in the two articles, that the economist, *qua* economist, is in no special position as to practical conclusions, having to rely for them on 'the common-sense and the moral judgment of the community' (Marshall, 1969, p. 200), on 'the judgment of common sense' (Marshall, 1925, p. 164), on 'our ethical instincts and our common sense' (Marshall, 1961, vol. I, p. 28), on 'individual judgement or ... the analysis of the ethical philosopher' (Whitaker, 1975, vol. II, p. 350).[5] Science, as we shall see, has to break reality in order to investigate it and is therefore concerned 'only with one side', while practical questions cannot be treated only by looking at 'a very one-sided view of a very one-sided part of the question', as he writes with a very cautious doubling due to the limited and didactic character of the *Lectures* (below, p. 88).

While keeping to the same clear-cut distinction between political economy and its possible practical applications, the *Lectures* unveil the mixing process in the making: the distinction, clearly stated in the first lecture, is afterwards intentionally set aside (below, p. 92), the stress being more on their strong connection, on their solidarity, than on their separation. This is not only because misbehaviour is often due to lack of knowledge (as the problem of helping the gouty person shows – below, p. 97), but also because the world is not given once and for all, irrespective of what actions will be deliberately performed. What looks like a slippery transition towards a neglect of the difference between ethics and social science is in fact nothing but a growing consciousness of their relatedness in an evolutionary perspective.[6]

The shift in stress between the *Lectures to Women* and the *Bee-Hive* articles is due to their different aims. What Kadish (1991) has shown of methodological passages of subsequent editions of *Principles of Economics* can be extended to these early texts: emphasis is laid on the theoretical elements which fit Marshall's practical purposes better. John Holmes and the readers of the *Bee-Hive* had to be reminded that there are objective laws of societ..y which cannot be defied; the Cambridge female audience had to be freed from the paralysing influence of absolute faith in those very laws.

The relation between the two texts, however, is not completely parallel: while the articles are intended to send a univocal message to the reader, the aim of the *Lectures* is wider and more in line with Marshall's well-known consciousness of the manifold nature of scientific and methodological problems. The first simply had to make the workers aware of the politically unbiased nature of economic science and to induce them to accept it as a language shared by contenders debating complex social issues. The second had to push middle-class women into the social arena, even at the price of some 'domestic disobedience' that he would not have conceived of in later years. This result could be achieved not only by proving that political economy did not prevent women from deliberately doing good, but also by exhibiting a better world and the way to it.

While both texts are undoubtedly limited by the need to be understood by lay people, the *Lectures to Women* seem to me to deserve precedence over the articles as a key to Marshall's broad methodological and philosophical opinions. They bring to the surface what in the articles is implicitly hidden: the social scientist who wants to be conscious of the effects of his message is compelled to take into account the perspectives of his audience.

Marshall himself avows that, were he lecturing to workers, he would tell a very different story (below, p. 90), while as the public widens, the message gets more complex, as any reader of *Principles* knows.[7] Audience-specificity is a steady Marshallian concern, related to the need to correct individual points of view. The cooperative social game implies knowledge of other people's knowledge in order to make different perspectives meet at some future point.

In the 1870s Trades Unions are significantly examined from both the 'Employers' side' and the 'Unionists' side', in view of a 'summing up, intended to be impartial' ('Fragments on trades unions', Whitaker, 1975, vol. II, pp. 346–9).

In 1884 his opposition to George's land-reform proposals was primarily due to the fact that the American radical was addressing the working classes, giving them 'just that advice which, if acted upon, would prevent them from rising from their low condition' and using his exceptional rhetorical 'power to instil poison into their minds'. Had George confined himself to the 'well-to-do class', Marshall would not have raised any objection (Marshall, 1969, p. 221).

In 1893 the existence of 'another side' which ought to be heard is forced into the mind of a reluctant member of the Royal Commission on the Aged Poor (RCOAP, Q. 10,433–4; in Marshall, 1926); Marshall denies the Commission the right to decide that the system of relief works smoothly without consulting the workers (Q. 10,193), whose 'dissatisfaction' (Q. 10,203) would be relevant even if it were unjustified (cf. also Marshall, 1892, p. 374).

In 1905 we come across the same concept in relation to one of Crooks's proposals of radical reform:

some years ago I read a good deal of Blue-book evidence for and against various schemes of Tenant compensation. I felt that I could form something of an opinion after hearing both sides, but none at all after hearing only one. (A. Marshall to E. Darwin, 24 September 1905, *Layton Papers*, 2.17; Trinity College Library)[8]

The framework of the relations between economics and politics is therefore much more varied than it looks at first sight. Its structure has three sides. Firstly, as political actions cannot share the abstractness of scientific enquiries, the economist's unavoidable one-sidedness must be integrated by 'the judgment of common sense'; 'for the present and for a long time to come that must be the final arbiter' in dealing 'with social problems as a whole' (Marshall, 1925 p. 164). Secondly, the lessons of economic science, taking part in a complex social game, influence the recipient's knowledge. Thirdly, opinions, at least when widely shared and firmly held, are a relevant component of the system itself and have to be known and carefully considered before deciding on any course of action; what men and women know is part of the world and, influencing what they do, may change the circumstances under investigation.

Readers of Marshall must make allowance for these ideas and avoid taking each perspective at face value.

III. The Wants-Activities Circuit

The constructive element of Marshall's work makes it difficult to disentangle his double nature of preacher and scientist.[9] It is not a case of split personality; giving a typically Marshallian answer, we may say that the two natures can be 'distinguished, but not separated'.[10] They branch from a common root: the view that society is a changing whole, open to different possibilities. The practical consequences of this view are stated nowhere as clearly as in these lectures.

Because of the pervading critique of 'leaving things to drift', this text could well deserve the title of forerunner of Keynes's *The End of Laissez-Faire*.[11] Even though the *types* of action are different, the *urge* to act is the same,[12] and the *motives* not very dissimilar. The main type of action urgently invoked by Marshall is education, the main motive for it, as for anticyclical Keynesian policies, is its ability to pay the expenses; activating unused human resources it increases production.

Education, in a broad sense, means not only schools, but also trade unions and cooperatives, a more stimulating environment (green commons, popular museums, playgrounds, etc.) and a plan of charity conceived as part of a wider system of social incentives rewarding merit.[13] Education improves the working men's pliability, elasticity (below, p. 140), versatility, readiness to adopt new ideas (below, p. 105), what he will later call plasticity and flexibility. The stress Marshall lays on these wonderful powers is a consequence of his dynamic conception of the human mind with its almost infinite ability of betterment.[14]

Moreover, social advantages are to be added to individual ones. New energies are made available, latent faculties are brought into the social context and 'the waste product' *par excellence* disappears (Marshall, 1925, p. 229, p. 237 and p. 255). Education is really investment in man, 'the finest instrument of production in the world' (below, p. 117), 'the most important productive machine' (below, p. 98). Society can afford it in the short run, as it can afford railways; while the long-run return is higher on this type of investment than on any other.

Lastly, education favours distributive justice as it raises the unskilled workers wages because: i) it reduces their numbers, making such labour scarce (below, p. 114); ii) it improves the quality of their labour and therefore increases production (below, p. 105).

This detailed discussion of the economic value of education clears the ground for Marshall's careful study of education economics in the *Principles*, of the growing importance of general education as an economic factor. For the first time, the need of State intervention in favour of general education is maintained on economic principles; as the parents, who do not 'reap the benefit of the increased expenditure', may lack forethought and self-sacrifice (below, p. 103), society is entitled to interfere and its action will be rewarded, even on strictly economic grounds (Bowman, 1990).

To convince his listeners that the remedy could work, that an initial push could be made permanent, Marshall had to show that it did not have to die away, that rising wages would neither be eaten up by an increasing population, nor end in drink, tobacco and other goods injurious to the labourers. The *Lectures* devote much space to these questions, with as few theoretical considerations as possible. Malthusianism is taken very seriously, being one of those cumulative processes to which Marshall paid close attention. It is seen as a real danger which the many theoretical critiques of it have left unshaken.[15] Here, as later on in the lectures on 'Progress and poverty', Marshall contends only that it *can*[16] be defeated by increased efficiency and by *conscious* restraint, which are themselves products of higher education.

The other objection is met with the help of statistics, brought in to prove that bad expenditure is proportionally diminishing, and with the hope and belief of attaining a better future, through the prospect of 'new sources of joy' shown to the workers.[17] While directly derived from Octavia Hill, the concept of joy had a precise philosophical meaning in the English associationist tradition which suited Marshall's purposes. Hobbes defined joy as a 'pleasure of the mind' which arises 'from the expectation that proceeds from foresight of the end, or consequences of things, whether those things in the sense please or displease' (Hobbes, 1839, I.vi), and therefore opposed it to the 'pleasures of sense'. This perspective relation to the future had been investigated in Bain's *The Emotions and the Will*, which Marshall knew fairly well. Here the joyful experiences are seen to require a superior exercise of the will, different from the immediate form of it which takes place in pursuing the pleasures of sense. Like deliberation and resolution, joy implies a 'suspense' (Bain, 1865, p. 419 and appendix C; cf. also Bain, 1864, pp. 524–5 and pp. 533–4),[18] a breakage of instinctive behaviours and the power of a telescopic intellect.

Having disposed of both objections, Marshall can be confident that 'the main purpose of these lectures', declared at the start, – 'not to urge Economic studies, but rather to defend the position which philanthropists are adopting' – has been reached.

The final aim, that everyone will *ultimately* (below, p. 107) be a gentleman,[19] is set and its possibility shown, provided men and women rise to the task and reject the idea that the existence of a proletariat is necessary, an idea similar to that upheld by the ancients with regard to slavery and already submitted to the verdicts of history (below, p. 126, p. 152 and p. 163).

A few months later, the argument is taken up in a Reform Club paper, 'The future of the working classes', which synthesizes the content of the *Lectures*. A man is there defined as a gentleman or a working man depending on 'the effect that his work produces on him rather than ... the effect that he produces on his work' (below, 'The future of the working classes', p. 158). 'When a man works – Marshall will repeat in 'The theory of foreign trade' – he produces two effects, one on his work and another on himself. The former alone is of direct pecuniary interest to the employer' (Whitaker, 1975, II, p. 55). Not what he does, but how his work shapes his life has to be considered, in particular whether culture, refinement, sense of responsibility and gentle social intercourse are promoted by it.[20]

However, even this relation of cause and effect between man's activities and his wants, on which Parsons insisted in his articles on Marshall, has to be seen as a circular one if we take into account the weight of those aspirations represented by the 'noble sources of joy' in pushing men into the activity-track. 'Hope' is 'the chief lever of all' and its 'energizing influence' is necessary to overcome poverty and destitution.[21]

Anxious to prove Marshall's Puritanism, Parsons developed his one-sided perspective, repeatedly quoting the sentence that 'work, in its best sense, the healthy energetic exercise of faculties, is the aim of life, is life itself', but relegating the other, 'the bad sense in which work crushes a man's life', to the discussion of a minor issue (Parsons 1931, footnotes 42 and 66. Cf. below, 'The future of the working classes', p. 169).

No ideology of work and sacrifice can be unreservedly derived from Marshall's teaching. The thorough acceptance of further reductions in working hours in those types of manual work which do not promote man's character – to which the *Lectures* adds a critique of Senior's 'last hour' that could have pleased Marx himself – is not to be forgotten. The term 'sacrifice' is indeed often used, but almost always in the negative sense that men are unduly and unnecessarily sacrificed to production; a sacrifice which had to be stopped as soon as possible.

Marshall's ethics were a compound of utilitarian and evolutionary elements, transcendental and religious values being useful mainly as working rhetorical devices.

IV. Telescopic Glances into the Future

The Marshallian progress towards making 'every man a gentleman ... every woman a lady' (below, p. 141) does not fulfil Mill's expectation that 'the condition of labouring for wages' would be superseded (Mill, 1965, IV.vii.4). Even though cooperation was highly valued, it was not going to displace wage labour. In 1899 Marshall confirmed this opinion; speaking to the Cooperative

Congress and exalting the results and future possibilities of this type of 'collective action' (Marshall, 1925, p. 227), he reminds the audience that there is no magic in it (ibid., p. 232) nor intrinsic degradation in working for hire under the direction of 'business ability in command of capital' (ibid., p. 245).

His picture of the future is that of a free enterprise economy with high wages and more leisure for culture and refinement, in particular for manual workers, and where poverty has faded away. Industrial conflicts would be resolved primarily by Boards of Conciliation ('A fair rate of wages', in Marshall, 1925, pp. 218–ff.); responsibility would be more diffused, both in the factory and in the socio-political field; Local Authorities would be engaged in town planning and social works aimed to improve 'the quality of human life' ('Where to house the London poor', in Marshall, 1925, p. 150); State Government would be stimulating and cooperative; there would be wider scopes for collective action, in particular by Trade Unions and Cooperatives; and general education would be extended to all the population. This is the 'fancied country' described in 1873 (below, 'The future of the working classes', p. 165) and enriched in later works. While resembling some socialist schemes, it does not require the 'subversion of existing arrangements' involved by them (ibid., p. 164).[22]

This imaginary country is similar to that depicted almost 50 years later in 'Ye route to ordered progress towards Utopia'. This and other short drafts of future 'scenarios' among Marshall's later papers bear witness to his concern for social perspectives and to the worth he attached to imagination in the social sciences.[23]

Marshall's ideal experiments of future possible societies are of two types: one, similar to the 'fancied country' and characterized by the adjective 'attainable', is for the near future, the other, an 'absolute Utopia' corresponding to Socialism and even Communism, can only be an outlook for posterity.[24] Although their institutional frameworks and requirements as to human nature are widely different,[25] they both lie near the same path and have the dignity of possible worlds. The fancied country is just one step in human evolution which at the moment looks the more promising of the two because it is 'attainable' and capable of eliciting the best human energies. While convergent with the other ambitious plan, it has the great advantage of combining imagination with knowledge of facts 'as they are' and is therefore protected from the dangers of a 'poetic imagination'

(Marshall 1925, pp. 228–9).

The first lecture helps us to understand the methodological standing of these 'imaginary worlds'. Like the beloved Kant's *Möglichkeit*, Marshall's possibility is not strictly related to experience of the external world. He sometimes likes to ask the reader to forget the world as it is, to think of one of those different possible worlds which fascinated him (Marshall, 1925, p. 64; Marshall, 1961, vol. I, p. 782 and various drafts). In a beautiful passage inviting women not to bow their heads to men's great experience of the world he writes:

> [men] are likely to know what will work, although for the very same reason they are unlikely to know what won't work, simply there is no precedent in their own experience of it. Therefore when practical men say a new scheme won't work, they are not necessarily right, seeing that they have but their own experience to guide them. (See below, p. 94. Cf. also RCOAP, Q. 10,365 in Marshall, 1925)

As matters of fact have no bearing on setting limits to what is possible, we have to resort to matters of reason, to abstract science. But if experience is silent, unable to disclose the future, abstract science cannot go beyond hypothetical criticism.[26] Marshall later insisted that economics is just an 'organon', 'not a body of concrete truth, but an engine for the discovery of concrete truth' ('The present position of economics', Marshall, 1925, p. 159). Even if it is the result of past experience, which it embodies, we are not bound by it to follow trodden paths. Its verdicts rely on given factual conditions which can be changed so as to make room for different possible types of 'Social Order'.

This methodological approach to social and political problems looks quite radical by any standard, making room for almost every possible outcome; but when we come to the present world Marshall's radicalism vanishes. As Biagini shows in his introduction, the practical proposals of the *Lectures to Women* are far from radical, even leaving aside Marshall's view of women's social standing.[27] The poetic imagination only is allowed to wonder as it works 'unmixed good', so long as it 'do[es] not profess to be practical' (Marshall, 1925, p. 329). The economist profits from such imaginative attempts to 'construct an edifice of pure crystal ... that will throw side lights on real problems', but 'such playful excursions ... seem to be productive only of good as long as their purpose is clearly understood' (Marshall, 1961, vol. I, p. 782). Science has a more difficult task:

> the responsible student of social problems ... must nourish the ideal in his heart ...; must resist every temptation to make a short cut to the ideal (Marshall, 1925, p. 84); [he] needs caution and reserve in order that his advocacy of ideals may not outrun his grasp of the future. (Marshall 1961, vol. I, p. 46)

A first answer to the question of how Marshall could combine radical telescopic perspectives with political microscopic moderation lies in the principle of continuity and the possibility of cumulative changes through the magic of the multiplication table and Taylor's theorem (Marshall, 1961, vol. I, pp. 843–4 and p. 559; Marshall, 1919, pp. 376–7).[28] Taking account of this, the main objective is not to rush towards the final end, but to make small self-growing steps in the right direction and let them work slowly; *Festina lente*[29] is the practical precept corresponding to *Natura non facit saltum*. If not the whole meaning of the principle of continuity, it certainly covers a relevant part of it, incorporating Lyell's and Darwin's philosophy of small causes producing large effects in due time. The stress on continuity is a pervasive, meandering stream of the Victorian age whose waters Marshall drew directly from the spring; he fully realized that the Industrial Revolution had shaken society to the ground, broken ancient customs and started 'the ordeal of economic freedom' (Matthews and Supple, 1991). To borrow Marx's expression, men and women had been thrown under the 'Juggernaut' of capitalism, but the Marshallian solution was to start processes capable of correcting past mistakes and overcoming the numberless faults of the social order rather than to subvert it again. He saw subversion as a primitive remedy of the past, not as an advisable one for the future.

According to Marshall, the initial greatness of a social transformation is unimportant; what does count is its self-growing character. Greatness can even cause damage to proposed remedies which have to be prepared carefully, investigating all the relevant present conditions under the microscope.[30] This attitude of course fits well also a conservative mood and provides excuses for it. Marshall's political positions were seldom far from 'the middle course'.

V. Microsurgery and Complexity

While undertaking his minute observations, the reformer has to remember that distant consequences can only be anticipated with the help of the telescope (Marshall, 1961, vol. I, p. 680).

Telescopic vision is a continuous concern to Marshall: 'the more we study history, the more we shall be convinced that it is not fair to say that because the world *has* gone on without some distinct forecasting of the future that therefore it may go on so now' (below, p. 116). 'The decade, the generation, the century', he later wrote ('Ye route to ordered progress towards Utopia', dated 27.4.1922), thus fixing a scale of outlooks which Keynes was to curtail. Marshall made it clear that on this point the economist, who 'looks beyond – not at the present only, but at the future' (Marshall, 1893, p. 384), had some special qualifications. Like Hobbes's moral and civil scientist, his telescopic view compares favourably with the 'emotionalist's' short one.

The need to look into the future is an obvious implication of the organicist conception of complex, evolving social systems, and no doubt exists as regards to the complex character of modern society in Marshall's thought.[31] It is not even a question of exactly defining complexity, because any conceivable meaning can match his opinions. Whether it be interdependence of causal links, changes in their operation or even refusal of causal explanations as such, Marshall would not refrain from maintaining it.

His insistence on complexity is proverbial and repeated on almost every page. Under all circumstances he opposes complex to simple, both in theory and in practice.[32] A simple explanation, for the very fact of being simple, is certainly wrong. Simple remedies to social problems are to be shunned. A piece of evidence before the Commission on the Old Aged Poor shows how the word 'simple' triggers negative associations in Marshall's mind:

> Q. (Broadhurst): Do you admit that one of the virtues of relief is that it should be immediate and simple in its form?
> A. (Marshall): I am not sure about its being simple. No, I want relief to be very complex. (Marshall, 1926, p. 239; Q. 10,335)

However, if society is a complex evolutionary structure, whose elements are interwoven and changing, inseparable and unfixed, what can be the uses of microscopical research, which involves cutting, separating and fixing?

The principle of continuity – metaphorically represented in the *Lectures* by the 'poetry of the multiplication table' (below, p. 148) – can do no more than assure us that *if* we can grow the 'little seed' we shall get the 'tree of boundless size' (below, p. 118).[33] But we know neither if the seed can be isolated, nor if easier ways of doing the job are open to us. This last doubt is given impressive and steady negative answers: science, while bold in inspiration, must take a 'humble line' when operative because its powers are limited and its task difficult (below, p. 87). Hence the need to divide problems and analyse each element individually:

> in all sciences there is one Method and only one; which when asked how to treat a complicated problem, simply answers 'don't treat it at all'. It is absolutely necessary to break such a problem into small portions. (See below, p. 87).[34]

Science has no privileged access to knowledge, its methods are simply a refinement of those of 'ordinary life'. It may look 'somewhat paradoxical', but 'there is nothing peculiar to science' (below, p. 87). No short-cut is conceivable; the more complex society is, the more cautious the scientist's steps must be. This message is not intended just for beginners, such as the Cambridge women, but also for trained scientists, as proved by the 1885 Cambridge inaugural lecture:

> the complexity and intricacy of social phenomena afford no reason for dispensing with the aid of the economic organon in its proper place: on the contrary they increase the necessity for it ... the fact which Comte seems to have ignored is that the human mind has no other method of inquiry than this; that a complex problem is broken up into its component parts, less methodically indeed but no less completely by common sense than by formal analysis. (Marshall, 1925, pp. 163–4)[35]

This echoes the *Lectures* warning that 'science must be uninteresting to those who do not see the special use of eliminating from our consideration for a time all but a very small portion of the question' (below, p. 87). Complex wholes must be broken in order to be studied and purposefully changed. This is another piece of the Kantian lesson which twists an otherwise completely nineteenth century Hegelian and Spencerian evolutionary thread.[36] The acknowledgement of complexity neither displaces modern scientific investigations nor forces radical changes of their methods; it merely reminds us of the simplified character of any scientific model.[37] The only method available to science is to build short deductive chains and to try to apply them to the real world ('the economic organon in its proper place').

This is where the sophisticated microscope is needed, in practice and theory alike, and where Marshall's limited positive answer to the first doubt comes to rescue. Breaking wholes and building small seed-traps is what science has always done and mainly consists in. The growing complexity of modern society makes the task even more difficult and more necessary, and microscopic detail is the only possible answer. It gives rise to abstractions which are not wild and to subtle and artificial concepts which do not claim to grasp 'the whole', but just for this reason are far from the simplicity implied by rough generalizations. Uncritical outsiders in economics are 'troublesome' precisely because:

> they run after simplicity in outward form, and become ardent disciples of those who are definite, simple and confident in their utterances. (*Marshall Papers*, 1890; quoted by Maloney, 1985, p. 41)

Dividing up, whose meaning is almost the contrary of simplifying, is an essential element of the Marshallian method of dealing with complexity, both in theory and in practice. Thinking in terms of 'pauperism', 'the working class' and similar general concepts must be overcome; they have to be divided up into poverties, working classes, and so on (Becattini, 1976). Marshall realized that undifferentiated aggregations, produced by the Industrial Revolution and nurtured by the Poor Laws, were dying away. As they were moral evils, persistence in theoretical adhesion to them was much more than an intellectual mistake.

Because the *Lectures to Women* deal with the practical side of the question, they remark on the absence of rules of social action to be applied unconditionally: there are no recipes for doing good, only general principles which have to be tuned in to specific situations.[38] If education partakes of the nature of a general principle, charity affords the best example of the need for discriminating application and dependence on individual conditions. Marshall is remarkably unconcerned in the *amount* spent on charity. The huge monetary cost was not the main negative consequence of the Speenhamland system, neither was its falling cost a criterion by which to judge the new Poor Law.[39] The true problem is the *quality* of dispensed charity, its relation to individual circumstances, its ability to give different answers to different situations. This is the reason why it has to be dispensed with personal knowledge and individual discriminating care, and the reason for Marshall's life-long support of the Charity Organisation Society, with its detailed investigations and far-reaching objectives. We can now follow Marshall's answer to Broadhurst to its end:

> the centre of relief, I think, should be the aim of raising a man out of the position of being a pauper; and that means, I think, a great variety of methods of treatment of individual cases. I would like it to be as quick as it can be, but I do not think I want to make it simple. (Marshall, 1926, pp. 239–40; Q. 10,335)

Stress on the complicated nature of individual cases of poverty was, however, the favourite argument through which some of the members of the Charity Organisation Society opposed any extension of State assistance. Marshall was not prepared to follow them on this point and when Bosanquet criticized his endorsement of State-aided pensions because 'public machinery operates on a large scale, under general rules' and 'is therefore restricted to very simple methods of work, and therefore again, as a rule, to very simple cases of distress', i.e. 'hopeless cases' of 'destitution' (Bosanquet, 1892), Marshall's answer was that

> 'simplicity' is a matter of degree; and the efficiency of public machinery is a matter of degree also, and it has risen in degree with the progress of time. (Marshall, 1892)

This quarrel brought Marshall to be suspicious of the 'oligarchic' basis of the COS (RCOAP: 'Preliminary Memorandum', Marshall, 1926, p. 203 and Q. 10,210, ibid., p. 211), and in favour of a mixed administration of assistance through semi-public bodies open to representatives of the working classes.[40]

Complexity does not constitute a conservative trench beyond which 'the old world' (ibid., Q. 10,210) and hierarchy could feel safe nor a valid reason for looking after wholesale remedies. Men are not forced to shun partial solutions: something can be done, here and now, and this something must be done without seeking refuge in global aims.

The same attitude is valid with regard to the intellect and its scientific products. This is the 'cool head' which prevents the 'warm heart' from putting forth 'hastily conceived plans which would often increase the evils that they desire to remedy'. But the 'warm heart' is likewise necessary if social problems are to be treated 'with weighty seriousness', and not in that 'amateur fashion' which recalls the 'dilettante' attitude which Christ came to supersede (below, p. 126).[41]

Marshall is undoubtedly in line with the Cambridge economic tradition of 'meliorism' (Keynes, 1972b, p. 447). Even if the stress on 'the long run' and the principle of continuity got lost, something of the Marshallian gist was preserved, together with the view that information and knowledge are active social forces. So many resemblances between the *Lectures*, aimed to promote women's philanthropy, and Marshall's later writings, especially the 1885 Cambridge inaugural lecture, aimed to establish a new scientific curriculum in economics, show how directions to beginners could reveal deeper methodological truths.

Notes and References

1. The author would like to thank John K. Whitaker for helpful comments on an early version of this paper.
2. Political economy is the term used by Marshall in this text and in the articles in the *Bee-Hive*. The change to the term Economics came just a few years later and was finally explained in *The Economics of Industry*. I use both, depending on the period in Marshall's life under consideration.
3. It is no surprise that subtle methodological themes were discussed in a text devoted to 'some economic questions directly connected with the welfare of the laborer'. The relations between the scientific status of political economy and the conditions of the working classes were hotly debated in the late 1860s and early 1870s. The Comtists, who supported the new Trade Unionism, were severely critical of the deductive method of political economy and its attempt to separate the economy from wider social issues (cf. Adelman, 1971). 'The limits of political economy' was the title of an article by Frederick Harrison who, here as well as elsewhere, assailed the pretention that real wages were 'naturally' determined by 'scientific' and 'immutable' laws (Harrison, 1865a, 1865b and 1865c). This marked the beginning of a double challenge to political economy. On the one hand Thornton, by concentrating his critiques against the applicability of 'the law of supply and demand' to the labour market, induced Mill to 'recant' at least one of the possible meanings of his theory of wages. On the other hand the methodological attack was successfully countered by Cairnes, who took up arms with the Comtists and restated the main tenets of political economy (Cairnes, 1870). Both Thornton and Cairnes are on Marshall's reading list for the course of lectures to women. Like Cairnes, Marshall thought that Thornton's scientific results were poor, but as an account of Trade Unionism he considered Thornton's book to be second only to Brentano's *Arbeitgilden* (cf. Whitaker, 1975, vol. II, p. 263).
4. The same concept is stated in Marshall (1961): 'economics are statements of tendencies expressed in the indicative mood, and not ethical precepts in the imperative' (vol. I, p. vi); while the necessity of a major premise which avoids the naturalistic fallacy of hedonism is stressed in the famous note on 'pleasure' and 'self-satisfaction' (vol. I, p. 17).
5. A difference of perspective is probably expressed by the change from the relation of sisterhood between ethics and economics (see below, p. 193) to that of mistress (ethics) and servant (economics) (Marshall, 1893, p. 389). The distinction is clear in both cases, but in the second one it is stressed by the emergence of serious doubts about the scientific character of ethics.

6. Marshall's view of historical, evolutionary change stands in the way of any absolute separation between what is and what ought to be. Beyond these two concepts lies what is becoming, 'tendencies' which the scientist has to grasp: 'from what *is* we have to learn what *is becoming*; from *das Sein* we have to learn *das Werden*' (Marshall, 1925, p. 300).
7. Cf. the 'bits of criticism' of Leslie Stephen for the absence of a clear distinction 'between the general principles and the modifications required by the complexity of actual circumstances' (L. Stephen to A. Marshall, 2 March 1891; *Marshall Papers*).
8. In the same letter Marshall states that Crooks, like George, deserves close attention as 'the mischief' done by such 'untrained thinkers', able to present 'the most vivid picture', 'varies as the product of their intellectual limitations and their oratorical efficiency' (*Layton Papers*, 2.17; Trinity College Library).
9. It was that double nature which Keynes both regretted as a hindrance to 'the ranging wings of an eagle' and praised as a 'pure advantage' (Keynes, 1972b, p. 173). (May we say that the advantage, and possibly the hindrance, were largely shared by Keynes himself?)
10. The two terms are consistently opposed in Marshall's writings. See below, p. 190. Another example is to be found in a passage from his letter to B. Kidd dated 6 June 1894: 'Indeed I regard the reasoning, the instinctive, and the moral sides of man's nature as capable of being distinguished, but not of being separated' (*Marshall Papers*).
11. Compare the radical tone of the *Lectures* with the moderate one of the late 'Social possibilities of economic chivalry', where, however, the substance of the critiques to *laissez faire* is very similar and anticipates many Keynesian ideas: both state that 'in Adam Smith's time Government was corrupt' but afterwards 'matters improved' (Marshall, 1925, pp. 334–5; Keynes, 1972a, p. 275) and both suggest that the State should concentrate 'on work which none but Government can do' (Marshall, 1925, p. 336; Keynes, 1972a, p. 291). Cf. also the second article in the *Bee-Hive,* where the need to investigate exceptions to the rule of *laissez faire* is thought to have become prominent (see below, p. 190). The widest treatment of the theme is to be found in *Industry and Trade*, which by no means supports an unconditional *laissez faire* policy (see in particular Appendix D for an historical perspective).
12. The urge to remedy social evils will be stressed in the 1885 Cambridge inaugural lecture: 'indeed the work is urgent' (Marshall, 1925, p. 172). The close similarities between this fundamental text and the *Lectures to Women* are examined below.
13. However important, schools, with their standardized methods, are by no means the main educational institutions (Marshall, 1919, p. 129 and p. 356).
14. On this point, reference has to be made to Marshall's early paper 'Ye Machine', in Marshall (1994).
15. Examples of this Marshallian attitude are the statement that the number of marriages grows with wealth and the idea that the birth-rate is a constant *by nature* which can only be checked *deliberately*. Both these theses had been strongly criticized by antimalthusian authors (Barton, Sadler, etc.). See also his Malthusian Lecture in Whitaker (1975).

For Marshall's critique of Malthusian ideas, cf. Marshall (1961), vol. I, pp. 509–10.

16. On this point, Marshall formulated what to my knowledge is his only critique of Spencer, who thought that the birth rate was *due* to become *necessarily* adapted to social and economic requirements. On the *possibility* of checking the growth of population, cf. also *Economics of Industry*, book I, chapter V.
17. This is one of Octavia Hill's favourite themes which Marshall took up in his *Lectures to Women* and in 'The future of the working classes', *passim*. Cf. also the negative expressions 'the joyless London sky' and 'houses ... devoid of joy' ('Where to house the London poor', Marshall, 1925, p. 144 and p. 146).
18. On these questions, and Marshall's early treatment of them, cf. Raffaelli (1994).
19. This attitude is an extension of the process by which Tocqueville had characterized the history of British society (Tocqueville, 1952, pp. 147–9).
20. The same opinion is held in the first page of *Principles*: 'man's character has been moulded by his every-day work'.
21. Marshall (1925), p. 311; cf. Reisman (1987), p. 39.
22. It was not only as a formal homage that T. H. Marshall took this article as the starting point of his 1949 *Alfred Marshall lecture* which centers on the notion of 'social citizenship' (Marshall, T. H., 1950).
23. On this subject see Becattini (1991). Very early in his life Marshall was aware of the functions of imagination in science. He derived this attitude from Buckle, whose famous pages on the subject he transcribed (Buckle, 1857–61, vol. II, pp. 502–5), but probably also from Kant. This is another of Marshall's differences from Mill's empiricist epistemology (cf. Raffaelli, 1991). Hints at his dislike of empiricism are to be found in the *Lectures* (cf., for example, the statement that 'All the results which are important we have before us but it is hard to know what they mean' – below, p. 97), and in 'The future of the working classes', below p. 165). In 1907 the need of scientific imagination made its appearance into his main work (cf. Marshall, 1961, vol. I, I.iv.5–6).
24. A reference to the Utopia of Communists is contained also in Marshall's lecture outlines (below, p. 144). Marshall's interest in Utopian movements brought him to visit Utopian communities during his journey through America in 1875 (cf. Whitaker, 1975, vol. II, p. 371 and Butler, 1993).
25. The human nature required by the second approaches 'perfection' and is therefore far beyond reality.
26. 'A law of science is simply a statement of the consequences which follow from a given set of causes' ('The laws of political economy', below, p. 180). 'There are two distinct points of view which are generally confused. i) If a science is perfectly abstract, its results are infallible. ii) Insofar as a science is abstract, its results are directly of no use whatever, and if a person, having learnt all that is purely abstract about a subject, attempts to give directions to the artist, he is quite out of his province' (below, p. 89). Again, in 1885, the concept is repeated: 'sometimes indeed the economist may give a practical decision as it were with the authority of his science, but such a decision is almost always merely negative or critical. It is to the effect that a proposed plan will not produce its desired result; just as an engineer might say with

authority that a certain kind of canal lock is unsuitable for its purpose. But an economist as such cannot say which is the best course to pursue, any more than an engineer as such can decide which is the best route for the Panama canal' (Marshall, 1925, p. 165).

27. No doubt Maloney was right in pointing out Marshall's 'lack of genuinely radical instincts' (Maloney, 1985, p. 39).
28. Science itself is characterized and distinguished from other subjects by its possibility of being cumulative (Marshall, 1961, vol. I, I.iv), a fact which makes old books superseded by new ones. This is the first part of the Baconian view of science that Marshall endorsed (the second one being the idea that scientific knowledge has practical relevance).
29. This expression was used in a draft concerning 'The future', dated 21.10.21: 'it is right to look eagerly far ahead: but it is not wise to move hastily on to perilous ground. Eagerness in testing progress is a duty: but the larger the venture, the more cogent is the rule *Festina lente*'.
30. 'Utopian schemes for renovating society ... do harm when put prematurely into practice; for their failure causes reaction' (Whitaker, 1975, vol. II, p. 342).
31. It would be much easier to consider him a forerunner of modern views of complexity than it has been to put Keynes in such a dress by some recent interpreters.
32. 'Economics can never become a simple science' (Marshall, 1961, vol I, p. 404). For the practical aspect, see his letters to B. Potter (11.7.1891) – 'You are constantly saying that there are two alternatives where there seem to me to be fifty' (quoted in Maloney, 1985, p. 36) – and to Bishop Westcott (24.1.1900) – 'I know of no simple means by which a fair wage can be assured to all workers' (Marshall, 1925, p. 386).
33. The image of the 'seeds of growth' is applied to the cooperative movement in 1889 (see Marshall, 1925, p. 228).
34. Cf. also Marshall, 1961, vol. I, p. 380, note. For a comment on this, see Boland (1990).
35. Cf. also Marshall, 1961, vol I, p. 510: 'A very difficult problem can best be solved by being broken up into pieces'; and p. 770: 'Their [of the physical sciences] rapid progress in the modern age is due to a breaking up of broad problems into their component parts'.
36. Spencer himself, in spite of his evolutionary optimism aiming at complete and absolute adaptation, was influenced by this Kantian lesson, mainly through Mansel (see Raffaelli, 1990 and 1994).
37. It may be interesting to compare Marshall's opinions with modern debates on 'the challenge of complexity', which by contrast have been characterized by the emergence of an epistemological revolution, maintaining that the study of complex systems requires new methods, which can overcome the limitations of 'Newtonian mechanism'.
38. Cf. below, p. 125. This is the practical correspondent to the theoretical warning that 'while attributing this high and transcendent universality to the central scheme of economic reasoning, we may not assign universality to economic dogmas. For that part of economic doctrine, which alone can claim universality, has no dogmas' (Marshall, 1925, p. 159). See above, p. 12.

39. The quantitative criterion was quite common in Marshall's time. He opposed it strenuously. See Marshall (1969) p. 189, (1925) p. 447 and RCOAP, Q. 10,386. Cf. also Reisman (1987), pp. 221 and 427, note 41.
40. Once more these remedies remind us of Keynes's preferences for autonomous semi-public institutions.
41. The concept of Christ as an anti-dilettante is probably taken from E. Renan (see below, lecturesnotes note 29).

Bibliography

Adelman P. (1971), 'F. Harrison and the "positivist" attack on orthodox political economy', *History of Political Economy*, vol. 3, pp. 170–89.

Bain A. (1864), *The Senses and the Intellect*, London: Longman, Green, Longman, Robert & Green, 2nd edition.

Bain A. (1865), *The Emotions and the Will*, London: Longman, Green & Co., 2nd edition.

Becattini G. (1976), 'Invito a una rilettura di Marshall', in A. Marshall e M. Paley Marshall, *Economia della produzione*, Milano: ISEDI.

Becattini G. (1991), 'Market and communism in the thought of Alfred Marshall', *Quaderni di Storia dell'Economia Politica*, vol. 10, pp. 161–88.

Boland L. A. (1990), 'The methodology of Marshall's "principle of continuity" ', *Économie Appliquée*, vol. 43, pp. 145–59.

Bosanquet B. (1892), 'The limitations of the Poor Law', *Economic Journal*, vol. 2, pp. 369–71.

Bowman R. S. (1990), 'Smith, Mill, and Marshall on human capital formation' in *History of Political Economy*, vol. 22, pp. 239–59.

Buckle H. T. (1857–61), *History of Civilization in England*, London: J. W. Parker & son.

Butler R. (1993), ' "To firm notions about men and manners": Marshall among the Americans', *Marshall Studies Bulletin*, vol. 3, pp. 3–20.

Cairnes J. E. (1870), 'M. Comte and political economy', *Fortnightly Review*, n.s. vol. 7, 579–602.

Harrison F. (1865a), 'The iron-master trade union', *Fortnightly Review*, vol. 1, pp. 96–116.

Harrison F. (1865b), 'The limits of political economy', *Fortnightly Review*, vol. 1, pp. 356–76.

Harrison F. (1865c), 'Good and evil of tradeunionism', *Fortnightly Review*, vol. 3, pp. 33–54.

Harrison R (1963), 'Two early articles by Alfred Marshall', *Economic Journal*, vol. 73, pp. 422–30; reprint in J. C. Wood (ed.) (1982).

Hobbes T. (1839) [1651], *Leviathan, or the Matter, Forme and Power of a Commonwealth, Ecclesiasticall and Civil*, in *The English Works of Thomas Hobbes*, ed. by Sir W. Molesworth, London: John Bohn.

Kadish A. (1991), 'University Reform and the *Principles*', *Quaderni di Storia dell'Economia Politica*, vol. 10, pp. 289–309.

Keynes J. M. (1972a), *Essays in Persuasion*, in *Collected Writings of John Maynard Keynes*, ed. by D. Moggridge, London: Macmillan, vol. 9.

Keynes J. M. (1972b), *Essays in Biography*, in *Collected Writings of John Maynard Keynes*, ed. by D. Moggridge, London: Macmillan, vol. 10.

Maloney J. (1985), *Marshall, Orthodoxy and the Professionalisation of Economics*, Cambridge: Cambridge University Press.

Marshall A. (1892) 'Poor-Law Reform', *Economic Journal*, vol. 2, pp. 371–9.

Marshall A. (1893), Response to the President's Address, *Economic Journal*, vol. 3, pp. 387–90.

Marshall A. (1919), *Industry and Trade*, London: Macmillan.

Marshall A. (1925), *Memorials of Alfred Marshall*, ed. by A. C. Pigou, London: Macmillan.

Marshall A. (1926), *Official Papers by Alfred Marshall*, ed. by J. M. Keynes, London: Macmillan.

Marshall A. (1961) [1890], *Principles of Economics*, ed. by C. W. Guillebaud, London: Macmillan, ninth (variorum) edition in two volumes.

Marshall A. (1969) [1883], 'Three lectures on progress and poverty', ed. by G. J. Stigler, *Journal of Law and Economics*, vol. 12, pp. 181–226; reprint in J. C. Wood (ed.) (1982).

Marshall A. (1994), 'Early philosophical writings', *Research in the History of Economic Thought and Methodology. Archival Supplement*, vol. 4.

Marshall T. H. (1950) [1949], 'Citizenship and social class', in Marshall T. H., *Citizenship and Social Class and Other Essays*, Cambridge: Cambridge University Press.

Matthews R. C. O. and Supple B. (1991), 'The ordeal of economic freedom: Marshall on economic history', *Quaderni di Storia dell'Economia Politica*, vol. 9, pp. 189–213.

Mill J. S. (1965) [1848], *Principles of Political Economy, with some of their Applications to Social Philosophy*, (1862 edition), in *Collected Works of John Stuart Mill*, ed. by V. W. Bladen and J. M. Robson, Toronto and London: Toronto University Press, vols. 2 and 3.

Parsons T. (1931), 'Wants and activities in Marshall', *The Quarterly Journal of Economics*, vol. 46, pp. 101–40; reprint J. C. Wood (ed.) (1982).

Raffaelli T. (1990), 'Gli studi filosofici del giovane Marshall', *Atti Accademia Nazionale dei Lincei, Rendiconti Classe di Scienze Morali*, series 9, vol. 1, pp. 121–60.

Raffaelli T. (1991), 'The analysis of the human mind in the early Marshallian manuscripts', *Quaderni di Storia dell'Economia Politica*, vol. 9, pp. 29–58.

Raffaelli T. (1994) 'Marshall's analysis of the human mind', *Research in the History of Economic Thought and Methodology. Archival Supplement*, vol. 4, pp. 53–93.

Reisman D. (1987), *Alfred Marshall. Progress and Politics*, London, Macmillan.

Thornton W. T. (1870) [1868], *On Labour. Its Wrongful Claims and Rightful Dues. Its Actual Present and Possible Future*, 2nd ed., London: Macmillan and Co.

Tocqueville A. de (1952) [1856], *L'ancien règime et la rèvolution*, in Tocqueville A. de, *Ouvres Complètes*, ed. by J.-P. Mayer, Paris: Gallimard, vol. 2.

Whitaker J. K. (ed.) (1975), *The Early Economic Writings of Alfred Marshall (1867–1890)*, London: Macmillan.

Wood J. C. (ed.) (1982) *Alfred Marshall: Critical Assessments*, London: Croom Helm, four volumes.

2. The Anglican ethic and the spirit of citizenship: the political and social context

Eugenio Biagini

I. Light of Liberalism?

Is it not remarkable that in Christopher Harvie's study of late-Victorian 'university Liberals' Alfred Marshall is included only in a cursory, incidental way (Harvie, 1976, pp. 200, 202, 215)? Even more surprising is the fact that he does not really feature in another, more recent work on Liberal intellectuals – Collini's *Public Moralists* (1991, pp. 921–3, 214, 215).[1] It would seem that, in contrast to Mill, T. H. Green and a later generation of intellectuals including Hobson and Hobhouse, Marshall is not perceived as a 'light of Liberalism'. Despite his pervasive influence, to Harvie he rather personifies the trend of 'economics and philosophy ... [to move] away from the unity of the 1860s ... [as economics became] a more technical, mathematically competent, profession' (Harvie, 1976, p. 202). And yet, to Marshall 'economics was a species of moral philosophy' (Himmelfarb, 1992, p. 285): ethics had led him to economics, which he saw first of all as the study of poverty and its remedies (Himmelfarb, 1992, p. 287). Indeed, it has been argued that part of his success and long-lasting fascination was due to the fact that 'he seemed to integrate ethics and economics into a single discipline' (Himmelfarb, 1992, p. 300).[2] His commitment to moralizing economics was such that for a while he even had a kind of 'socialist' reputation (McWilliams Tullberg, 1990a, pp. 75–111).

So why is he not more readily identifiable with the early trend towards the 'New Liberalism'? Part of the explanation may lie in his style and temperament; it is well known that Marshall lacked Mill's taste for political controversy and his enthusiasm for engaging with the 'hot' issues of the day,[3] he was first and foremost an 'academic'. However, given Marshall's intellectual stature, psychological factors can hardly be seen as more than marginal. A fuller picture requires a contextualization of his thought and of the way it contributed to the contemporary political and social debate.

The works published in this volume can help us to see more clearly into this problem. They are important both because of the topics dealt with, and because they belong to the delicate period of transition from *laissez-faire* optimism to various experiments in public control. They are significant also for the role they played in Marshall's early career: for, '[l]ike Toynbee, whose influence derived from his lectures and personal appeal rather than his writings, Marshall [first] acquired his reputation on the basis of lectures, courses and the acclaim of students and colleagues' (Himmelfarb, 1992, p. 282). The main thrust of these *Lectures* and articles is social; and yet few of the reforms advocated by Marshall can be referred to as evidence in support of the traditional claim that he was a 'Radical', at least in the sense in which the word was used in the last quarter of the nineteenth century.

For example, when in the *Lectures to Women* Marshall emphasized education and trade union organization, he echoed what was then being recommended by most politicians (Smith, 1967, pp. 198–325; Spain, 1991, pp. 109–33) and labour leaders (Biagini, 1987, pp. 811–40). In 'The future of the working classes' Marshall seemed to go farther, mapping a brave new world of industrial relations characterized by 'economic chivalry', shorter working hours, and gentrified working men. This programme was definitely inspired by a 'radical' *ideal*; however, since he did not prescribe any *means* whereby it could be brought within the realm of practical politics, it had the feel of a largely utopian scheme. With the exception of Marshall's commitment to the movement for women's university education – a Radical cause in 1873, as Rita McWilliams Tullberg shows (see below, p. 52–ff.) – these works do not convey the impression that he was particularly 'advanced'. Even if he was developing his views along lines broadly parallel to those of contemporary Liberal thought – i.e. in acknowledging the limits of market economy and the priority of moral over purely economic concerns (Coats, 1990, pp. 155–7) – he steered clear of the most controversial (and urgent) issues of the time.

This observation can be substantiated with a few examples. Marshall's recipes for social reform started from the (correct) assumption that the labour movement accepted the market system and industrial capitalism, rejected class struggle, and believed that the interests of industrial employers and factory workers were ultimately coincident (Biagini, 1987, pp. 838–9). On these premises, Marshall tried to address the disturbing question of why – after almost thirty years of free trade – the economic system did not seem to be workable without keeping a large section of the labouring poor in a state of permanent distress, degradation and unemployment. He argued that this state of affairs could be improved by the combined action of state-supported mass education, and centralized, well-disciplined, trade unions.

This approach was very similar to the strategy which had been adopted by the Trades Union Congress (TUC) since its foundation in 1868. Theoretically it did not involve any major revision of Dunning's and Fawcett's analyses, published in 1860 (Dunning, 1860; Fawcett, 1860; Mill, 1862, p. 932). In the 1870s the TUC's leadership aimed at establishing collective bargaining by extending arbitration and conciliation as the means of settling industrial disputes, as well as by various 'sliding-scale' agreements. Following a series of early successes, prominent labour leaders and industrialists looked forward to creating a sort of 'corporate liberal' version of the market (Biagini, 1987, pp. 836–7). They hoped that increasingly representative trade unions would co-operate with large and 'enlightened' employers' organizations in planning for growth and preventing social strife and the disruption of industrial productivity (Applegarth, 1869; Potter, 1870, pp. 550–61). Such convictions and hopes were enthusiastically shared by Marshall (McWilliams Tullberg, 1990a, pp. 80–1; Harrison, 1982, p. 120).[4] He genuinely admired the labour leaders of the 1870s, the trade unionists 'of the old stamp' with whom, in later life, he would identify himself (A. Marshall to E. Caird, 22 Oct. 1897, in *Memorials*, p. 398; cf. Roberts, 1958, pp. 92–172).

What he said was definitely not 'radical', not so much because he had not 'analysed the core problem of poverty' (McWilliams Tullberg, 1991, p. 264), but because he deliberately steered clear of the then current Radical discussion of possible solutions. While the latter – even in the early 1870s – concerned redistributive taxation and various schemes of land reform, Marshall preferred uncontroversial and 'non-political' policies, such as education, 'scientific' poor relief, paternalist factory legislation, and moralized capitalism. In the early 1870s the moderates of both parties supported these policies to such an extent that Liberals and Conservatives co-operated both with each other and with the TUC in preparing new reform Bills – a trend culminating in the bipartisan legislation passed under Disraeli's government in 1874–76 (Spain, 1991, pp. 109–33). Even when Marshall sounded highly emotional, as in his peroration on child rights (e.g., see below, pp. 93, 95 and 99), he knew that he was addressing issues, and proposing reforms, for which there would be a large consensus. In other words, he focused on economic and social remedies which did not involve a political dimension.

II. Moralizing Capitalism

It is even more remarkable that, after criticizing the impractical proposals of 'utopian socialism' (see below, 'The future', pp. 164), Marshall proceeded to produce the equally utopian-looking scheme of working-class 'gentrification'. However, in the context of the contemporary academic debate his ideas were actually less eccentric than we might suppose. For one thing, his emphasis on transforming working- into gentle-men was in tune with the then current conviction that the 'social question' was also the question of the 'disposition', the 'thoughts, beliefs and feelings' of the working man. Thus, in 1874 J. E. Cairnes had concluded that no improvement in their lot was possible 'without substantial change in [their] moral character' (cit. in Stedman Jones, 1984, p. 4). While Cairnes was pessimistic about the likelihood of change, Marshall personified the then prevailing optimism: wages had risen and were still rising (Himmelfarb, 1992, p. 38), while '[a]ll ranks of society [were] raising; on the whole they [were] better and more cultivated than their forefathers [had been] ...' (see below, 'The future', p. 144).

This strong expectation of economic and social progress represents an interesting contrast with Mill. The latter was resigned to the imminent onset of the 'stationary state'; as a consequence – just like the Chartists in the 1840s – in the 1860s Mill saw resolute political action as the only way to achieve greater social justice. In contrast, sustained economic expansion could become a disincentive to political action and militancy: such had been the case in the early 1850s, when Chartism, wounded by the 1842–47 factory legislation, was eventually killed off by the mid-Victorian economic boom (Stedman Jones, 1983, pp. 171–8). As Cobden had predicted, political revolution and economic progress were inversely related.

Marshall went well beyond a Cobdenite faith in progress, and offered an elaborate economic system built upon the hypothesis that *continuous* growth was possible. This was then a new development in economic thought, and was bound to play a major role in the way Marshall looked at social problems. As the economy continued to expand, economic growth, rather than political action, would provide the real source of the solution to the problems of society. He regarded this 'incessant evolution' as 'an *a priori* good ... the progressive realization of the value system immanent in free enterprise' (Stedman Jones, 1984, p. 6). The latter included 'an ethical obligation to be rational' and the progressive transformation of labour from 'a necessary pain' into 'a creative activity ... the result of which was to develop character' (Stedman Jones, 1984, pp. 6–7). *Working*-men could become *gentle*-men: to Marshall this was not a utopia, but a forecast, very much like the 'stationary state' to Mill: a realistic expectation on the basis of his understanding of the economic system. In this sense – as well as in others – Mill and Marshall really belonged to two different eras. With T. H. Green, Marshall emphasized

> moralized capitalism ... Both relied on some conception of evolution as a central explanatory mechanism in their systems. They were thus able to escape the problem that had so baffled Mill – that is, how will men come to strive for the higher rather than the lower pleasures. For the new thinkers, history itself solved the problem. Both Marshall and Green saw history ... as a transition from self-interest to self-sacrifice and altruism. (Stedman Jones, 1984, p. 7)

In their formative years both had been impressed by the display of self-control and moral and political maturity which had allegedly characterized the Lancashire workers during the 1861–5 Cotton Famine, and which played such an important role in the rhetoric of Gladstone's popular Liberalism. 'Set in evolutionary context beside signs of increasing thrift, sobriety and rationality, exemplified by the growth of co-operatives, penny savings banks, and friendly societies, the prospect of working class improvement was seen as infinite' (Stedman Jones, 1984, p. 8). Marshall could speak of the workers becoming gentlemen because, as a consequence of economic liberalism and education, the working class 'would increasingly become a middle class in working class dress' (ibid.).

This faith also explains his expectation that a future drastic limitation of the hours of work would be accompanied by a moral and intellectual 'reformation' (see below, 'The future', p. 165; cf. Hutchison, 1969, p. 245). Like Green and Toynbee, Marshall postulated that the working class as a whole would come to share some version of that 'Protestant ethic' which almost invariably inspired his beloved 'trade unionists of the old stamp' (Reid, 1991, pp. 214–43). He believed that the new State education would provide an equivalent of the 'Protestant ethic'; properly educated workers would desire 'higher' and 'nobler' forms of recreation, while their wages would grow on account of their increased skills and productivity. Both arguments were then widely accepted even among trade unionists.[5]

The prevailing opinion was that ignorance was the main cause of both crime[6] and pauperism (Fawcett, 1876, p. 232). In contrast, cultivated people would be not only morally, intellectually and socially 'superior' (West, 1964, p. 170; Parry, 1986, p. 105),[7] but also civically aware (Halliday, 1976, p. 98), socially useful, and economically efficient (Fawcett, 1876, p. 237). Expectations as to the economic effects of mass education had been voiced time and again since 1850–51 by a number of economists and reformers, including Richard Cobden (Cobden, 1870, p. 605). In the early 1870s this idea was proposed by Stanley Jevons and Fawcett (Fawcett, 1871, pp. 122–63), while Charles Booth fully subscribed to Marshall's mottoes of 'Promote education at the expense of capital. Educate first. Attend to its effects on capital afterwards' (see below, p. 98; cf. Himmelfarb, 1992, p. 82 for Booth in 1870). Indeed education was increasingly becoming of central concern to industrialists as well, because it seemed related to the questions of national performance and 'efficiency', which from the 1850s were causing headaches to observers of international trade trends (Cobden, 1870, p. 606; Jones, 1977, p. 113).

Marshall's emphasis on the urgency of State primary education could hardly sound radical in 1873. Already in 1870 an important Education Act – passed by the Liberal government with Conservative support – provided for the gradual establishment of rate-supported schools throughout the country. It must be stressed that nobody at the time considered State-funded education to be a breach of *laissez-faire*; on the contrary, in 1867–70 one of the main advocates of national schooling for the poor had been Robert Lowe, the intransigent 'high priest' of the Victorian minimalist State (Briggs, 1990, pp. 263–6).[8] Gertrude Himmelfarb has argued that in recommending a 'nonutilitarian, nonvocational' syllabus for working-class children Marshall 'went well beyond most of the reformers of his time' (Himmelfarb, 1992, p. 296): however, it would be more accurate to say that he espoused the traditional *curriculum* favoured by self-taught 'old stamp unionists' – such as his friend Thomas Burt (Burt, 1924, pp. 113–27; Biagini, 1992, pp. 33–4) – who were concerned with both emancipation, and the fostering of 'civic virtue'.

Thus, this was an old platform. Yet it acquired a different significance in the context of Marshall's emphasis on a new kind of full, active citizenship which included *social* rights and duties, as well as political ones. For the novelty of Marshall's approach was his genuine expectation that a socially-guided economic progress would rid society not only of pauperism, but of poverty as well (Himmelfarb, 1992, pp. 288–90). What was really advanced and 'radical' in the writings under discussion was Marshall's commitment to economic reform as a means to moral regeneration, his targeting the working classes for 'abolition' (Himmelfarb, 1992, pp. 291–3). If it was the effect of labour which determined whether one became either a 'working' or a 'gentle' man, then conceivably – by means of technological progress and economic reform – it would be possible to ensure that ordinary manual labour would become no more degrading than 'professional' manual labour, such as the work of a surgeon (see below, 'The future', p. 158).

Thus, in 1873 Marshall began his long march towards what Himmelfarb describes as his 'great achievement ... to humanize economics without losing its scientific character' (Himmelfarb, 1992, p. 298). This journey was arduous and not without casualties, one of which was the political militancy typical of the previous generations of economists who had been influenced by J. S. Mill. Sustained economic progress made 'short-term' political reform redundant. This also applied to economic proposals, such as land reform, which were politically controversial. Consequently, land reform does not figure in Marshall's agenda, despite the fact that in 1870–3 – in the aftermath of Gladstone's first Irish Land Act – it was quite popular among Liberals, and advocated by J. S. Mill. Marshall's well-known psychological reluctance towards getting involved in controversies was reinforced by the results of his scientific analysis and by what he saw as rational policy-making: progress and immanent evolution seemed to be squaring the circle of creating 'scientific' politics, politics without passion.

In political terms this had conservative implications – it implied setting aside methods of agitation, and trusting in the rule of the intellectuals rather than the deliberations of the demos. Towards the 'layfolk' Marshall felt a typically 'clerical' diffidence. In this too he was at odds with the 'Saint of Rationalism': Mill had no objection to plunging headlong into controversy, neither did he fear to address the man in the street against both educated public opinion and Parliament itself, as he did in 1868–73 (Collini, 1991, pp. 121–69; Biagini, 1996). By contrast Marshall's vehement hostility to Henry George in the 1880s was inspired not by the theoretical concerns which moved Toynbee,[9] but by his revulsion towards George's preference for expounding his subversive ideas to ordinary working men, rather than academics.[10] Marshall's attitude resonates with the irritation felt by most Whig and Erastian Anglican Liberals against Gladstone during the 1879 'Midlothian Campaign',[11] when he exposed to the judgment of 'the mob' matters considered to be the sole preserve of Parliament and gentlemanly opinion (Jenkins, 1984, pp. 337–60; Parry, 1986, pp. 140–4).

III. The Limits of Marshall's Radicalism

The parallels exist and are important. From a political point of view it is insufficient merely to say that Marshall was not a Radical; for he both fitted the contemporary Liberal-Anglican agenda (Parry, 1986, pp. 105–12), and shared some of the attitudes which were typical of moderate opinion. The best example is his discussion of education.

In the 'The future of the working classes' Marshall invoked compulsory education, denouncing the supporters of 'voluntary' systems.[12] These were often old-fashioned Nonconformists, zealous for theological purity in religious education, or stern and unbending Anglicans, who rejected any prospect of secular interference with their schools.[13] However, 'voluntary' education drew support as well from a vocal group of working-class spokesmen, including eminent trade-union leaders (Biagini, 1992, p. 201). The latter were concerned less with theology than liberty, especially freedom from 'state interference' (then a code-word for social control: ibid., pp. 195–7, 253) in working-class family matters. This was a real issue with two important aspects. First, it involved the preservation of the community-centred 'dame schools' and other similar 'voluntary' institutions; in these private schools children were offered only a rudimentary education, but parents appreciated their flexible schedules, personalized *curricula*, low fees, and responsiveness to family demands (Gardner, 1984, pp. 95, 100, 157–8). Second, it affected religious freedom: in the 1870s, especially in rural towns and villages, 'compulsory' education would inevitably mean Anglican instruction for the children of Methodist farmworkers and artisans. This possibility generated bitter controversies also because at the time working-class Nonconformity was a way to articulate social issues and raise political questions. Thus, the issue at stake was not only diluted theological substance, but diminished political articulation. However, Marshall displayed a certain insensitivity to this part of the problem, despite its ample representation in the *Bee-Hive* (which he read), and in most other popular newspapers.

The impression that he was leaning towards the position of the established church is strengthened by various statements in the *Lectures*. There, though he waxed lyrical about the benefits of public education, he did not even mention the then hotly debated religious question. While the need for a national system of primary schools was widely recognized, Radicals, Liberals and Conservatives were then viciously attacking each other in Parliament and in local school boards, as they debated whether the new State education should be denominational or 'unsectarian', Christian or secular, and (in the rural districts) controlled by elective boards, or by magistrates. Of such polemics there is no echo in the *Lectures*, though they were delivered the same year that the second school-board elections were held.

It is not to be supposed that 'a scientist' like Marshall would shun these diatribes as sectarian strife, for he was convinced that education should address the spiritual as well as the intellectual sphere. This meant that the education which he had in mind had strong *ethical* content. However, in the context of the contemporary debate it is hard to see how such content could be discussed without facing the 'religious question', especially as the latter was felt to be crucial not only in Britain, but throughout Europe.[14] In the last analysis, the choice was between a strong ethical function for the State (a Radical platform), and a continuing role for the established church. The former is never mentioned in the writings here published, and there is no evidence that Marshall objected to the preservation of the latter. Thus, by avoiding the *political* side of the question, he virtually took up the line of the Anglican party.

Also on the more technical question of whether national schools should be fee-paying, Marshall rejected the Radical proposal of a fully free system of public education, in favour of traditional views. Yet the 'free school' platform was far from being perceived as 'socialist' even in 1873: in fact as early as 1851 it had been endorsed by Cobden himself (Cobden, 1870, p. 605). Marshall opposed free education on the 'moral' ground that the responsibility and authority of working-class parents would be weakened were they to be completely relieved of the payment of their children's school fees.[15]

IV. Anglican Civic Virtue

There are other aspects which suggest that Marshall's Anglican background played some role in shaping his attitudes. Admittedly, in the early 1870s his was a fading, non-dogmatic, purely 'ethical' version of Anglicanism, such as was then becoming common among Churchmen affected by historical criticism and 'liberal' theology. Like many other lapsed Christians, Marshall believed that humanity was now 'mature' enough to retain the ethical part of Christianity after rejecting its theological message (Reisman, 1990, pp. 5–6, 16; Himmelfarb, 1992, p. 303).

By 'Christian' ethic he meant 'Protestant' ethic: he had lost his Christianity but not his Protestantism. The *Lectures* are the best instance of what Mary Paley Marshall meant when she described her husband as 'a preacher'. Elsewhere I have explored certain similarities in the structure and rhetorical devices between classical Protestant expository homiletic and his *Lectures to Women* (Biagini, 1991, pp. 334–54). Anglo-Protestant culture imbued not only Marshall's style, but also his *Weltanschauung*.[16] The most conspicuous indication of that was his persistent anti-Catholicism. The latter – then deeply rooted in Anglicanism, as shown by the 1874 anti-Ritualist uproar and 'anti-Vaticanist' polemics (Machin, 1987, pp. 78–84) – is well attested to in the *Lectures*. There Marshall explicitly identified Christianity with the Reformation, and contrasted it with both Paganism and Roman Catholicism: Protestantism had rescued the world from 'that despotism of mental sluggishness which ruled Europe before the Reformation'.[17] It is remarkable that similarly negative remarks on the Church of Rome occurred even in writings of a later period, despite the fact that his own Anglican heritage was progressively fading away.[18]

Moreover, Marshall shared the classically Protestant belief in the centrality of 'character' (Collini 1985, pp. 29–50; Raffaelli 1990, p.

143), which epitomised Evangelical social policies throughout the century and across the political spectrum, from Thomas Chalmers to James Keir Hardie (Tholfsen, 1976, p. 348; Himmelfarb, 1992, pp. 348; Bebbington, 1981, pp. 37–60). This belief was accompanied by a moderate anthropological pessimism which saw human nature as shaped by both sin and grace – a view as yet only marginally modified by the new emphasis on evolution, 'ethology' and the 'national' character (Becattini, 1991, pp. 165–7; cf. below, p. 168). Significantly, when Marshall praised the unions' educative functions, he emphasized their tendency to train the workers 'to sacrifice individual interests for a common object ... to bind [themselves] to treaties and adhere to them' (see below, p. 145). It was a step towards the hoped-for transformation of all labourers into 'gentlemen' – almost a second 'Reformation', a mass moral regeneration (see below, 'The future', pp. 165 and 168). 'Regeneration' was the only real answer to the social question: the labourers had to be 'born again'.

His practical proposals did not go much beyond what many of his contemporaries would have accepted as plain common sense. Yet, as we have already seen, he presented them with a strong emphasis on a new, extended concept of citizenship. The latter was a further manifestation of the 'Anglican ethic' which inspired him. In this connection the affinities between Marshall and Arnold Toynbee (whom Marshall replaced at Balliol in 1883) are worth noting. They shared a missionary approach to the problems of modern industrial society, within the framework of a civically-minded social Christianity (Reisman, 1990, p. 223; Stedman Jones, 1984, pp. 10, 42–3). They personified that 'equation between religious feeling, active self-sacrificing philanthropy, and science' (Stedman Jones, 1984, p. 6) of which J. R. Seeley had written in his *Ecce Homo* (1866). While Toynbee's attitude was actually inspired by Anglican Puritanism (Himmelfarb, 1992, p. 279), in Marshall's case – as in the case of T. H. Green – the 'doctrine of citizenship and reform ... can best be understood as a surrogate faith appealing to a transitional generation' (Reisman, 1990, p. 48).

Their attitude provides a further instance of the inadequacy of the old stereotype contrasting the 'republican' tradition of 'positive liberty' with the 'liberal' one of 'negative liberty'. Like Green, Marshall was a standard-bearer of the Victorian crusade for 'civic virtues'. Though he was a much more moderate Liberal than Green, in his writings there is no trace of any 'crucial moral opposition' between economic individualism and the 'classical republican' concept of active citizenship which – according to A. MacIntyre and others (MacIntyre, 1981, p. 241; Lasch, 1991, pp. 14–5, 59) – should have characterized these allegedly different political traditions. As I have suggested elsewhere (Biagini, 1996), this dichotomy is just not applicable to British Liberalism – or, in all probability to *any* other Liberal tradition as such.[19]

In the *Lectures* Marshall stressed participatory citizenship[20] and the civic duties of ordinary citizens, and in particular of *women* – then not the most obvious recipients of 'republican' calls to civic virtue. He argued that they had a special calling to social care and social reform: '[t]o make every man a gentleman ... [e]very woman a lady' was 'peculiarly a woman's question' (see below, p. 141). However, only academically educated women could play this role – one which Marshall described as 'a female priesthood':

> A highly educated, mentally, morally, haestetically [sic] cultured staff of strong emotion joy imparting beings exists in the ladies of modern civilisation.
> They are by nature of the case the priestesses of the highest culture – the priestesses of joy. (See below, p. 148)

One of their main fields of action was poor relief. The theme of joy, which recurs twice in this short quotation, was then an important component of the new Evangelical and idealist strategies which inspired the Charity Organization Society (COS). As Octavia Hill put it in 1869, 'The poor of London need joy and beauty in their lives' (cit. in Himmelfarb, 1992, p. 215). Like Toynbee (Reisman, 1990, p. 43) and many other Anglican intellectuals, Marshall endorsed her approach to poor relief,[21] based on the conviction that charity ought to be guided by knowledge, rather than 'sentimentalism' (Mason, 1974, pp. 291, 297). Women like Hill were acting their role of 'priestesses of joy' as they sought to counteract the general tendency towards wasteful, 'unscientific' forms of charity and almsgiving.

Marshall argued that in order to be able to do that effectively, civically-minded women required proper education – which again, as with working men, was to be Nature's 'multiplication table' (see below, pp. 118 and 101). A true Victorian, Marshall maintained that – when considered from a 'scientific' perspective – there was no contrast between maximizing profits and improving the working conditions and quality of life of the labourers. His favourite example was the early factory legislation which, despite bitter opposition from 'unenlightened' factory masters, proved in the end to be both morally just and economically sensible. Yet the coming to fruition of the benefits of this immanent harmony between ethics and economics was delayed because the employers were merely 'practical' men, without any real grasp of the economic science. It was their ignorance, rather than their hardheartedness, which was responsible for this evil. Lack of 'scientific' education had also prevented their wives and daughters – who according to Marshall had first-hand knowledge of the social evils of the day – from articulating their views effectively and bringing their opinions to bear on their male kinsfolk.

V. Deaconnesses and Priests

This was the central argument in Marshall's advocacy of women's education. In it he offered a fine example of a moderately progressive application of the Victorian ideology of 'separate spheres' (cf. below, MacWilliams's introduction, sections II and III). Marshall corrected the current understanding of the 'angel-of-the-hearth' role by arguing that women ought to look after their 'extended' hearth, the social environment. He suggested that in the 1830s their request to improve working conditions in factories and mines were rejected because they lacked economic education, being seen as 'well-intentioned people who know nothing of the subject with which they profess to deal' (see below, p. 94).[22] The urgency of women's university education arose from the necessity of avoiding the recurrence of similar mistakes.

It is clear from the text that Marshall's role-model was Octavia Hill (see below, pp. 119, 127 and 120; Darley, 1990, pp. 209–10). He admired her approach to the treatment of poverty through 'scientific charity', her campaigns for the preservation of the commons (Marsh, 1982, p. 39–ff.), and the way she ran the most successful Victorian scheme of working-class housing. In addition, he admired the example she personally set as an educated, energetic 'priestess of progress'. She must have been particularly inspiring to him also because she shared his Protestant sense of a civic calling, the urge 'to be of ... use in the world' (Reisman, 1990, p. 53, about Marshall's very Protestant and Evangelical servant, but applies to her employer too), a 'religious' zeal for social reform, hope in individual regeneration, and a Protestant dislike for indiscriminate almsgiving (Boyd, 1982, p. 138; cf. Hilton, 1988, pp. 81–2, 101–4).

To her true charity consisted in helping people to help themselves (Hill, 1869, p. 130). Through the COS Octavia Hill was deeply involved in a movement which wanted 'to reform the spirit not only of charities but of society' (Darley 1990, p. 116) – a 'splendid work', according to Marshall (see below, p. 121). Her emphasis on the close links between 'real charity' and 'economic science' sounded very 'Marshallian' indeed (Boyd, 1982, p. 139). She wanted middle-class men and women to get involved in a work of continuous social and moral care for the very poor (Hill, 1869, p. 222), thus elevating both their tastes and lifestyle, and, as Marshall put it, 'open[ing] up to the people noble sources of joy' (see below, p. 127).

Another affinity between the two was the fact that Hill's commitment to social reform did not lead her to adopt socialism. Indeed – again like Marshall – she became increasingly hostile to Marxist and Fabian ideas as their influence began to be felt in intellectual circles at the turn of the century. She persisted in her advocacy of local initiative and private endeavour, and maintained that 'the disciplining of our immense poor population must be effected by individual influence ... this power can change it from a mode of paupers and semi-paupers into a body of self-dependent workers' (Hill, 1869, p. 219). While she was effective in organizing private philanthropy, 'she was always suspicious of national politics and State interference. She hated bureaucracy with its inhumanity and inefficiency' (Boyd, 1982, pp. 140–1).

Civic responsibility and citizens' involvement were the solutions, and she went on 'preaching' cleanliness, independence, self-discipline and the love of beauty to the London labourers. She was convinced that self-help was the only way out of pauperism. The latter could be eradicated not by increasing living standards by action from above, but only by instilling into the poor the powerful seed of 'the dignity of independence' (Hill, 1877, p. 130); this was her version of Marshall's regenerational scheme. In due course this attitude was to have important democratic implications, for, by treating the poor as *citizens* – rather than outcasts – it led to the demand that they be made citizens in reality as well as in name (Himmelfarb, 1992, p. 205). Ultimately, although unwittingly, it opened the door to State welfare policies, by emphasizing that the poor could actually be *deserving*: if such was the case, they 'deserved' not so much private charity, but public relief, and 'as a matter of right, rather than compassion, as a legal obligation of the state' (Himmelfarb, 1992, p. 203).

Though Hill personified Marshall's 'priestess of progress', his sacerdotal metaphors did not fit her own more modest ambitions. The latter fell short of a 'priesthood' of any sort, finding a more appropriate ecclesiastical parallel in the 'diaconate'. In the church this is the position of the practical organizer and the social worker, who neither exercises the ministry of the Word, nor presides over the church assembly, but concentrates on the community's material needs. It is quite evident that 'diaconate' was what Marshall really meant by 'female priesthood' (McWilliams Tullberg, 1991, pp. 235–68).

Perhaps his choice of the latter expression was a reminiscence of the then popular Comtian terminology, or, less likely, a further testimony of the pervasive influence of Carlyle (Carlyle, 1993, pp. 133–68). Alternatively, it may have been borrowed from Harriet Taylor, whose writings Marshall may have known (cf. below, p. 156): but it is significant that she used this expression not to idealize, but to condemn what she saw as a situation incompatible with women's self-fulfilment.[23] Her point was that the 'priesthood' (and, she might have added, the 'diaconate' too) implied some form of separation from the rest of society – indeed, implied 'separate spheres'. While she and later feminists wanted to pull down the barriers which preserved such 'separation', Marshall was trying to make them more modern and functional.

And yet, within these limits his enthusiasm for the women's cause was genuine. In this sense the *Lectures to Women* not only reveal Marshall's ambivalent view of women's role in society, but are also representative of what was then, and what would long remain, a widespread attitude in British society. While Marshall emphasized that 'women had work to do *outside* the home' (McWilliams Tullberg 1991, p. 247), all what he said was compatible with both his later conservatism and the understanding (and practice) of a woman's public role as a social worker in the 1870s. Though their admission to local government in 1869 had great potential for future developments, it was originally an extension of their 'angel-of-the-hearth' activities.

It must be said that in 1873 this view of limited political emancipation and 'civic diaconate' was likely to be acceptable to a large part of Marshall's female audience, for, as Patricia Hollis has suggested (Hollis 1987, pp. 476–80), the activism of Victorian women in local government and charity organizations contrasted with their apparently less marked interest in national politics, and to this extent seemed to confirm contemporary assumptions. Nothing of what Marshall said in 1873 undermined the latter; he simply suggested that the modern, 'extended', 'angel-of-the hearth' required scientific training. As he was to explain in 1883,

> Man is the perfection of nature, but woman is one step further still. Progress in general and the abolition of poverty depend above all things on the strength, and gentleness, and purity and earnestness of the women of England. It is they who form character when it is most plastic. If the mothers of a nation are ignoble, that nation must fall; if they are noble it must rise.[24]

Significantly in the 'The future of the working classes' he referred neither to liberty nor equality of opportunity as the aim of woman's education, but simply to 'giving her free scope *womanfully* to discharge her duties to the world' (see below, p. 156, my emphasis). In other words, Marshall suggested that she should look after her 'natural' sphere of interest in a more effective and competent way.

Though arguably in 1873 this was just one of the purposes of a broader commitment to the movement for women's university education, it is significant that by 1881 Marshall had already restricted his understanding of the legitimate purpose of women's studies to the training of social workers and refined wives (McWilliams Tullberg, 1990b, pp. 217, 219). The new 'local', 'provincial', and not-too-academic universities were the institutes of higher education really suitable for gifted women, who could thus be tutored without leaving home. Home was the place for them, it was there that their 'mission' was primarily to take place. This was the 'separate sphere' in which the greatly admired Octavia Hill excelled.

Once again she provided a model for the Marshallian 'educated woman', especially because she combined commitment to social causes with 'an ideology of domesticity' (Darley 1990, p. 111), which involved the idealization of marriage and Victorian family roles. Not surprisingly, she shared Marshall's hostility to parliamentary franchise for women, reiterating, to the end of her life, the 'separate sphere' argument (Boyd, 1982, pp. 140–1). The latter formed both the cornerstone of 'anti-suffragism' (Harrison, 1978) and the main polemical target for the women's movement (Kent 1987, pp. 22, 85–6, 223–5) until their final enfranchisement in 1928.

Academia, just like Parliamentary politics, was to remain men's preserve. When considered in this light, Marshall's later resentment against woman 'competition' at Cambridge (McWilliams Tullberg, 1990, p. 222) comes as much less of a surprise. While this does not imply that already in 1873 he endorsed the restrictive view of female education he later came to express, his exhortation to social activism cannot be taken as a sign of 'advanced liberalism'. We should not forget that by 1873, for over three years, women had been sitting on important elective local councils, which were in charge of the implementation of most of contemporary social legislation (Hollis, 1987, p. 31).

Neither Marshall nor Octavia Hill were 'conservatives', except in the very general sense of the word: on the contrary, from the point of view of *economic and social* reform they were both quite 'advanced'.[25] Ambiguous as their *political* position may appear nowadays, it was not uncommon at the time. Indeed, in their basic attitudes they were 'typical' liberal-minded late Victorians: people generously committed to improving the lot of the poor by developing the potential of the existing economic and social system, while unwilling or unable to accept the agenda of *political* radicalism.

It would be unfair to charge them with hypocrisy because they were not 'feminists' and were later to become anti-suffragists. There is evidence to suggest that throughout their lives they were remarkably consistent both in supporting a certain degree of women's emancipation, and in resisting what they saw as an excessive and inappropriate extension of their presence into the sphere of public life. In the 1870s both Marshall and Hill were progressive enough to set an example for the generation which was then being educated, and moderate enough to be persuasive.

Their understanding of woman's role in society and politics lost credibility only when the distinction between the local-government 'diaconate' and the parliamentary 'priesthood' was made obsolete by the growth of State intervention and by changes in the political climate. For 'as the responsibilities of central government expanded in the field of social welfare up to 1914, the argument that the municipal and the national represented two separate spheres grew implausible'; and consequently 'the notion that women could participate in one but were fundamentally unsuited for the other became practically untenable' (Pugh, 1980, p. 13; cf. Pugh, 1993, pp. 1–42). During the same period the Tariff Reform campaigns meant that economic and social issues again became, for the first time since 1846, hot questions in national *politics* – and questions about which most women felt they had something to say. Marshall's economic ideas had shaken Mill's heritage. However, as far as the implementation of social reform was concerned, his trust in evolutionary economic progress did not survive the test of the new century. His analytical and theoretical contribution had to be supplemented by a Millite political activism in order to become effective: and it was Mill's 'Chartist option' which carried the day in 1905 as in 1910.

Notes and References

1. In this introduction I have used 'Liberal', with a capital initial, when referring to policies and people formally associated with the Liberal party; and 'liberal' with a small initial when meaning the more broadly defined attitudes associated with free market economics, social reform, and equality of civil rights. Similar criteria have been applied to other political terminology, such as 'Radical' and 'Conservative'.
2. Himmelfarb has suggested that 'Marshall's economics appears a corollary of Green's positive liberalism – and as a practical alternative to socialism' (p. 303).
3. Cf. his reply to the Secretary of the Unionist Free Trade League ('Free trade a vital necessity for England', 23 Nov. 1904, in Marshall Papers, Newcsuttings Volume, f. 170): 'I have ever acted on the principle that academic economists should avoid joining leagues, and should not belong to political parties'; as for his own support for free trade, this was purely the outcome of thirty years of economic inquiry – a 'scientific', rather than a political, conviction.
4. Though arbitration was not discussed in the *Lectures*, Marshall's reading list included Thomas Brassey's *On Work and Wages* (1872), then the sacred text of industrial arbitrators.
5. Cf. G. Howell, 'Technical education', MS, n.d., in Howell Collection (Bishopsgate Institute, London), *Letter Books*, 880; and [leading article], 'Lord Shaftesbury's scholars', *Lloyd's Weekly*, 19 Nov. 1871, p. 6. More generally see W. P. McCann, 1970.
6. Letter by the shoemaker Edwin Hiley, in *Leeds Mercury*, 26 Jan. 1869, p. 7. On the same theme see also Adams, 1875, p. 250; and Chamberlain, 1877, p. 72.
7. W. E. Forster – the Liberal minister of education – declared in 1870: 'I am not one of those ... who say that knowledge is virtue; but this I do say, that ignorance is weakness; and, as weakness to resist temptation fills our prisons, so weakness for the struggle of life fills our workhouses' ('The Government Policy in Education', *Bee-Hive*, 22 Jan. 1870, p. 4).
8. Indeed, from the 1830s national education had been supported by the Whigs as well as some high-Tory reformers: Mandler, 1990, p. 182.
9. For Toynbee motivations see Himmelfarb, 1992, p. 278. Marshall's theoretical attitude was different: McWilliams Tullberg, 1990a, pp. 85–6.

Indeed, from a purely theoretical point of view Marshall 'sanction[ed] radical land reform in the future': Paul 1979, p. 266.

10. For Marshall's motivations see Raffaelli's introduction, above, p. 6. Cf. also 'Lectures on progress and poverty', Lect. 3 (6 Mar. 1883), 23–4, in *Marshall Papers, Newspaper Cuttings*. Cf. 'The radical view of the land question' in 'Press reports on "Progress and poverty", Bristol, 1883' (*Marshall Papers*, 3/5 [5.1.g], now in Wood, 1982). The speaker, one Henry Rogers, on behalf of the Irish tenant farmers, advocated some sort of land nationalization reminiscent of Mill's 1868 proposals.
11. Though, on the theme of foreign policy, Marshall's 1873 denunciation of 'perverted patriotism' has a certain Gladstonian flavour: see below, *Lectures*, Lecture IV, p. 144 and footnote 15.
12. See below p. 171.
13. See note 1 to 'The future of the working classes'.
14. *E.g.* in the case of the Third Republic in France: Thompson, 1949, pp. 144–7.
15. It must be said that, though this view was increasingly old-fashioned by the mid–1870s, as late as 1869 it had been endorsed even by Mill and Fawcett, whose argument Marshall reproduced in the *Lectures*: see J. S. Mill to H. Fawcett, 24 Oct. 1869, in Mill, 1869, p. 1658.
16. Cf. *Lectures*, Lecture VI, below p. 126. For the strong links between Protestantism and the Liberalism of many intellectuals – especially historians – see Burrow, 1991.
17. See below, p. 126. In the 'Lectures on the method and history of economics', p. 26, in *Marshall Papers* 3/ (formerly 5.1.f) – now in Marshall, 1990 –, Marshall complained of 'the utter absence of the sense of duty' among the Chinese.
18. Cf. the Bristol lecture on 'The economic conditions of America', from *The Western Daily Press*, 15 Jan. 1878, in Marshall Papers, 3/5): 'Almost all the wanton outrage and destruction of property was committed by the scum of the large cities, who consist, almost exclusively, of Irishmen and Roman Catholic Germans.'
19. Italian Liberals, for instance, were deeply concerned about participation, self-government and 'civic virtue': Romanelli, 1983, pp. 35–84; Urbinati, 1990, pp. 26–33.
20. See below, p. 115.
21. Though not without reservations: cf. above, Raffaelli's introduction, p. 6. Yet, as late as 1893 Marshall recommended the selective and 'personalized' approach to the relief of old-age people proposed by the COS – suggesting that the COS itself 'should be semi-established' to manage the system – in preference to any of the pensions-for-all schemes then debated: see his printed memo *The Aged Poor*, 5 June 1893, p. 4, in *Marshall Papers*, Newscuttings Volume.
22. Marshall refers to debates which are supposed to have taken place at family level between employers and their wives and daughters. He does not specify his source, but it is not otherwise evident that women played any significant role in the early movement for factory legislation.
23. She once declared: 'What is wanted for women is equal rights, equal admission to all social privileges; not a position apart, a sort of sentimental

priesthood.' Cit. in Kent, 1987, p. 191.

24. 'Lectures on Progress and Poverty', Lect. 3 (6 Mar. 1883), pp. 23–4, in *Marshall Papers, Newspaper Cuttings*: reprinted in Wood, 1982.
25. It should not be forgotten that in the 1900s Marshall supported Lloyd George's social reforms: Paul, 1979, p. 267.

Bibliography

Adams F. (1875), *The Free Schools of the United States*, London.

Applegarth R. (1869), *Annual Report of the Amalgamated Society of Carpenters and Joiners*, London

Bebbington D. W. (1981), *The Nonconformist Conscience. Chapel and Politics, 1870–1914*, London: G. Allen and Unwin.

Becattini G. (1991), 'Market and communism in the thought of Alfred Marshall', *Quaderni di Storia dell'Economia Politica*, 9, pp. 161–88.

Biagini E. F. (1987), 'British Trade Unions and popular political economy, 1860–1880', *Historical Journal*, vol. 30, pp. 811–40.

Biagini E. F. (1991), 'Marshall's 1873 "Lectures to Women" ', *Quaderni di Storia dell'Economia Politica*, vol. 9, pp. 335–54.

Biagini E. F. (1992), *Liberty, Retrenchment and Reform. Popular Liberalism in the Age of Gladstone, 1860–1880*, Cambridge: Cambridge University Press.

Biagini E. F. (1996), 'Liberalism and Direct Democracy. J. S. Mill and the Model of Ancient Athens', in E. F. Biagini (ed.), *Citizenship and Community. Liberals, Radicals and Collective Identity in the British Isles 1865–1931*, Cambridge: Cambridge University Press.

Boyd N. (1982), *Josephine Butler, Octavia Hill and Florence Nightingale*, London: Macmillan.

Briggs A. (1990), *Victorian People*, Harmondsworth (Middlesex): Penguin Books, (first ed. 1955).

Burrow J. W. (1981), *A Liberal Descent. Victorian Historians and the English Past*, Cambridge: Cambridge University Press.

Burt T. (1924), *An Autobiography*, London, T. Fisher & Unwin.

Carlyle T. (1993), *On Heroes, Hero-Worship, & the Heroic in History*, The Norman and Charlotte Strouse Edition of the Works of Thomas Carlyle; introduction and notes by M. K. Goldberg, J. B. Brattin and M. Engel; Berkeley, Los Angeles and Oxford: University of California Press.

Chamberlain J. (1877), 'Free Schools', *Fortnightly Review*, vol. 21, pp. 54–72.

Coats A. W. (1990), 'Marshall and ethics', in R. McWilliams Tullberg (ed.), *Marshall in Retrospect*, Aldershot (Hants.): E. Elgar.

Cobden R. (1870), *Speeches by Richard Cobden*, ed. by J. Bright and J. Thorold Rogers, vol.II, London.

Collini S. (1985), 'The idea of "character", in Victorian political thought', *Transactions of the Royal Historical Society*, London: The Royal Historical Society, pp. 29–50.

Collini S. (1991), *Public Moralists. Political Thought and Intellectual Life in Britain 1850–1930*, Oxford: Clarendon Press.

Darley G. (1990), *Octavia Hill*, London: Constable.

Dunning T. J. (1860), *Trades Unions and Strikes. Their Philosophy and Intentions*, London.

Fawcett H. (1860), 'Strikes. Their tendencies and remedies', *Westminster Review*, n.s., vol. 18, pp. 1–23.

Fawcett H. (1871), *Pauperism: Its Causes and Remedies*, London, Macmillan & Co.

Fawcett H. (1876), *Manual of Political Economy*, London, Macmillan & Co., (first edn 1863).

Gardner P. (1984), *The Lost Elementary Schools of Victorian England. The People's Education*, London: Croom Helm.

Halliday R. J. (1976), *John Stuart Mill*, London: G. Allen and Unwin.

Harrison B. (1978), *Separate Spheres. The Opposition to Women Suffrage in Britain*, New York: Holmes and Meier.

Harrison R. (1982), [introduction to] 'Two early articles by Alfred Marshall', in *Alfred Marshall Critical Assessments*, ed. by J. C.Wood, vol. 4, London: Croom Helm.

Harvie C. (1976), *The Lights of Liberalism. University Liberals and the Challenge of Democracy, 1860–1886*, London: Allen Lane.

Hill O. (1869), 'Organized work among the poor; suggestions founded on four years' management of a London court', *MacMillan's Magazine*, vol. 20, pp. 219–26.

Hill O. (1877), 'A more excellent way of charity', *MacMillan's Magazine*, vol. 35, pp. 126–31.

Hilton B. (1988), *The Age of Atonement*, Oxford: Clarendon Press.

Himmelfarb G. (1992), *Poverty and Compassion. The Moral Imagination of the Late Victorians*, New York: Vintage Books.

Hollis P. (1987), *Ladies Elect. Women in Local Government, 1865–1914*, Oxford: Clarendon Press.

Hutchison T. W. (1969), 'Economists and economic policy in Britain after 1870', *History of Political Economy*, vol. 1, pp. 231–55.

Jenkins T. A. (1984), 'Gladstone, the Whigs and the leadership of the Liberal Party', *The Historical Journal*, vol. 27, pp. 337–60.

Jones D. K. (1977), 'Socialization and social science: Manchester model secular school 1854–1861', in P. McCann (ed.), *Popular Education and Socialization in the Nineteenth Century*, London: Methuen & Co.

Kent S. K. (1987), *Sex and Suffrage in Britain 1860–1914*, Princeton: Princeton University Press.

Lasch C. (1991), *The True and Only Heaven. Progress and Its Critics*, New York and London: Norton.

McCann W. P. (1970), 'Trade unionists, artisans and the 1870 Education Act', *British Journal of Educational Studies*, vol. 18, pp. 138–41.

Machin G. I. T. (1987), *Politics and the Churches in Great Britain 1869–1921*, Oxford: Clarendon Press.

MacIntyre A. (1981), *After Virtue*, Notre Dame: University of Notre Dame Press.

McWilliams Tullberg R. (1990a), 'Marshall's "tendency to socialism" ', *History of Political Economy*, vol. 7, pp. 75–111.

McWilliams Tullberg R. (1990b), 'Alfred Marshall and the "Woman question" at Cambridge', *Économie Appliquée*, vol. 43, pp. 209–30.

McWilliams Tullberg R (1991), 'Alfred Marshall and the male priesthood of economics', *Quaderni di Storia dell'Economia Politica*, vol. 9, pp. 235–68.

Mandler P. (1990), *Aristocratic Government in the Age of Reform. Whigs and Liberals 1830–1852*, Oxford: Clarendon Press.

Marsh J. (1982), *Back to the Land. The Pastoral Impulse in England from 1880 to 1914*, London and New York: Quartet Books

Marshall A. (1990), *On the Methods and History of Economics*, ed by P. D. Groenewegen, Sydney: The University of Sydney.

Mason, J. W. (1974), 'Thomas Mackay: the anti-socialist philosophy of the Charity Organization Society', in K. D. Brown (ed.), *Essays in Anti-Labour History. Responses to the Rise of Labour in Britain*, London: Macmillan 1974.

Mill J. S. (1862), *Principles of Political Economy*, (1862 edition), in *Collected Works of John Stuart Mill*, vols. 2 and 3, ed. by V. W. Bladen and J. M. Robson, London and Toronto: University of Toronto Press, 1965.

Mill J. S. (1869), *Collected Works of John Stuart Mill*, vol. 18, 4, *Later Letters*, ed. by A. R. Robson and J. M. Robson, London and Toronto: University of Toronto Press, 1972.

Parry J. P. (1986), *Democracy & Religion*, Cambridge: Cambridge University Press.

Paul E. F. (1979), *Moral Revolution and Economic Science. The Demise of Laissez-Faire in Nineteenth-Century British Political Economy*, Westport (Conn.) and London: Greenwood Press.

Potter G. (1870), 'Conciliation and arbitration', *Contemporary Review*, vol. 15, pp. 550–61.

Pugh M. (1980), *Women's Suffrage in Britain 1867–1928*, London: The Royal Historical Society.

Pugh M. (1993), *Women and Women's Movement in Britain 1914–1959*, London: MacMillan.

Raffaelli T. (1990), 'Gli studi filosofici del giovane Marshall', *Atti Accademia Nazionale dei Lincei, Rendiconti Classe di Scienze Morali*, serie 9, vol. 1, pp. 121–60.

Reid A. J. (1991), 'Old Unionism reconsidered: the case of Robert Knight', in E. F. Biagini and A. J. Reid (eds), *Currents of Radicalism. Popular Radicalism, Organized Labour and Party Politics in Britain 1850–1914*, Cambridge: Cambridge University Press, 1991.

Reisman A. D. (1990), *Alfred Marshall's Mission*, London: Macmillan.

Roberts B. C. (1958), *The Trades Union Congress 1868–1921*, London: G. Allen & Unwin.

Romanelli R. (1983), 'Autogoverno, funzioni pubbliche e classi dirigenti locali', *Passato e Presente*, 4, 1983, pp. 35–84.

Smith P. (1967), *Disraelian Conservatism and Social Reform*, London: Routledge & Kegan Paul.

Spain J. (1991), 'Trade unionists, gladstonian liberals and the Labour Law Reform of 1875', in E. F. Biagini and A. J. Reid (eds), *Currents of Radicalism. Popular Radicalism, Organized Labour and Party Politics in Britain 1850–1914*, Cambridge: Cambridge University Press

Stedman Jones G. (1983), 'Rethinking Chartism', in *Languages of Class*, Cambridge: Cambridge University Press, pp. 90–178.

Stedman Jones G. (1984), *Outcast London. A Study in the Relationship Between Classes in Victorian Society*, London: Penguin.

Tholfsen T. (1976), *Working-Class Radicalism in Mid-Victorian England*, London: Croom Helm.

Thompson D. (1949), *Democracy in France since 1870*, London: Oxford University Press.

Urbinati N. (1990), *Le civili libertà*, Venezia: Marsilio.

West E. G. (1964), 'The role of education in nineteenth century doctrines of political economy', *British Journal of Educational Studies*, vol. 12, pp. 161–5.

Wood J. C. (1982), *Alfred Marshall: Critical Assessments*, London: Croom Helm, four volumes.

3. Marshall's contribution to the women's higher education movement

Rita McWilliams Tullberg

I. Introduction

The lecture notes published here for the first time were taken down by Mary Paley at a series of six lectures given by Alfred Marshall in April and May 1873 within the framework of the Lectures for Women in Cambridge scheme of which Marshall had been a founder member. Advertised in the University *Reporter* for 22 April 1873, Marshall's lecture series was intended as an introduction to Political Economy for women students:

> These Lectures will be introductory to a systematic course on Political Economy which will be commenced in October; but they will also be adapted to the wants of those who do not propose to make a special study of Political Economy. No papers will be set in connexion with this course: no fees will be charged to those who attend it. (*Reporter*, 22 April 1873)

The lectures should therefore not be confused with the teaching Marshall gave women students in preparation for the Political Economy paper in Group D of the Higher Local Examinations nor his coaching for the Political Economy papers in the Moral Science Tripos. In both those cases, Marshall was bound to some extent by the requirements of a syllabus and lists of recommended reading matter.

In his introductory lectures, Marshall was free to interpret the topic of Political Economy as he saw fit and to adapt the subject-matter to his audience of women of varying educational backgrounds, many of whom did not intend to take up formal study of the subject. This accounts for the non-technical, general-interest nature of the lectures.[1]

Marshall seems to have had two goals in mind when preparing his lectures. First, he wanted to convey what he felt middle-class women in general ought to know about the relevance of economics studies to an understanding of society's ills and to the possibilities of social progress and industrial peace:

> The main purport of these lectures is not to urge Economic studies, but rather to defend the position which philanthropists are adopting. ... I want to come to the main proposition which is this, that if a philanthropist gives himself intelligently to the work of raising the working classes, the conclusions he will come to will be the same as those arrived at by P[olitical] E[conomy]. (Lecture V, p. 117)

Since his listeners were drawn from the middle-classes, he proposed to illustrate social problems from the point of view of the working-classes; he explained that had he been talking to working-men, he would have emphasised the claims of capital and dangers of union power (Lecture I, p. 90). Second, he wanted to inspire women with a bold vision of what they could contribute to society, to urge on them the importance of purposeful study as a preparation for this work and to convince them that they could rightly place their obligations to society above many of the duties which contemporary opinion felt they must perform for their families.

The strange sight of Marshall addressing an audience of middle-class women in the male and almost totally celibate Cambridge of the 1870s needs to be explained, both in the light of the University's general disregard for the education of women at this time and Marshall's own ambivalent attitude to the issue of women's higher education.

II. Background

Throughout the 19th century, changing social, religious and economic pressures dictated a number of different modes of approved behaviour which shaped the lives of middle-class women.[2] Among urban, middle-class families of the industrial age, the number of idle women supported by a man had become a status symbol. Such women were generally regarded as physically, intellectually and morally-enfeebled humans in need of the guidance and protection that could only be supplied by husbands or male relatives. Their lives were dominated by the need to make a 'good' match; consequently, they had to develop talents which would be valued in the marriage market and result in their 'sale' to a suitably rich and well-placed male. For a time it seemed as if an attractive appearance and a supply of drawing-room accomplishments was all that a woman needed.[3]

However, the spiritual and moral renewal which swept the Church of England in the early decades of the century (and which was fundamental to the Non-Conformist churches) helped to create a new role for middle-class women. The new Victorian woman was to be a creature of modesty and piety, absolutely pure and unworldly. Her innocence was to be guaranteed by her ignorance, thereby assuring that this 'Angel of the Hearth' would create a haven of peace, a home for her husband and children, unstained by the evils and worries of the outside world. This vocational ideal was championed by some of the artistic and literary figures of the day who felt revulsion for the ugliness, aggressiveness and vulgarity of the industrial revolution. Positivists of the Comtist persuasion, saw women as domestic goddesses.[4]

In the second half of the century, awareness grew within the Established Church of the temporal as well as the spiritual needs of the 'lower-classes' and solutions to the problems of poverty began to be sought beyond the traditional one of personal acts of charity. The duty of the middle-classes to guide those they considered not only economically but also morally less fortunate than themselves was preached from the pulpits, in the Public Schools and at Oxford and Cambridge. Those too, for whom biblical reinterpretation, theological reformulation and the mid-century revelations of Darwin had resulted in a loss of faith, found they could ease their wandering spirits with secular good works. Yet earnest men felt helpless when faced with the formidable social problems of bad housing, malnutrition and disease that characterised the domestic lives of the poor, together with the perceived problem of their moral turpitude. Many felt, and Marshall was one of these, that the call to duty encompassed both men and women, and that middle-class women had a clear role to play in helping the poor overcome at least their practical difficulties.[5] This was clearly at odds with the doctrine of the 'Angel of the Hearth'; a middle-class woman regularly witnessing dirt and despair in the homes of the poor, as well as open prostitution, drunkenness, wife beating and child abuse, found it difficult to accept the role of innocence and ignorance thrust on her within the confines of her home. Women and their supporters therefore accepted the need for some degree of education and training to fit women for their new role in society.

A third and perhaps most significant pressure, that of economic necessity, combined with these religious and social demands to inspire the movement for improved education for middle-class women. The number of unmarried middle-class women was high for a variety of demographic and economic reasons. In the large, Victorian family, death, illness or failed investments could often leave a woman and her daughters with little or no means of support. Unmarried men placed in such a situation might choose to leave the district or emigrate, looking for opportunities elsewhere and shunning the expense of marriage. Social pressures did not permit such mobility for women,[6] and their middle-class status ruled out all forms of work except teaching. They found themselves obliged to open their own school, if they had any capital, or seek employment as an assistant teacher or governess. Such women were unwilling teachers, unprepared and ill-equipped to take on pupils. Their working conditions were often abysmal and their pay at or below subsistence levels.

In 1841, a Governesses' Benevolent Institution was founded in London 'to afford assistance privately and delicately to ladies in temporary distress'. From the pathetic case histories which poured in from applicants for grants, it became clear that the major cause of their low status and pay was their incompetence. These women needed to raise their own educational levels and acquire pedagogical skills, not waiting until teaching was forced on them by family tragedy but earlier, when they themselves were schoolgirls and young women. Schemes for the improvement of girls' secondary education sprang up and through the work of many dedicated volunteers, both men and women, within such bodies as the Royal Commission on Secondary Education 1864–67 (the Taunton Commission), Queen's and Bedford Colleges, London, the Girls' Public Day School Company (later Trust) and the High School movement, a massive improvement in educational standards for a great many girls of middle-class families was achieved. A major part was played in the setting of recognised standards in girls' secondary schools by the opening to them of public examinations run by the universities and originally intended for the exclusive use of schoolboys. Cambridge took the lead in agreeing to accept schoolgirls as examination candidates in 1865 (McWilliams Tullberg, 1975, chapters 2–4).[7]

It was also appreciated that women needed training beyond school standard if they were to become proficient professionals. Pressure built up from a number of directions for women to be given access to tertiary education. One prominent case was that of Elizabeth Garrett

(Anderson) who, with the support of Emily Davies and others, sought to qualify as a doctor. From the difficulties which Garrett encountered, Davies concluded that women should have the same rights as men to university examinations, degrees and membership. She had supporters within the National Association for the Promotion of Social Science, a radical organisation which welcomed women into its membership, founded in 1857 by her brother, among others.

Initially Davies directed her efforts towards London University but their reply was to offer examinations 'specially adapted' for women. Davies and her supporters firmly rejected such 'women's examinations' as a method of trapping women in inferior forms of education offering second-rate qualifications. With an unerring instinct for quality, she drew up a plan for a residential college for women, modelled on Trinity College, Cambridge, where women would be educated to degree standard. Ideally, the college would be 'a dependency, a living branch of Cambridge [University]' although for reasons of propriety it was not to be located in the town. In 1869 she opened her college for women in a rented house in Hitchin, about 45 kilometres south of Cambridge, and persuaded her supporters among the Cambridge Fellows to make the train journey out to the college to teach five young women in the subjects of the University's preliminary and degree examinations. No allowances were made for the gaps in the women students' elementary and secondary education, nor for the inadequacies of the examination syllabuses which at that time were being questioned and criticised by a number of reform-minded dons.[8] When asked by Davies if the women students could make use of the University's examination papers, the answer was that while no official permission would be given, the University did not object to a private arrangement being made with examiners. In 1872/73, two women were, unofficially, successful in the Classical Tripos and one in the Mathematics Tripos. The college was moved to Girton, five kilometres from Cambridge, in 1873 and Davies continued to develop her educational ideal of offering women a university education under identical conditions with men.

Meanwhile in Liverpool, Anne Jemima Clough was seeking to organise lectures for senior girls and their teachers drawn from a number of schools in a district.[9] A scheme was conceived covering a number of the major northern industrial towns and employing an itinerant lecturer to give lectures to large groups of women. Anne Clough contacted Henry Sidgwick at Cambridge for suggestions as to whom the job should be offered.[10]

The success of these lectures led to the formation of the North of England Council for Promoting the Higher Education of Women, with responsibility for the organisation of lectures in the major northern towns. At its first meeting in November 1867, the Council members 'expressed sympathy' for Emily Davies' proposed College for Women but devoted their attention chiefly to two objectives: the institution of lectures on literary, historical and scientific subjects; and, the promotion of an examination for women over eighteen at a level higher than that of the Cambridge Local Examinations, which had recently been opened to schoolgirls, 'with the intention of setting up a carefully chosen standard to be aimed at in their education, and with the further purpose of improving the training of teachers' (*Oxford University Gazette*, August 1895). Unlike Emily Davies, this group of women felt that they were not yet ready to attempt honours degrees, while their Cambridge advisors strongly disapproved of the low standard of the University's Pass degree and did not want to see it used by women as a stepping-stone to higher education. Initially a private examination board consisting of men from both Oxford and Cambridge was planned, which would run examinations for governesses and schoolmistresses. However, the North of England Council successfully petitioned Cambridge University to undertake examinations testing the higher education of women. The plan was approved in October 1868 with very little opposition. The first Higher Local Examinations for Women over eighteen years were administered in 1869.[11] In May 1869, Marshall was appointed examiner for the Political Economy paper of Group D (Moral Sciences) that year (Rough Minutes Book, p. 59, LES 1, Cambridge University Archives).[12] Encouraged by her father, Mary Paley decided to study for these 'Higher Locals', to relieve the boredom created by the disappearance of her fiancé to India on a three-year tour of military duty and by the marriage of her sister. Taking different groups of subjects in 1870 and 1871, she received distinctions in both Divinity and German.

III. Marshall's Early Involvement in the Women's Education Movement

Although Marshall was certainly familiar with what became the 'Girton model' of women's education at Cambridge, there is no evidence to suggest that he took an active part in Emily Davies's scheme. His own interest in higher education for women was most probably roused by his association with Henry Sidgwick and through membership of the Grote Club, a gathering of mainly young reformist dons who met to discuss speculative and social questions.[13] Henry Sidgwick, who was four years Marshall's senior, was at this time active in a number of schemes for educational reform involving not only the education offered at the University itself but the role it played in shaping secondary school education and its capacity to provide tertiary education in the new industrial centres. He sought higher standards of teaching and scholarship in the Cambridge Colleges, the abolition of the Previous Examination and the Pass degree, which he held were of dubious educational merit, and a modernisation of Tripos subjects. For a number of years, Marshall clearly acted as a willing lieutenant in Sidgwick's reform campaigns.[14]

The Higher Local examinations proved very popular but they also highlighted the need for teaching for women beyond school level. Lecture schemes were started in a number of towns and calls were made for the universities to provide lecturers. Clearly, lectures given in Cambridge itself could make good use of the ready supply of underemployed College Fellows. Following a private gathering held in the home of Henry Fawcett, Professor of Political Economy (his wife, Millicent was the sister of Elizabeth Garret who had sought medical qualifications),[15] a meeting was held in January 1870 to form a General Committee of Management of the Lectures for Women in Cambridge. The committee included Alfred Marshall and a number of other Grote Club members: F. D. Maurice, W. K. Clifford, J. B. Mayor, J. F. Moulton and J. Venn. Sidgwick was one of the Committee's two Secretaries.[16]

A circular was issued with the first syllabus of lectures outlining the purpose of the lectures:

> For some time past, a great and growing desire had been felt and expressed in many quarters for some improvement and extension of the Education of Women.
>
> To meet this demand, several schemes have been organised in London, Edinburgh and other towns of the United Kingdom: schemes differing widely in detail, but all having in view the same subject.
>
> These schemes have proved more or less successful: and progress and experiment are still being made in the same direction. It has seemed to many persons resident in Cambridge, that this town offers exceptional facilities for

> an attempt of this kind since it contains a large number of trained and practised teachers, who are willing to extend the sphere of their instruction. Such persons delivering Lectures in the special subjects with which they are familiar, may supply fully any demand that exists among Women for higher education: while, owing to the small amount of preparation that such lectures will involve, the fee charged may be low, and yet not unremunerative. Again, the present juncture seems a favourable one for the experiment as the University has recently instituted an examination for women in various subjects, and it appears natural and desirable that members of the University should offer instruction on the same subjects to all who may be disposed to avail themselves of it. Accordingly a Committee has been formed of resident members of the University engaged in education, who have adopted the following scheme of arrangements for lectures. (Text of circular copied into the North Hall Diary, Newnham College Archives)

The first lectures were given in February 1870 and at the end of that Lent Term, the committee was able to report that:

> The success of these lectures during the present term has equalled the most sanguine expectations of the originators of the scheme. Between seventy and eighty ladies are now attending eight courses of lectures, the number of attendances [counting each lecture separately] being in all 115. The Committee feel themselves now in a position to announce that the lectures will be continued permanently during term-time. (ibid.)

Under the scheme, Marshall lectured three times a year from Lent 1870 until Lent 1875 with the exception of Lent 1873.[17]

By January 1871, the scheme was such an obvious success that the committee confidently published a lecture list for the following two terms. As a result, students came to reside in Cambridge, living in private homes, for the purpose of attending lectures. That same year, Mary Paley was awarded a scholarship on the results of her efforts in the Higher Local Examination for Women. A condition of the scholarship was that she should come to Cambridge to attend lectures given under the Lectures for Women scheme. The existence of this scholarship, awarded as it was on the *results* of the Higher Local examinations, suggests a certain ambivalence on the part of some of the organisers of the lecture scheme. What exactly was the purpose of bringing women to Cambridge who had already proved themselves in the Higher Locals, the only post secondary-school examinations open to them at that time? With the benefit of hindsight, Millicent Fawcett claimed that there was indeed a 'hidden agenda', a plan to found a college for women in Cambridge. However, it seems the plans were more *ad hoc*; a few women, like Mary Paley, were initially invited to Cambridge to broaden their knowledge by following lectures for other groups of subjects within the Higher Local examination scheme. Five young women came 'into residence' in Cambridge in October 1871 in a house rented and furnished by Sidgwick and watched over by Anne Clough. One, Mary Kennedy, a talented woman four years older than Mary Paley, had boarded in the town with a private family and had already followed the lectures for two terms. She became Mary Paley's close friend and responsible for turning her interests towards economics:

> When I first arrived, I attended lectures for 'general cultivation', such as Latin, literature and history etc., but [Mary Kennedy] insisted on my going with her to a Political Economy lecture.[18] I said that I knew all about it, for it had only to do with wages, etc. which everyone understood. However, she was determined so I went, and went to stay. (Marshall, M. P., 1940, p. 50)

The two young women studied the Moral Science subjects for Group D of the Higher Local Examinations in 1872, passed with a First Class and divided the Group D exhibition and Alfred Marshall's essay prize between them. Mary Paley had gained distinctions in Logic and Political Economy.[19]

It was Marshall who then took the scheme a significant stage further and introduced the idea of Tripos examinations to the women. Although thoroughly familiar with the basic aim of the women's supporters to raise, broaden and test the academic accomplishments of women teachers and prospective teachers as quickly and cheaply as possible, Marshall realised that some students already had such educational backgrounds, intellectual talent and the necessary financial resources to be able to benefit from the in-depth study of a few subjects as required by the Tripos syllabuses. The idea was not a new one, three students at Emily Davies' college having already been informally successful in the Cambridge Mathematical and Classical Triposes. Davies regarded this as 'proof' of their academic equality with men and Marshall was quite certainly aware of the symbolism involved in a Tripos triumph. As their lecturer in Political Economy, Marshall persuaded his two best women students, Mary Paley and Mary Kennedy, to study for the Moral Sciences Tripos, at that time the degree examination which included papers in Political Economy:

> One day Alfred Marshall ... stopped Mary Paley and me in the street and asked us if we had ever thought of working for a Tripos examination. He explained that this would mean at least three years' study, specializing in one or two subjects. We accepted the challenge lightly, not realizing what we were undertaking. Mary and I decided on the Moral Science Tripos for which we

> were devotedly coached by Henry Sidgwick and Alfred Marshall. (Phillips, 1988, p. 3)

Mary Paley sat her Tripos examinations, on an informal basis, in December 1874 (examinations were taken after ten terms at that time). The Tripos examiners, Herbert Foxwell, W. S. Jevons, P. G. Gardiner, and J. B. Pearson, who had all been persuaded to look over her papers, were unable to agree whether to place her in the First or Second Class and, in the absence of a chairman to cast a deciding vote, she was 'left hanging between heaven and hell' (Marshall, M. P., 1947, p. 17).

It is important to emphasise the part Marshall played in raising the academic aspirations of the women and their supporters. In her memoirs, Mary Paley Marshall reminisced that she and her fellow students had no 'coaching or supervision' for the Tripos (M. P. Marshall, 1947, p. 17, although on the previous page she mentions the 'immense deal of trouble' Sidgwick took in coaching them). This recollection is not correct as far as Political Economy is concerned; records in Newnham College clearly demonstrate that 'advanced courses' were given, among them courses in economics. In June 1874, the Association for the Promotion of the Higher Education for Women reported that advanced classes had been fairly small, except for Political Economy (Report presented at the Annual Meeting, 11 June 1874) and the following year the Association informed its members that 'a certain quantity of private instruction has been given to advanced students, whose requirements were not sufficiently met by the lectures'. This coaching was subsidised by the Association, so that the students did not have to pay more than three guineas[20] (Report presented at Annual Meeting, 30 October 1875). Rather ambiguously, the Committee felt the money was well spent *on account of the great importance of developing advanced studies*, but did not intend to encourage the practice of private tuition. Three advanced students had been successful in the Tripos, two in Moral Sciences and one in Classics and Mathematics (Report presented at Annual Meeting, 30 October 1875).

When coaching women for the Moral Sciences Tripos,[21] Marshall probably prepared the women as he did his students at St John's College. Few students came to Cambridge at that time with any knowledge of economics and, in this respect, there would be little difference between the male and female Moral Sciences students. Women students, however, generally lacked experience in regular study and examinations. Mary Paley and Mary Kennedy had remedied this by tackling the Moral Sciences papers of the Higher Local Examinations during their first years at college; this possibly put them ahead of their male contemporaries who had had to study for the Previous examination.[22] It is known that Marshall as their Tripos coach in economics taught them his 'curves'. Mary Paley in her obituary of Mary Kennedy remembered the following incident:

> There was the incident of the blackboard, which seemed to Mary [Kennedy] and me to have got too old and greasy for all the complicated economic curves. So we put our money together and bought a large handsome one. However, it refused to let the curves be rubbed out and was ignominiously set aside for the old one. What an impression those curves must have made on her; for only a few days before she died she wrote me a long letter on some fallacy in the subject which they illustrated and which I had quite forgotten. (M. P. Marshall, 1940)

In 1873, in order to attract women to the study of economics in Section D of the Higher Locals or in the Moral Sciences Tripos, Marshall gave a series of introductory lectures on the subject. He wanted to demonstrate that there was an important role for women to play outside the home, but to fill their new function properly, they needed to study. Many women, perhaps attending Cambridge lectures without the whole-hearted support of their parents, needed reassurance.[23] He encouraged them to ignore the constraints placed on them by their families and to overcome their own feelings of guilt. Women must stop 'tatting their tatting and twirling their thumbs' (Lecture V, p. 119); they must work as 'Miss [Octavia] Hill works or as teachers in schools, or in private – but not in general contented with a few hours wastefully spent over their near relations' (Lecture Outline VI, p. 153).[24] This might seem immoral: 'I am aware that there is this paradox "I ought to do what is wrong". Sometimes (such is our social education) it is not thought unreasonable that a person should prevent others from doing important work' (Lecture V, p. 120; see also Marshall's lecture outlines, Lecture IV, p. 144 and Lecture V, p. 148). Above all, they must not drift but must attain 'knowledge of what difficulties there are to be overcome and of how to overcome them; this can seldom be done without study, and can always be done most rapidly by its help' (Lecture VI, p. 128).

This was a giant step for many of them to take – and in this sense, the tone of Marshall's 'Lectures for Women' were far more radical and inflammatory than his plea, delivered in 'The future of the working-classes' to the Cambridge Reform Club, that its members should be aware of the poverty of the poor and their potential for improvement. His message in the *Lectures* was that women had a duty to work outside the home and that they could and should train themselves for such tasks. It is not surprising that their new roles should initially be seen as an extension of their domestic role as 'carers', assisting the work of men. There was, at that time, no question of women taking men's jobs as clergymen, lawyers, politicians, business leaders etc., and more than ordinary vision and optimism would have been required to see them in such positions.[25] Yet in the one profession where women had already challenged the male monopoly – medicine – Marshall supported them. Discussing the prevalence of restrictive practices – 'actions in limitation of trade' – in all classes of society Marshall wrote:

> Those ... who condemn most fiercely the refusal of a workman to teach many apprentices are those among whom are to be found the most ardent supporters of the doctrine that medical men 'have a right' to exclude women from their profession. (Article in the *Bee-Hive*, 2 May 1874, below, p. 191)[26]

The continued success of the Cambridge lectures meant that pressure for more residential accommodation grew, as did the need to develop a programme of studies for women who had already passed the Higher Local Examinations. These problems were taken in hand by the Association for Promotion of the Higher Education of Women in Cambridge formed in October 1873, of which Marshall became a member. Its primary object was 'to maintain and develop the system of lectures for women instituted in 1870 in the subjects of the Cambridge Higher Local Examinations and in other branches of Academic study' (Newnham College, North Hall Diary). Here again, the ambivalence among the supporters of the scheme as to their precise intentions *vis à vis* the University is evident.

Land was taken in Newnham, at that time on the outskirts of Cambridge and residential accommodation built. Mary Paley Marshall recorded how Marshall, a member of the Building Committee, had assisted the architect, Basil Champneys, in measuring out the ground for the new building (Newnham Notes: Talk, p. 32/15, see McWilliams Tullberg, 1993b). Newnham Hall was opened in October 1875. Mary Paley returned the same term to take over the task of lecturing to economic students from Alfred Marshall who wished 'temporarily to withdraw from the work' (Minute Book of the Association for the Promotion of the Higher Education of Women in Cambridge, 30 October 1875, Newnham

College Archive).[27] However, Marshall maintained his interest in the project, generously donating £60 to the Newnham Hall Company in 1877 (Newnham Hall Company, *Report*, 1877).

In 1877 Alfred Marshall married his successful student, Mary Paley, and left Cambridge to embark on what proved to be a lack-lustre career as Principal of the recently-founded University College, Bristol. (The years 1877 until his return to Cambridge in December 1884 have been discussed in Whitaker, 1972, Groenewegen 1995; and McWilliams Tullberg, 1995.) Marshall's enthusiasm for the Newnham scheme for improving the educational standard of school-teachers and governesses seems to have waned in the years which immediately followed this move.[28] Evidence for this can be gleaned from an undated address book of the Association for the Promotion of the Higher Education of Women in Cambridge of which Marshall became a member at its formation in October 1873 (Newnham College Archives). Initially, Marshall is given with his St John's College address. This is then deleted and his Bristol address given. Then the whole Marshall entry is deleted and Mrs Marshall's name and Bristol address are given below. Since the Association was amalgamated with the Newnham Hall Company to form Newnham College Association for Advancing Learning and Education in 1879, it would seem that Marshall began to reconsider his position on women's education quite soon after his departure from Cambridge.

Later in the century, Marshall was an outspoken critic of any plan which might encourage women to come to Cambridge for their higher education or to allow them access to Cambridge degrees (McWilliams Tullberg, 1975, chapters 6–8; 1990b; 1991; 1993a and 1995). His preferred model for womankind reportedly became that of the German *hausfrau* (Phillips, 1988, p. 47). Some brief explanation must therefore be offered as to how and why he had a change of heart.

IV Marshall's change of heart

It has been argued (Biagini, 1991), that the young Marshall's reputation for radicalism is undeserved, and that, despite his commitment to the causes of labour and women's education in the 1870s, he was no more advanced than mainstream Liberals. This assessment requires a little modification. Within the ranks of educational liberals in the early 1870s, it has been demonstrated that

Marshall was among the vanguard who felt not only that all middle-class women should be educated, but that some women could benefit from the most advanced education then available to men. He demonstrated this by the encouragement and assistance he gave several women students to attempt a Tripos, and the public support he gave women who wanted to enter the medical profession.

He also voiced the opinion of middle-of-the-road liberals who, shocked by the co-existence of idle wealth and abject poverty, sought to bridge these unfortunate features of the industrial revolution by voluntary efforts, spurred on by earnestness and calls to duty. He spoke out very firmly against the view that women's only role was to 'embellish the existence' of their families. Women, he believed, had a particular role to play outside the home, rejecting luxury and idleness and bringing instead discipline and joy into the lives of the poor. It was self-evident that the first steps into the public sphere would be taken by women based at home, working locally within some extension of the traditional definition of women's duties, economically supported by their male relatives. No special significance should be attached to the particular tasks which he encouraged his women students to take up at this early stage in their educational and professional development.

Of greater significance is the way Marshall ignored and then rejected the central *economic* argument of the women's case. In lauding the good works of Octavia Hill and presenting her as a role model for his women students, he did not explain who was paying her bills.[29] The battle for women's educational rights 1850–1950 was not primarily an ideological one about careers for all women, whether married or not. It was a pragmatic struggle, first for the right to a meaningful and economically secure spinsterhood and then, as the century wore on, the right to a respectable alternative to what for many women was the thraldom of a Victorian-type marriage.[30] Mary Paley Marshall understood this aspect of the women's emancipation movement very clearly. In her review article of Clara Collet's *Educated Working Women*, she reports favourably the view that economic independence was good for a woman's character and self-respect, and that to be obliged to marry for a living was a destructive humiliation (Mary Paley Marshall, 1902, p. 256). A year earlier, Marshall expressed doubts as to the wisdom of allowing women into his classes, wondering whether women modelled on the German *hausfrau* would not serve the nation better (Phillips, 1988, p. 47). As to marriage, Marshall held that a woman was a subordinate being and that men would refuse to marry women who demonstrated their 'strength, courage and independence' (6 March 1889, Microfiche typescript of diaries of Beatrice Webb). Such women, he implied, deserved to remain unmarried (ibid., 7 June 1887).

The first sign of Marshall's waning enthusiasm for a new role for women appears in his evidence before the Committee on Intermediate and Higher Education in Wales. He argued that women's needs could be provided for in a local college like Bristol and that because of their domestic duties, they could only study part-time. Only a very few women, he told the Committee, could or should be educated away from home. And these were not the 'best' women, since such women have duties to perform for their families in making the home more cheerful and sometimes educating younger brothers and sisters. Only an 'unimportant' woman could be spared (McWilliams Tullberg, 1990b, p. 19). His evidence seems to have been anecdotal – an examination of the facts does not support his claim as to the specifically feminine nature of part-time studies – and the normative element of his argument represent a complete reversal of his views as expounded in his *Lectures to Women* in May 1873.

Marshall's observation that 'women do not, as a rule, take so many classes as men' (Q. 18,306) is not correct in general terms, although it is certainly true that those few Bristol students who were studying many subjects were men.[31] Marshall also asserted that 'the tendency is for [women] to study to a less extent than men in a given time' (ibid.) and that 'a woman can give up half her time for six years much more easily than a man can, she cannot give up her whole time for three years so easily as a man can' (Q. 18,304). No data from Bristol was presented to support this claim and Marshall had, at the time of giving his evidence, been Principal for only three academic years and one term. Furthermore, Marshall gave the impression that the College ran three-year degree courses (Q. 18,304), which it did not.[32] Bristol University College was typical of the widespread movement to provide opportunities of study beyond school level for the disadvantaged of both sexes cheaply and close to their homes.[33]

Perhaps the most interesting of Marshall's remarks to the Enquiry are those concerning women's family duties which, he believed, must be expected to take up a great deal of her time and reduce the time she could spend studying:

> With regard to women (and this has been overlooked in discussions with regard to colleges for women at Oxford and Cambridge), the best women generally are those women whose families require part of their time; generally they have duties to perform to their father and mother and sisters and brothers that take up some part of their time: and while a woman can give half of her time for six years much more easily than a man can, she cannot give her whole time for three years so easily as a man can. I am [not speaking of middle-aged women but] of women of the ordinary college age of 17–23. Many of the best women from the fact that they are the bright lights in their families are unable to go away for a long time together; of two sisters, one may be unimportant to the family and the other important; the former may go away to study, but the latter carry on her studies at home or not at all. (Q. 18,304–5)

Asked whether he meant that such women were important to their families because they were pleasant company, Marshall agreed and explained: 'Her family like her to be at home because she makes the home more cheerful and very often she educates the younger brothers and sisters' (Q. 18,306; cf. below, p. 153 and footnote 24).

This romanticised view of women students overlooked the harsh facts of life facing students of both sexes at local colleges. When Marshall looked at the enrollment figures for that year and the number of subjects taken by the men and women students, he might have reflected on the problems which many students were facing in finding the money for courses and books, and in some cases getting time off from their jobs to attend classes and then coping with the subsequent loss of income. From his experience in Cambridge, Marshall knew that one reason for women cutting short their studies was the cost of courses and of living expenses. In many cases, women were wanted by their families not because they were 'pleasant company' but because they were supporting a widowed mother and younger brothers and sisters with their tiny wages as teachers or governesses. While it is true that some women with financially sound backgrounds attended the Cambridge lectures, their ability to pay full fees was essential to the scheme and helped to subsidise the studies of the poorer students. Even reduced fees were beyond the reach of many and scholarships, awards, grants and loans were an essential element in financing students. In Newnham in 1875–76, these amounted to £260. That year, tuition fees were £464 (Accounts of the Association for the Promotion of the Higher Education of Women).

The situation was no different in Bristol:

> Some of the 'young ladies' attending courses were drawn from the wealthier classes living in Clifton and tended to regard the College as an intellectual

'finishing-school'. Others, however, had more serious ends in view, and were training to become teachers and governesses. (Bird, 1993, p. 28)[34]

Here, however, the scholarship situation was meagre. Seven General Scholarships of £15 each were available in October 1877–78, four of which were specifically for women and help was offered with other expenses. Scholarships offered for 1880–81 reflected the malaise which was affecting all the College's finances: three General scholarships of £25, £15 and £10 were available, but the women's scholarships had been reduced from four to two and no help could be given with other expenses.

Marshall's close familiarity with the women's education movement should also have alerted him to the fact that women in general had a far poorer basic education on which to build than men. It therefore made good sense for them to limit themselves initially to the study of only one or two subjects. Had he so wished, Marshall could have examined and assessed the impact of these economic and pedagogical aspects of women's study habits and presented them to the Committee. He chose instead to present, as evidence, his views on what he felt *should* be the behaviour of women.

Returning to Cambridge in 1884, Marshall began to oppose every effort made by the authorities of the women's colleges to gain the University's recognition of their academic achievements. Marshall's opposition was very persistent, sometimes petty, showed a marked disregard for facts and figures and was crowned with some considerable success (McWilliams Tullberg, 1975, Chapters 7 and 8; 1990b; and 1991).[35] There appear to be two aspects of Marshall's retreat from his earlier position; one relating to his character and based on childhood and domestic experiences about which we know very little, and the other relating to pseudo-scientific ideas of the time which reinforced and allowed him to justify his behaviour.

Accounts of Marshall's father describe him as 'despotic': 'the nearest objects of his masterful instinct were his family, and their easiest victim his wife; but their empire extended over the whole of womankind' (Keynes, [1933] 1985, p. 162; see also Guillebaud, 1971 and Coase, 1984, 1990). Keynes held that Alfred Marshall's attitude to women was the result of the 'mighty' influence of this heredity and that 'he did not altogether escape the influence of the parental mould' (Keynes, ibid.). Initially Marshall demonstrated a determination to cast off his father's dominance by turning down a valuable Classical scholarship at Oxford, choosing instead to study mathematics at Cambridge on borrowed money. This was followed by the abandonment of his religious faith and the clerical career which his father is said to have planned for him. He took a further step towards independence by associating, as a young Fellow, with a group of radicals who challenged conventional opinions on such topics as the importance of classical studies, the position of the Established Church at the universities, the celibacy requirement for Fellows and the role of women in society. Marshall no doubt tried hard to eliminate the reactionary elements of his father's attitude to women from his own personality and succeeded in suppressing them for a while under the strong influence of Sidgwick and his Grote Club friends. They provided him not only with causes to work for but also with the social and intellectual recognition and comradeship he had probably lacked as an undergraduate.

Following his move to Bristol, Marshall now became an important person in his own right, chairing meetings, making public speeches which were reported in the press and even giving expert evidence before a government inquiry. He became the close friend of the powerful master of Balliol College, Oxford, Benjamin Jowett. At the same time, he came to hate his work at Bristol and his exile from Cambridge. He had wasted his time helping his wife write a worthless little text-book (Marshall, A. and Marshall, M. P., 1879; Mc Williams Tullberg, 1992), and while she flourished as 'lady lecturer', his energy was sapped by administrative affairs which made him ill and interrupted his constructive work. All this seemed to have been forced on him by his marriage.[36] Had it really been worthwhile?

When, after eight years in the wilderness, he returned, via Oxford,[37] to his beloved Cambridge as the Professor of Political Economy, Marshall no longer felt any social and intellectual dependence on Sidgwick and may even have been embarrassed by his earlier allegiance. Almost immediately he attacked Sidgwick, whose proverbial even-handedness and fussy ideas about syllabus reform stood in the way of Marshall's declared ambition to create a separate school of economics in Cambridge with its own Tripos (Sidgwick, 1906, p. 394–6, p. 402). Sidgwick continued to support the further education of women, even allowing his wife's appointment as Vice-Principal and later Principal of Newnham College to determine where the couple lived. Marshall had in the meantime developed views on women and their place in society which were now quite opposed to those of Sidgwick and his former friends.

Later in life, Marshall recalled how 'a saying of Spencer sent the blood rushing through the veins of those who a generation ago looked eagerly for each volume of his as it issued from the press' (Scott, 1924, pp. 449–50).[38] Herbert Spencer was an early supporter of the women's education movement. He wrote in *Social Statics* 1850 that social convention (Marshall's 'custom') 'had always stifled the avenues of feminine intellectual achievement' and that the 'alleged inferiority of the female mind' was by no means 'self-evident'. However, in his *Principles of Biology* 1867, Spencer claimed, on the basis of a difference which he believed he observed in the birth-rate between upper and lower classes, that the development of a girl's intellect reduced her reproductive powers and threatened the 'welfare of posterity'. In his later works, Spencer insisted on the central importance of the family in which the woman dedicated herself exclusively to the welfare of its members for the sake of the future progress of the race.[39]

Spencer's work fuelled the late 19th century concern with evolutionary characteristics and the quality of the race. Dyhouse has noted how people who were interested in 'questions of national efficiency and social progress were frequently drawn into contemporary debate over the status and education of women' (1976, p. 42). Attention was focused on women solely in the role of child-bearers 'pregnant with the destiny of races'. Two perceived problems were discussed: education did physical damage, leaving women unable to bear children or breast-feed them; and, education would render women unwilling to marry and bear children. As the chairman of the British Medical Association put it in 1887:

> I think that it is not good for the human race, considered as progressive, that women should be freed from the restraints which law and custom have imposed upon them and should receive an education intended to prepare them for the exercise of brain power in competition with men. And I think this because I am persuaded that neither the preliminary training for such competitive work, nor the subsequent practice of it in the actual strife and struggle for existence, can fail to have upon women the effect more or less (and rather more than less) of indisposing them towards, or incapacitating them from their own proper function – for performing the part which ... nature has assigned to them in the maintenance and progressive improvement of the human race. (Quoted in Dyhouse, 1976, p. 45)

Two years later, Marshall's own view on the same subject was recorded by Beatrice Webb:

> [I]f women attempt to equal men and be independent of their guidance and

> control, the strong women will soon be ignored and the weak women simply starved: it is not likely that men will go on marrying, if they are to have competitors as wives – *Contrast* – is the only basis to marriage and if that is destroyed we shall not think it worth our while to shackle ourselves in life with a companion whom we must support and must consider. (7 June 1889, Microfiche typescript of diaries of Beatrice Webb, no. 1057)

Marshall repeated his uneasiness over 'the present drift towards new-womanhood' in a letter to Benjamin Kidd (14 February 1898, Cambridge University Library, Add Ms 8064.M254). Edgeworth, in his 'Reminiscences' confirmed that it was an issue which concerned Marshall profoundly (Pigou, 1925, p. 72).[40] There was a public outcry over the 'physical deterioration of the race' revealed by the medical examination of recruits to the Boer War; the fact that girls were taught academic rather than domestic skills at school was held to blame. Marshall concern with racial 'quality' deepened as he recognised the growing military threat from Germany.

Groenewegen has argued that Marshall's chain of reasoning – that the race progress and national survival depended on the family and the nurturing role played by women within it – did not rest on prejudice but on the empirical and scientific evidence which he gathered on the science of heredity:

> The subjection of women to the needs of the family and the limitations on their freedom which that implied arose from his social Darwinist vision of race survival, race preservation and race progress. In that sense, as in others, Marshall reflected the spirit and the knowledge of his time. (Groenewegen, 1994)

Like other social Darwinists and many of his contemporaries, Marshall missed the fundamental lessons of Darwin's theory – that evolution is random, it does not necessarily result in 'progress' and there is no guarantee that 'intelligence', for example, is beneficial to survival.[41] But it also seems legitimate to ask whether Marshall was not using Spencer as a convenient peg on which to hang some preconceived ideas. There was no statistical evidence to suggest that girls educated at Oxford or Cambridge were any less inclined than their sisters to marry and have children, although it did seem to be the case that girls from families of that social standing had less than a 50 per cent chance of marrying, whether or not they were college educated (Sidgwick, 1890). A detailed analysis of census returns made in 1892, showed that spinsterhood was a function of much the same demographic forces at the end as it had been in mid-century when women had first pressed for better education opportunities, that is, age discrepancy, middle-class expectations, migration and marriage into a lower class (Collet, 1892).[42] Had Marshall chosen to study them – and it seems likely that he had received copies of both enquiries – he might have been led to conclude that if a college-educated woman refused a particular offer of marriage, then the fault lay not with her education but with the marriage relationship as then defined by many men.

Marshall's discussion of the education of middle-class women was also coloured by the evidence he listened to during his service on the Royal Commission on Labour 1891–94. Like many other observers, he firmly believed that working-class women should stay at home with their children, since:

> the things she can buy with her earnings are of far less importance for the health and happiness of the family than the mere material services she could have rendered them if she had stayed at home, to say nothing of her moral influence in educating the children, in keeping the household in harmony and making it possible for her husband to be cheered and soothed in his evenings at home (Marshall, 1890, Bk. IV.v.5).[43]

To this end, Marshall felt that women's education should emphasise domestic science skills. Although Collet's statistics showed that the majority of working-class women could expect to marry, Booth's inquiry (1892–93) revealed that there were many cases where the man's income was inadequate, uncertain or totally absent. In these circumstances, women needed to work, the choice and remuneration of which was limited by their level of education. The ideal of women staying at home to look after their families was one which could only be logically combined with radical views on improving pay, conditions, safety standards and job security for male workers. For middle-class women, the argument for a sound academic education was even stronger, since so many of them would remain unmarried and it was in recognition of this that many of Marshall's contemporaries pressed the claims of women to the best possible, properly attested education. Through his close connection with Newnham, Marshall was very well placed to see that the women's cause was still primarily that of worthwhile and economically sound job-opportunities for middle-class women before marriage or, for those who did not find a partner, throughout life.

Twenty-five years after the arrival of the first women students in Cambridge, there was a big difference in the expectations of many of the younger women and dons. It was this, I believe, which Marshall found so difficult to accept. Cambridge women who had once been mere 'guests' at the University, gratefully accepting the 'freewill offering of higher Culture made to Women by Members of the University' were now claiming they had won the right to at least the title of their degrees.[44] They revelled in the intellectual stimulation of the Cambridge Tripos examinations, at which they were so successful. They found collegiate life, which Marshall so much opposed for women, offered them the same elements of mutual support and convenience of communal living as did the men's colleges for males. In the wider sphere, women who once had to be urged to 'do their duty' outside the home were beginning to demand their share of social, political and economic power, access to jobs and a choice of life-style. Despite his faith and hope in 'progress', Marshall found it difficult to conceive of social change which involved any genuine expansion or shift of democratic power. This is perhaps not unexpected in a man whose ideal world was one in which there were duties but no rights,[45] where the relationship between classes would be governed by chivalry on the part of those with economic power,[46] and the relationship between the sexes would be characterised by the subordination of the woman and, in marriage, by the 'devotion, body, and soul, of the female to the male'.[47]

Notes and References

1. The differentiated reading-lists given for various categories of student on p. 134 of Marshall's lecture outlines further illustrate this point.
2. The description given here of issues relevant to the revolution in middle-class female education is, of necessity, brief. For fuller analysis, see, for example, Bryant, 1979 and Vicinus, 1985.
3. Old habits die hard. Men were still demanding and families still supplying such girls for marriage at the end of the century.
4. Small groups of people rejected this view of the ignorant and therefore, 'innocent' woman. They claimed that women shared a common humanity with men and should be encouraged to realise their intellectual and moral potential. Such radicalism could be found among followers of the humanist Sydney Smith ('[E]very human being must do something with their existence ... Let any man reflect ... and he must feel convinced that the happiness of a woman will be materially increased in proportion as education has given her the habit and the means of drawing her resources from herself' (Rev. Sydney Smith, *Writings,* 'Female Education', quoted Bryant, 1979, p. 28) and in certain religious communities, in particular the Unitarians and Quakers, who encouraged their daughters to study and to accept responsibility for their lives. However, the fundamental principle of a common humanity, equal to both sexes, never attracted many adherents.

5. The source of Marshall's early inspiration and ideas on the contribution which women could make to society cannot be identified with certainty, but it was unquestionably reinforced by Sidgwick and other members of the Grote Club, including Maurice, and by reading Mill.
6. In 1862, the chronicler, W. R. Gregg asked why 750,000 women were 'redundant'. His own answer was that they were not fulfilling the essentials of a woman's being, not ministering to and being supported by a man. His solution was that half of them should emigrate to the better marriage market in Canada and the remainder should resort to coquetry to catch their man (Vicinus, 1985, p. 4).
7. Marshall superintended these school examinations on two occasions, in Windsor, December 1871 and in Birmingham, 1876 (Rough Minute Book of the Local Examinations Syndicate LES 1/1 pp. 117 and 189, Cambridge University Archive).
8. These included Alfred Marshall who wrote to the University *Reporter* on the subject. He was also a member of the Syndicates (committees) revising the Previous Examination and the Law and History Triposes.
9. Anne Clough also had the advantage of a brother, the poet Arthur Hugh Clough, who before his early death in 1861 had made many friends among radical intellectuals in London.
10. It was eventually given to James Stuart and the project can be seen as the beginning of the important adult education movement by means of Extension Lectures given by university men. Marshall does not appear to have lectured under the Extension Lecture Scheme, but acted on several occasions as examiner of those students who submitted papers on completion of lecture series on Political Economy (Yorkshire District Jan.–April 1874), and on the Social History of England (Northern towns, 1875) (Archives of the Board of Extra-Mural Studies, Items 59.1, June 1874 and Item 66, 12 June 1875, Cambridge University Archives).
11. The examinations were opened to men candidates in 1874 and during the century became the normal route to matriculation (see Appendix A, p. 76).
12. This appears to have been the only occasion on which Marshall acted as examiner, probably being barred from the post while lecturing in economics for the Lectures for Women scheme in Cambridge.
13. He had been introduced to this small discussion society by H. G. Dakyns of Clifton College, Bristol, where Marshall spent a couple of terms as a temporary mathematics master in 1865. It seems also probable that Marshall was introduced to Henry Sidgwick by Dakyns when Sidgwick came to Clifton College as an examiner in the same year.
14. In the absence of a full biography of Sidgwick, it is not possible to give details of this alliance. However, age and social and academic standing would suggest that Sidgwick was the leader in these schemes.
15. A hand-written description of a proposed scheme of lectures for women, including residence in private houses for those not living in Cambridge, and a printed call for support was circulated by T. Markby of Trinity Hall on 15 December 1869 (scrap-book of mainly printed items, Newnham College Archives).
16. It was stipulated that 50 per cent (four of eight members) of the Executive

Committee should be women.

17. The preliminary lecture schedule for Lent Term 1877 notes Marshall as giving a course in economic history, but these lectures were not included in the definitive lecture list (*University Reporter*, 1 October 1876 and 30 January 1877).
18. In *What I Remember*, she also mentions taking logic which her father advised was such a *safe* subject (Marshall, M. P., 1947, p. 13).
19. The Political Economy paper taken by Mary Paley for which she received a distinction is given in Appendix A, p. 76. Details of the Marshall Essay Prize are given in Appendix B, p. 81.
20. In 1876, when he no longer lectured to the women students, Marshall was paid £4 for 'private tuition' (Accounts for the Association for the Promotion of the Higher Education of Women, 13 June 1876).
21. These were Mary Paley, Mary Kennedy and Amy Bulley, who migrated from Girton College, and possibly three others (see note 27). Although Mary Paley Marshall commented in *What I Remember* that the Moral Sciences Tripos was felt to be especially suitable for women, the choice of Tripos among Newnham women was quite even-handed in the early years, 1871–80 – 12 Classics, 10 Maths, 13 Natural Sciences, 13 Moral Sciences, 12 History. This suggests that they were less inclined to choose a subject that was 'suitable' for them than one which interested them. The Moral Sciences Tripos became less popular later in the century.
22. Though offering a wider choice of subjects, the Higher Locals were at least on the same level as the University matriculation examination, and possibly higher (see Appendix A, p. 76). This matriculation examination, popularly known as the Previous or Little-Go, was at that time an examination of Latin, elementary Greek, mathematics and the doctrines of the Church of England. Most Cambridge male students took the examination after they entered the University. As the century progressed, passes in the Higher Locals were gradually accepted by the University in lieu of the Previous Examination. For many men, the Previous Examination was the *only* examination they took while at Cambridge. Between 1851 to 1906, for every 100 male students at Cambridge, on average 41 took an Honours degree (Tripos), 34 took the Pass or Ordinary degree and 25 took no degree, the figures for students taking Triposes improving towards the end of the century (Royal Commission on Oxford and Cambridge Universities 1922 x Cmd. 1588). All women students were barred from using the Pass degree papers from 1881. Sidgwick had never permitted their use by Newnham students. By the end of the century, over 80 per cent of women students in Cambridge were taking Triposes.
23. Mary Paley, for example, received the support of her father, but not of her mother (McWilliams Tullberg, 1995).
24. Marshall also felt that teaching at home could sometimes be wasteful (Lecture Outline VI, p. 153).
25. The commonest profession for a university man at that time was that of clergyman in the Established Church, a career which remained closed to women until 1993! Vicinus, who is primarily concerned with the initiatives taken by single women to find meaningful occupations, points out: 'At first women did not claim arenas already controlled by men, such as politics;

rather, they captured unclaimed areas and pushed out from there' (Vicinus, 1985, p. 15).

26. Marshall was presumably thinking of the cases of Elizabeth Garrett and others who were refused permission to qualify in England. Garrett finally took her M. B. at the Sorbonne.
27. It seems unlikely that Mary Paley coached the three Newnham students who took the Moral Sciences Tripos in the years 1875–77, in which case Alfred Marshall may have continued with the task. These included Mary Martin (Mrs James Ward) who got a First. In her report to the Newnham Shareholders, June 1877, Anne Clough spoke of Mary Paley's successful work in lecturing to Higher Local Examination candidates, but made no mention of Tripos candidates.
28. Marshall's final service for the Local Examinations scheme was to act as Presiding Examiner for the Higher Locals in Bristol in 1878 for a fee of £10. Although these examinations had been open to men since 1874, the candidates were still mainly women (Local Examinations Syndicate Rough Minute Book of the Local Examinations Syndicate, LES 1/1, p. 208b, Cambridge University Archives).
29. Marshall could perhaps not have been expected to know the particular story of Octavia Hill's shaky finances but it was a familiar one and repeated, often with a less happy outcome, in a great many middle-class families. Hill was born into a family of great economic instability made worse by her father's bankruptcy and mental illness. The family was supported by loans from her grandfather and income from her mother, Caroline Hill's, work as a teacher. After giving them some education at home, Caroline Hill had planned further training for her daughters but the need to repay loans and debts made this impossible. Octavia's working life began at 14, running a toy-making co-operative for poor girls and women founded by the Christian Socialists. She started a school with her sisters in 1862 but found that teaching showed up her own ignorance. In 1864 she gained a certificate in mathematics from Queen's College. Supported by rich patrons, her voluntary engagement with slum housing grew, while the school, which was presumably the source of household income, was gradually taken over by her sisters. In 1874, friends set up a generous trust fund to provide for her and she later received an inheritance from a well-wisher. However, 'personal poverty was a constant reality in Octavia Hill's childhood and endured well into her adulthood; the worry of repaying debts and living on the genteel brink of disaster was a spectre which haunted her all her life' (Darley, 1990, p. 20).
30. The question of whether a woman with a secure income was justified in taking a paid job began to be discussed at the end of the century; prior to that, the issue was almost entirely one of incomes for unprovided spinsters or widows.
31. Looking at academic year 1879–80 (Marshall gave his evidence in December 1880), 53 day and evening women students and 48 men students attended classes regularly and passed the subject examinations organised by the college at the end of each term. Although by no means a perfect measure of enrollments, these figures can be taken as an indication of the number of 'serious' students working at the college that year. Of these, 92 per cent of

women students and 88 per cent of men students took one or two subjects. It can also be noted that for all practical purposes, the engineering and applied science courses (almost one third of the courses available in 1879–80), were not open to women. One year's intake of about a hundred students is a poor basis for statistical analysis, but in previous years, the number of women students examined so greatly outnumbered the men students that comparisons between them cannot be made. Maybe Marshall was irritated because the College attracted so many middle-class women and few of the working-class men as he had perhaps hoped for. If so, he was forgetting the close connections between the movement for the higher education for women, the extra-mural teaching schemes and the local Colleges, and the way in which the two former had spawned the latter (see footnote 10).

32. Marshall told the Enquiry that examinations were a great waste of examiners' time, required a large body of specialists to conduct them; financial constraints meant that the staff at Bristol would always be too small for both teaching and examining. He neither then nor later wanted Bristol to become a degree-awarding university, refusing to support Bristol's efforts to become a full university in the 1900s (Travers, correspondence and manuscript of autobiography, Bristol University Archives). The College introduced Honour Certificates for three terms' study in individual subjects for students who had satisfied an External Examiner, only after Marshall left the College.
33. Specifically, the College aimed to 'supply for persons of either sex above the ordinary school age the means of continuing their studies in Science, Languages, History, and Literature, and more particularly to afford appropriate instruction in those branches of Applied Science which are employed in the arts and manufactures. A special course of instruction has been arranged for students intending to become Engineers, Surveyors, or Architects. Special attention is given to class teaching and laboratory work. To afford opportunities of improvement to those who are engaged during the day, there are evening courses of lectures and classes, at low fees' (University College Bristol *Calendar* 1878–79).
34. 'Young men, too, who had perhaps entered a family business, came in for as little as a term to improve a chosen subject' (Bird, 1993, p. 28).
35. Cambridge women were not given the titles of their degrees until 1923 and not awarded degrees proper until 1948.
36. The fact that the union was childless may have contributed to the difficulties. Without further knowledge of who could not, or would not, have children, it is impossible to assess the importance of the childlessness. But see below p. 65 for the view that study damaged women's reproductive organs.
37. Through his friendship with Jowett, Marshall had here moved in quite exalted political and intellectual circles (Mary Paley Marshall, 1947, p. 37). However, even at Oxford, Mary Paley Marshall appears to have be far happier than her husband (McWilliams Tullberg, 1995).
38. This excitement had not been shared by Sidgwick who after an early admiration for Spencer (1862), became critical of his results and of his metaphysics (Sidgwick, 1906, p. 277).
39. Marshall had thirteen of Spencer's works in his library, several of them multi-volume.

40. See also Pigou, 1925, p. 468 on Marshall's fear for family life 'under the influence of aggressive womanhood'.
41. Nor is there any clear definition of what 'intelligence' is, nor proof that it is genetically transmissible.
42. Among the middle-classes, men often waited until they were in their 30s or 40s before marriage, but then married a women in her early 20s, causing an imbalance of numbers. This problem was exacerbated by parents insisting that future sons-in-law should be able, literally, 'to keep their daughters in the style to which they had become accustomed', normally an impossible task for a young man at the beginning of his career. More single middle-class men emigrated than did women, or migrated from their home districts where, freed from social pressures, they might marry a girl from the 'respectable' working-classes (as Marshall's father seems to have done). A man could also choose not to marry at all, free to pursue his career, travel and recreational activities without any social stigma, and able to purchase whatever domestic comforts he required.
43. Earlier, in the *Economics of Industry* which he wrote together with his wife, Marshall held that family life was a distraction to some women at work; but education could fit women for more responsible jobs, and it was hoped that the employment of women in business management would increase (Marshall, A. and Marshall, M. P., Bk III 3. 7).
44. Marshall described women students as temporary 'guests' in a letter to Sidgwick rejecting proposals asking for degrees for women (Alfred Marshall to Henry Sidgwick, early June 1887, Newnham College Archive). Earlier, A. J. Clough in a report to the Association for the Promotion of the Higher Education of Women in Cambridge called the lecture scheme a 'freewill offering of higher Culture made to Women by Members of the University'.
45. 'I hold that the ultimate good of all endeavour is a state of things in which there shall be no rights but only duties'. 'How far do remedial causes influence prejudicially (a) the continuity of employment (b) the rates of wages?' (Talk given at the The Industrial Remuneration Conference, 1885, and reprinted in the Annual of the Wholesale Co-operative Society, 1888).
46. 'Social possibilities of economic progress' (Pigou, 1925, pp. 323–46).
47. 6 March 1889, microfiche typescript of diaries of Beatrice Webb.

Bibliography

Biagini E. (1991), 'Marshall's 1873 "Lectures to Women" ', *Quaderni di Storia dell'Economia Politica*, vol. 9, 2–3, pp. 335–51.

Bird E. (1993), 'Lectures for ladies', *Nonesuch: the University of Bristol Magazine*, Spring.

Booth C. (1892–93), *Life and Labour of the People of London*, 4 vols., London: Macmillan & Co.

Bryant M. (1979), *The Unexpected Revolution: A Study in the History of the Education of Women and Girls in the 19th Century*, London: University of London Institute of Education.

Coase R. H. (1984), 'Alfred Marshall's father and mother', *History of Political Economy*, vol. 16, no. 4, pp. 519–27.

Coase R. H. (1990), 'Alfred Marshall's family and ancestry', in McWilliams Tullberg (ed.), 1990a, pp. 9–27.

Collet C. (1892), 'Prospects of marriage from women', *Nineteenth Century*, April.

Darley G. (1990), *Octavia Hill: A Life*, London: Constable.

Dyhouse C. (1976), 'Social Darwinistic ideas and the development of women's education in England, 1880–1920', *History of Education*, vol. 5, no. 1, pp. 41–58.

Groenewegen P. D. (1994), 'Alfred Marshall – Women and economic development: labour, family and race', in Groenewegen P. D. (ed.) *Feminism and Political Economy in Victorian England*, Aldershot: Edward Elgar.

Groenewegen P. D. (1995), *A Soaring Eagle: Alfred Marshall 1842–1924*, Aldershot: Edward Elgar.

Guillebaud C. W. (1971), 'Some personal reminiscences of Alfred Marshall', *History of Political Economy*, vol. 3, Spring, pp. 1–8.

Keynes J. M. (1985) [1933], 'Alfred Marshall', in *Essays in Biography*, D. Moggridge, ed., *Collected Writings of John Maynard Keynes*, London: Macmillan for the Royal Economic Society, vol. 12, Ch. 14, originally published in *Economic Journal*, September, 1924.

Marshall A. and Marshall M. P. (1879), *Economics of Industry*, London: Macmillan.

Marshall A. (1890), *Principles of Economics*, London: Macmillan.

Marshall M. P. (1902), 'Educated working women by Clara E. Collet', *Economic Journal*, vol. 12, pp. 252–57.

Marshall, M. P. (1940), Obituary of Mary Wright (Kennedy), 1871–75, *Newnham College Roll Letter*, January 1940.

Marshall M. P. (1947), *What I Remember*, Cambridge at the University Press.

McWilliams Tullberg R. (1975), *Women at Cambridge – a Men's University, though of a Mixed Kind*, London: Gollancz.

McWilliams Tullberg R. (ed.) (1990a), *Alfred Marshall in Retrospect*, Aldershot: Edward Elgar.

McWilliams Tullberg R. (1990b), 'Alfred Marshall and the "woman question" at Cambridge', *Économie Appliqueé*, vol. 43, no. 1, pp. 209–30.

McWilliams Tullberg R. (1991), 'Alfred Marshall and the male priesthood of economics', *Quaderni di Storia dell'Economia Politica*, vol. 9, 2–3, pp. 235–68.

McWilliams Tullberg R. (1992), 'Alfred Marshall's attitude to the Economics of Industry', *Journal of the History of Economic Thought*, vol. 14, Fall, pp. 257–70.

McWilliams Tullberg R. (1993a), 'Marshall's final lecture, 21 May 1908', *History of Political Economy*, 25:4, pp. 605–16.

McWilliams Tullberg R. (1993b), 'Material in the Archive of Newnham College, Cambridge', *Marshall Studies Bulletin*, vol. 3, pp. 36–47.

McWilliams Tullberg R. (1995), Chapter on Mary Paley Marshall in Dimand, M-A. and Dimand R. (eds), *Women of Value*, Aldershot: Edward Elgar.

Phillips A. (ed.) (1988), *A Newnham Anthology*, Cambridge: for Newnham College at the University Press.

Pigou A. C. (ed.) (1925), *Memorials of Alfred Marshall*, London: Macmillan.

Scott W. R. (1924–25), 'Alfred Marshall 1842–1924', *Proceedings of the British Academy*, vol. 11, 446–57.

Sidgwick A. S. and Sidgwick E. M. (1906), *Henry Sidgwick, a Memoir*, London: Macmillan.
Sidgwick E. M. (1890), *Health Statistics of Women at Cambridge and Oxford and their Sisters*, Cambridge: Cambridge University Press.
Vicinus M. (1985), *Independent Women: Work and Community for Single Women 1850–1920*, London: Virago.
Webb B. (1873–1943), *Microfiche Typescript of Diary*, Cambridge: Chadwyck & Healey Ltd.
Whitaker J. K. (1972), 'Alfred Marshall: The years 1877 to 1885', *History of Political Economy*, vol. 4, 1, Spring, pp. 1–61: Reprinted in Wood, 1982, vol. 1, item 8.
Wood J. C. (ed.) (1982), *Alfred Marshall: Critical Assessments*, London: Croom Helm, four volumes.

Appendix A. The Cambridge Higher Local Examinations

The Higher Local Examinations run by Cambridge University were introduced in 1869 as the result of a petition from the North of England Council for Promoting the Higher Education of Women and their supporters. Initially available only to *women* over 18, they were opened to male candidates in 1874. Since at that time no degrees were open to women, the examinations were primary conceived as providing a qualification for school-teachers and governesses, beyond the level of school examinations.[1]

The examinations tested groups of subjects; success in Group A was essential before a certificate could be awarded. The original subjects groups are given below; the groups subsequently underwent many changes. Some idea of the standard which the examinations held can be judged from the discussion which preceded the acceptance of passes in the Higher Locals as part of the matriculation qualification for Cambridge University in place of the Previous Examination. The Minutes of a meeting of the Local Examinations Syndicate in February 1877 concluded that:

> With regard to the Higher Local Examinations, the Syndicate felt that the standard of that examination was rather that of a degree examination than of the Previous Examination, but that it might be convenient to provide that those who obtain its certificates be excused the Previous Examination. (Local Examination Syndicate Minute Book, 26 February 1877, p. 158)

This recommendation was sent, with roughly the same wording, to the Council of the Senate. No serious objections were raised to the proposal, which was then confirmed (Cambridge University *Reporter* 12 March 1877).[2]

Subject groups

University of Cambridge Regulations of Examinations for Women 1870.

Group A: Religious Knowledge; Arithmetic; English History (incl.

geography where relevant); English Language and Literature; Essay.

Group B: Latin; Greek; French; German; Italian.

Group C: Euclid; Algebra; Plane Trigonometry; Conic Sections; Statics; Astronomy; Dynamics.

Group D: Logic; Political Economy.

Group E: Botany; Geology & Physical Geography; Zoology; theoretical and practical Chemistry .

Group F: Music; Art

Group A was compulsory in order to receive a pass in the other groups. Distinctions could be obtained in the individual subjects of all groups. For Groups B, D, and E, a Pass Certificate was awarded for success in one subject, a Certificate of Honour for success in two subjects. For Group C, success in Euclid and Algebra was required for a Pass, two more subjects were required for a Certificate of Honour.[3] *Proficiency in Group F subjects did not entitle candidates to a Certificate of Honour, but distinctions in either subject were noted on the Certificate.*

The suggested reading for Group D Political Economy for the June 1870 examination was Mill's *Political Economy* and Smith's *Wealth of Nations*. In 1872, the year in which Mary Paley took Group D, Cairnes' *Logical Method of Political Economy* was added to the list, and candidates were informed that two-thirds of questions on the examination papers would have reference to these books (From information in the Association for Promoting the Higher Education of Women Box file, Newnham Archives). English and European Constitutional History were added to Group D subjects in 1875 (Local Examination Syndicate Minutes, 22 February 1875, p. 117, Cambridge University Library).

Higher Local Examination Papers[4]

The following paper was taken by Mary Paley at the end of her first year in Cambridge. No indication here or elsewhere is given as to choice, and it must therefore be assumed that candidates were expected to attempt all questions.

Group D

Thursday, *June* 20, 1872. 4 to 6½.

Political Economy

1. WHAT is the province of Political Economy? What definitions of the science have been suggested? State which you prefer, and give reasons for your preference.

2. State the requisites of production: and distinguish between productive and unproductive labour.

How would you class the labour of Actors, Literary Lecturers, Professors, Barristers?

3. Define Capital, fixed Capital, circulating Capital.

What phenomena may be expected to be exhibited during the rapid conversion of circulating Capital into fixed Capital and subsequent to that conversion?

4. Establish the principle:
'Demand for commodities is not demand for labour.'

Can you mention any case in which this principle is not applicable?

5. Examine the effect on production caused by the separation of employments.

Account for the different rates of wages in different employments, and for the different rates of gross profits in different trades.

6. What was 'the mercantile system'?

Give a brief account of the agricultural systems of Political Economy as they are described by Adam Smith.

7. State Ricardo's theory of rent. What objections have been made to it? Examine their validity. How does Adam Smith's theory of farm-rents differ from Ricardo's?

8. 'It may and often does happen that a country imports an article from another, though it might be possible to produce the imported article with less cost in the importing country than in that from which it is imported.'

How do you explain this seeming paradox?

9. What is the Malthusian doctrine of population?

What result do you consider would follow in England if the mortality among young children of the labouring class were very materially reduced?

10. 'Ireland pays dearer for her imports in consequence of her absentees.'

Establish this proposition.

11. Discuss the policy of the English poor-law from an economical point of view.

12. 'There are no public institutions for the education of women, and there is accordingly nothing useless, absurd, or fantastical in the common course of their education.'

What was Adam Smith's opinion with respect to endowments for educational purposes? To what extent do you conceive that he was influenced in making the foregoing statement by his individual experience?

13. Discuss *one* of the following assertions:

(1) A country will always have as much pauperism as it chooses to pay for.

(2) Educational endowments are employed more advantageously in assisting learners than in paying teachers.

Notes and References

1. For a brief history of the Cambridge Junior, Senior and Higher Local Examinations, see McWilliams Tullberg, 1975, chapters 2–4. Degrees were awarded to women for the first time in England by London University from 1878.

2. Holders of Higher Local Examination certificates in Religious Knowledge, Greek and Latin would be excused Part 1 of the Previous Examination; holders of Higher Local Examination certificates in Religious Knowledge, in Group A and Sections 1 & 2 of Group C would be excused Part II of Previous; holders of Higher Local Examination certificates in Sections 2, 3 and 5 of Group C would be excused the Additional Subjects of the Previous. It is interesting to note that the University gradually adopted Newnham College's approach to matriculation, via the Higher Local Examinations.
3. These classifications were changed to First, Second and Third Class. Thus, in successive years, Mary Paley was awarded a 2nd Class in Group A, with Distinction in Divinity, a 1st Class in Group B, with Distinction in German, a 3rd Class in Group C and a 1st Class in Group D, with Distinctions in Logic and Political Economy. The Political Economy examination paper taken by Mary Paley is given below.
4. Cambridge University Library, Cam.c.11.51.27

Appendix B.

The Marshall Essay Prize for successful women candidates of Group D of the Cambridge Higher Local Examinations

A scribbled note in the rough Minutes book of the Local Examinations Syndicate records that Marshall first proposed this prize in May 1872. The full Minutes state that: 'A prize of £20 having been offered for the best essay on some subject of Political Economy, the competition to be limited to women who have passed Group D, the Syndicate determined to undertake the appointment of an examiner' (Local Examinations Syndicate Minutes, 3 May 1872, Cambridge University Library). The prize was publicly announced the following August:

DIRECTIONS TO CANDIDATES

> A prize of £20 has been offered by a Member of the Senate for the best Essay on some social problem into which economical considerations enter as an important element. The choice of a subject is left to each Candidate. The prize will be open to all women who shall have passed the Examination in Group D. The Essays must be sent in under cover to the Secretary on or before November 30, 1873, and will be returned to the Candidates. A similar prize will be given in 1874, for which the successful Candidate in 1873 may compete, but her Essay must be on a different subject (Examination Papers for Higher Local Examinations June 1872 and Regulations for June 1873, p. 7 [published August 1872]).

The same announcement was made the following year, giving the candidate only four months in which to complete the essay. It was on this occasion that Mary Paley and Mary Kennedy shared the essay prize for the best essays.[1] Marshall continued to offer the prize for three more years but began to guide candidates in their choice of subject. The regulations for the 1874 prize were as follows:

> The choice of a subject is left to each Candidate; but the *donor suggests the following*, (i) Means whereby such of the moral and social effects of division of labour as are evil may be diminished; (ii) The influence of luxury on progress; (iii) The principle of co-operation in its present applications and probable

> development. (Papers and Regulations for Higher Local Examinations, August 1874)

Marshall clearly felt this first topic on certain negative moral and social effects of the division of labour was an important one for the women to consider, since he repeated it the following year. In addition, candidates could choose to discuss 'The houses and gardens of the working classes' (Papers and Regulations for Higher Local Examinations, August 1875). Finally, the suggested subjects for the 1876 prize were: (i) The functions of the State in offering facilities for recreation; (ii) The division of the work of education between men and women (op. cit., August 1876).

Marshall withdrew his prize in 1877, probably in view of his impending marriage and the subsequent loss of his Fellowship income from St. John's. His award of £20 annually for four years had been exceptionally generous; he clearly gave back to the women's education movement a large part of what he earned teaching women students. Other prizes offered in 1873, for example, amounted to £119 and were subscribed to by groups of people. The women students of economics were fortunate in that 'Mr. Sidgwick expressed a wish to continue the essay prize' (Local Examinations Syndicate Minutes, 20 March 1877). His offer was accepted, and Sidgwick followed Marshall's practice of suggesting essay topics.[2]

Notes and References

1. J. B. Mayor, like Marshall a member of the Grote Club, was examiner.
2. Examples of these are: (i) The economic and other social conditions favourable to national art; (ii) The functions of private organization in the relief of the poor (1877); (i) Education considered in its economic aspect; (ii) the disadvantages incident to an industrial system organized on the basis of free competition, and their remedies (1879); An investigation of the actual differences in the earnings of different classes of persons engaged in industry in England at the present time, together with an analysis of the causes of these differences, and an estimate of the amount of effect attributable to each cause (1881); The precise meaning and application of the proposition that 'equality ought to be the rule in matters of taxation', the difficulties in the way of applying the principle under the actual conditions of English Society, and the best means of overcoming these difficulties (1883).

Part II

4. Lectures to Women

Easter Term 1873 Mr Marshall's Lectures on

'Some economic questions directly connected with the welfare of the laborer'[1]

Lecture I: 25 April. Method; complicated questions must be broken up into simpler ones; no royal road to the solution of social problems. What Political Economy cannot do and what it can do. Need for accuracy of language. 'Capital'. The fallacy 'Lavish expenditure is good for trade'.

Lecture II: 2 May. Our rapid progress in science and the arts of production might have been expected to have prevented to a great extent the sacrifice of the interests of the laborer to the interests of production. Importance of the inquiry why it has not done so. The wages-problem. Laws of increase of capital and labor.

Lecture III: 9 May. The wages problem continued. Fluctuations in the supply of capital and labor, in profits and wages, of individual trades. Connexion between various parts of wages problem.

Lecture IV: 16 May. Trade Unions; their origin, present purpose and organisation: the extent of their control over the supply of labor. 'Free-trade in labor'; its good and evil effects. Co-operative associations. Summing up of the circumstances of 'the labor market'.

Lecture V: 23 May. Economic legislation; factory acts; education acts; poor laws. Charitable societies – how to select those whose benefits are liable to the least drawbacks.

Lecture VI: 30 May. The influence of private individuals; the pursuit of wealth; the true meaning of 'wealth'. The harmony between true Political Economy and Ethics; luxury, its direct and indirect effects. Rightful luxury and wrongful luxury. Conclusion

Books Recommended[2]

Thornton on Labour (omit chapters 2 and 3 book 2)
Ludlow and Jones – Progress of Working Classes since '32.
Brassey – Work and Wages.

(In case of more thorough study)
Hearn's Plutology
Macdonell's Survey of Political Economy
Mill's Political Economy
Fawcett's Pauperism
Brentano's Guilds (translated from German)
11th report in Blue Books.

Cairnes' book on Method.

Heads of Lecture I

Method; complicated questions must be broken up into simpler ones; no royal road to the solution of social problems. What political economy cannot do and what it can do. Need for accuracy of language. 'Capital'. The fallacy 'Lavish expenditure is good for trade'.

Lecture I [25 April 1873]

In these lectures we can only consider a part of a part of a subject.

Today I wish to speak simply of method. Now what we have to do is to ascertain what it is that marks off the method of a specialist from the method of other people, what it is that makes his work uninteresting to others, but nevertheless of great value when he has attained his results. In talking of method there is a great advantage in taking some simple case. Here for instance we find that the laws of the cricket field exemplify almost every principle in Mill's Logic, and the method which ladies employ in talking over dress is precisely the same as that employed in political economy. In all sciences there is one method and only one; which when asked how to treat a complicated problem, simply answers 'don't treat it at all'. It is absolutely necessary to break up such a problem into small portions; wherever science has attempted to solve complicated problems it has failed, it has only succeeded when it has forced itself rigidly to break up a complicated problem into simple ones. Now what is meant by this breaking up? It is classing together those enquiries which have many properties in common, and neglecting for the while the rest: in a word, it is abstracting. All who have tried to solve complicated problems except by this method have failed; the only result of their work being, that they have shown the impossibility of solving them, and they have left a heap of material which may be useful to those who following them are content to take a humble line. In all physical science advance has been made by that method only, and in social science so little progress has been made because it has been found almost impossible to split up the problems to be solved. Science must be uninteresting to those who do not see the special use of eliminating from our consideration for a time all but a very small portion of the question. There is nothing peculiar to science. All that the scientific man does is done by all in ordinary life; he has nothing more to teach in principle than what you may gain from observing the events of ordinary everyday life. This statement seems simple in itself but must be regarded as somewhat paradoxical, because so many people appear not to be able to see it.

Economists are generally found fault with for discussing only one side of a question; but no blame should be attached to them for not doing what they do not attempt to do. The only harm is when they look upon that side as determining all practical questions.

We must bear in mind the grand distinction between the method of procedure of a person who wishes to obtain certain ends, and of one who merely seeks to obtain knowledge. Art is really the mode of procedure employed to obtain certain ends though it is vulgarly used as nearly synonymous with the fine arts. There is a great distinction between a scientific man and an artist. The two may be combined in one person, a scientific man may be an artist just as a chancellor may be a landlord, but yet he must be kept distinct, the man of science and the artist. The former seeks to obtain knowledge; he brings a number of facts together which bear on all sides of the question, but he must be able rigidly to exclude all which prevent his obtaining an accurate result. At any one time the scientific man must be at liberty to ask a specific question and receive a specific answer, and to reject all else as irrelevant to the subject under consideration, however valuable it may be in itself. If ordinary people would only bear in mind the necessity for this abstraction, we should hear none of that nonsense one so frequently hears about the hard-heartedness of economic science. I will now pass on to a general account of what Political Economy can do. What it cannot is to supply the social artist with complete directions; the political economist is concerned only with one side and consequently cannot give directions to the artist who wants to know all sides in order to obtain certain ends and must take into consideration all the light to be obtained from all sides. I have insisted at length on this point in this course of lectures because it will only be possible for me here to give a very one sided view of a very one sided part of the question, and I should be very sorry if those who hear them should therefore think themselves able to treat any practical question.

Political Economy suffers from the great misfortune of being interesting to a great many people who have no taste for scientific method. These people have done an enormous amount of harm. Sciolist[s][3] – those who have read a little and therefore speak a great deal – are more common in Political Economy than in any other Science except Theology. It is in consequence of the immense amount of nonsense talked by such people that working men have a saying: 'If Political Economy is against us, we are against political economy'; and they would be right if Political Economy were nothing but this.

Political Economy enables us to determine what will be the results of certain courses of action. The word is used in a narrower and in a wider sense. In the narrower sense political economy considers the decision of such questions as this: 'if such and such conditions be given, what results will follow?' These conditions being all that is necessary for the consideration of the subject, Political Economy is in this sense a purely abstract science, and in this respect will be exactly like mathematics. Every problem of political economy in this narrower sense must start with an 'if', and the results will necessarily follow. Although as it stands they will be no use whatever; but if our data are right and our reasoning right, the results must be true.

There are two distinct points of view which are generally confused. I. If a science is perfectly abstract, its results are infallible. II. In so far as a science is abstract, its results are directly of no use whatever, and if a person, having learnt all that is purely abstract about a subject, attempts to give directions to the artist, he is going quite out of his province.

What then is the use of abstract science? As it stands it is simply critical (engineer's calculations reviewed by the mathematician, data being given). Thus a political economist is quite within his sphere when criticizing those portions of an act of parliament (in itself concerning rather the political artist) which depend on the results necessarily following certain given conditions.

Such a work as mere criticism, whilst extremely healthy and educationally of singular value, has perhaps but little interest, and is never likely to be pursued alone; indeed there is no work on Political Economy which confines itself entirely to this province. In Political Economy there are many questions which can be discussed *almost* entirely without taking into consideration any but pure economic questions, and on such points a political economist is likely to glide from the scientific to the artistic and therefore one desirous of not being misunderstood is careful on such points to guard against the assumption that he is treating purely economic questions (Title of Mill's Book).[4] With regard to the questions we shall discuss in these lectures this is true; but although we cannot even discuss that side thoroughly in such a short time and to a mixed class [sic].[5] Hence many considerations must be entirely omitted; for instance in discussing a question thoroughly, we have to guard about objections and misapprehensions. All this must here be omitted.

But again, these questions are those mainly referring to the relation of capital to labour; and as you are likely to hear elsewhere all that capital has to say for itself, I shall generally confine myself almost entirely to what labor has to say. If I were lecturing to labouring men, I should omit almost entirely what I say to you, I should show them the danger of the abuse of the power they are obtaining and the necessity for establishing a new code of morality, one lying between private morality and international morality, the morality between class and class. All this I shall leave almost untouched here.

There is a hint I wish to give you before I close about the necessity of accuracy of language – I don't know [how] far you are aware of this fact, that excepting in so far as a person may have observed inaccurately, every mistake that is committed is an inaccuracy in language;[6] neglecting mere slips all errors are capable of being reduced to this source. Errors which have perverted the whole course of the world have been simply due to people's talking about a word in one sense and reasoning from it in another. The large progress which political economy has made in late years is almost entirely due to the constant repetition of the monotonous phrase 'Now you know you didn't mean that at all'. The very greatest minds that have ever existed have made mistakes of this kind. Even Bacon has made mistakes that would be laughed at now if put in their baldest form. There is one of these as atrocious as any which is hardly crushed out yet, viz. that 'lavish expenditure is good for trade'.[7] Now what do we mean by *expenditure*? Spending money, I suppose you will say. Now the mistake is mainly due to our using the word *money* instead of *capital*. Never use the word money if you can possibly help it. There are certain things which must be supplied to carry on any business; these are capital. Now having this, someone proposes that he should add to his expenditure, and so improve trade. Setting aside the case of a man shutting up his money in a strong box which practically never occurs and which we therefore will not consider now, if a man saves, how does he invest his money? There are roughly only two ways: 1. in Government bonds, in which case he takes a bond from someone else and sets that person's money free to be employed in other ways;

2. in some productive company, when he simply gives someone else his money to spend for him. In either case the money is as much spent as if he actually bought things with it himself. To increase expenditure, you must withdraw capital from somewhere else. The mistake of the phrase in question arises simply from treating a partial proposition as if it were true without limitations. Lavish expenditure in one place increases the trade in that place, but not of the world at large; it is false to say that such expenditure is good for trade in general. You can't increase your expenditure though you can your consumption; *saving* is simply a diminution of expenditure in one place and an increase of it in another.

Heads of Lecture II

Our rapid progress in science and arts of production might have been expected to have prevented to a great extent the sacrifice of the interests of the laborer to the interests of production.

Importance of the inquiry why it has not done so. The wages problem. Laws of increase of capital and labour.

Lecture II May 2nd [1873]

In my last lecture I discussed the question how much it was possible to do in these lectures. We found it was impossible to obtain any thorough and practically valuable knowledge in a discussion in which there is no room for enquiry into exclusively abstract questions. I consider it of the greatest importance that people should understand that it is impossible to make any serious progress in social science without giving much time to the consideration of abstract theories quâ abstract theories without allowing any thought of practical results to disturb their judgement. In the last lecture the question was raised of lavish expenditure. This is quite different from the question: what expenditure is *right*. This will be discussed in my last lecture, and a great deal of what we have to say in the following lectures will tend to the solution of this question.

This explained, I do not wish in the rest of the lecture to keep any clear line of demarcation between abstract reasoning and its application.

Some time ago when people wanted to grind their corn, they worked at the mill themselves, and very hard work it was. Then the water mill was discovered, and the Greek poet sang about it, 'Rest from your labour, the nymphs have undertaken it, hour after hour, year after year' etc.[8] Since then we have a more powerful servant than water: steam. Steam carries us from place to place, transports our burdens and does our weaving incomparably better and faster than we could. Now suppose you had told an intelligent man 100 years ago, that all manual labour would thus be dispensed with, he would have looked forward to a time of perfect freedom, a perpetual Sunday, when work would be so entirely subordinated to what was more important, to the growth of a man and of his character, that it would almost have been forgotten. This might have been expected but now, let us see what has been done? And first let me say that I do not agree with those who see nothing but retrogression. I think if you want to see the greatest misery and the worst forms of vice you must look to backward times in England and backward nations now. I think that the accounts of the growing depravity of the race are absolutely inconsistent with truth. For instance, you hear that the raising of wages only increases the amount spent in beer, that the laborers don't give any more to their wives and children. Now this is one of the few statements that can be stated by statistics; and we find from them that since 1750 the consumption of spirits per head has scarcely increased; that of beer is only half as much, whereas that of luxuries, those little things which go to make up the comfort of the working man's family (such as tea, sugar, currants) has in some cases doubled trebled, increased tenfold. Thus I do not mean to say that we have gone backwards, but I do mean to say that in so far as we have allowed things to drift, it has been found a bad method of procedure, that in so far as things have been allowed to take their course, men women and children have been sacrificed to production. If we want to see what would result from the natural course of things, if we remained always apathetic, we must look back to that period in the manufacturing districts, when machinery had nearly reached its present state of perfection, but had not roused men from their apathy. First to look at purely physical evils: there was no one occupation without its own disease peculiar to it, and some had many. A distorted leg was the result of some, viz the potteries; curvature of the spine of many; and consumption of most. Much of the work was necessarily unhealthy, but leaving this out of the question as not giving us our strongest side, the large majority of these diseases was mainly due to over work and bad food. For instance in one place, in order that the looms might be kept constantly at work, they had relays of children, and consequently only one set of beds for two sets of children. But worse than all, looking merely at the physical side, was the enormous amount of work the children had to do; they had to work till nothing but the fear of ill treatment could make them move their weary limbs, and so on from day to day till some disease prematurely stopped their hurried lives. But what was the world about all this time? Were the masters different from the rest of mankind? Was there nothing human in them? There is no evidence that they were more hard-hearted than the rest of the world. When a commission was instituted to inquire into the state of things in the potteries, many of the masters freely came forward to give their evidence as to the existing evils. They acknowledged that the work necessarily caused disease and absence of education but they said: If we endeavoured single-handed to remedy these evils we should be undersold by others. Now there are two meanings to this world 'undersold': first, that the masters must lose part of their profits; second (and this is what most meant, though it is not quite clear whether such a result would have followed), that they would have been compelled to retire altogether from trade, and hand over their factories to hard-hearted men. They said: Unless legislation comes forward, this state of thing must go on, we can't afford to help it. There were only a few however who thought like this; the great majority were occupied with the work before them, and acted up to the truly English maxim: Charity in play hours, business in work hours. They had no time to see if they could find a wholesale remedy for the wholesale evil around them. The men were busy, but what were the women doing? Probably carrying round mutton broth and beef tea to isolated sick persons, and their fathers and brothers approved of this work, and listened to any opinion they had to give on such matters. But if they complained of the wholesale evil around them and said that it ought to be checked, they would receive the answer, and it was a just one: You know nothing about these things. There is much talk nowadays about women's rights; there is one right which, if they have, all the rest must certainly follow, and that is to have their opinion respected on such points as these; and there is but one way to get this right; to get these opinions worth having. The immense majority of projects heard from well intentioned people are perfectly impracticable, and there could be few calamities graver for the world than that the control and management of its affairs should get into the hands of well intentioned people who know nothing of the subject with which they profess to deal. And this advantage men certainly have over women in matters such as we are discussing; they are likely to know what will work, although for the very same reason they are very unlikely to know what won't work, simply there is no precedent in their own experience of it. Therefore when practical men say a new scheme won't work, they are not necessarily right, seeing that they have but their own experience to guide them.

Now the world has gone on for a long time with all this amount of misery growing almost incessantly in one direction. The men were all apathetic because they had too much to do; the women because they did not know what to do.

The history of the factory act taken alone is one of the most marvellous things we have. But things have bettered themselves since then; people have roused themselves from this apathy, and there is much less physical injury than there was. Physical evils however are not the greatest; a cramped spirit is the worst. And the evidence on the moral side of the question is at least as startling. Until you have read the blue books, you can have no idea what the state of things was in this respect: horrors, few of which I can even hint at here, were on a scale of gigantic magnitude.[9] When talking to foreigners we are offended at the way in which they arrogate to themselves a softer heart than the English and say that the English have coined their hearts with gold, but we can't blame any foreigner, German or American, who says this, if he knows what things used to go on in our English mines. Even of the agricultural groups now things could be told which would be by no means pleasant to hear. Of the moral side, perhaps the best idea I can give you is a hint at the intellectual side. Of the few children who were put down as being able to read, notably in Scotland, few could read more than monosyllables. Of those who could write, only a very few could write their own names and fewer still could write it so that anyone but themselves could read it. A few specific answers to questions are quoted. Who is the devil? Answer 'He was a good man'. 'I don't know where he lived'. Who was Jesus Christ? 'A bad man'. They had never heard of God; didn't know where London was, said they didn't live in England: All they knew was their way about the mine. They had just been kept at work as long as they had any faculties left, and then went to sleep.

Gradually it dawned on the mind of the English nation that such evils must be checked. Of the various remedies suggested all had for their object two things; to shorten the hours of labour, and to increase the precautions taken by the employers. To the last only a passive resistance was offered; to the former there was but one answer: 'We can't afford it'. And this (after the improvements of science had helped us to do much more in an hour than ever before), (after the introduction of steam) and at a time when more and more people were simply occupied in directing the energies of that great servant.

A certain man of the name of Senior, who may well wish now that all the first part of his career were blotted out, put forward an elaborate and deliberate treatise to prove that it was the last hour the mills were kept going which alone gave the profits, and that if this last hour were taken away, all the profits would be gone.[10] His arguments are plausible, and for those situated as most practical men are, forced to look at the matter from a narrow point of view, in details and not broadly, his reasons seem tolerably conclusive, and there was much difficulty raised when the matter was first discussed. Looking at the thing in a broad way, it is easy to see its fallacy, but the manufacturers are not to be wondered at, considering the lights they had. However gradually the doctrine that we could afford to give the children rest, to let them work only ten hours a day, gained ground. Now if we had got over all these difficulties there would be little need to discuss the question; but it is not so. The same sacrifice of man to production still prevails; the same arguments are still brought forward. We shall get over it in time, the world is moving on, but the pace at which it moves depends upon how much we think for ourselves.

And it is the particular province of woman to pay particular attention to those evils to which she is naturally more sensitive than man, and practically to suggest how they may be remedied.

I claim then to have shown what pressing reason there is for showing why the development of our arts of production has done so little to prevent the sacrifice of man to production. And it is not easy to say why things are as they are, not easy to see why the hopeful prophecy we imagined a man of a hundred years ago to have uttered has not come true. Why every day is not a Sunday, devoted to culture, with just so much work perhaps, as is necessary for the health of the body, with time to learn and to think, to be educated to science and art.

I must now break up the question and examine each part separately. The question I will take first is the growth of population. Many people will give the answer glibly 'Well population has grown faster than capital'. *Ans.* 'No, not so.' 'Well then, population has grown faster than it should in proportion to capital.' Their answer contains truth, but a very small portion of the whole truth.

Statistics show that under the most favourable circumstances, population doubles itself in 15 years. At the present time in England, at the present rate, it would double itself in about 60 years. Now allowing a margin for possible errors, I will take it to increase at such a rate that it would double itself in 100 years. Would food increase at an equal rate? If population doubled itself once in a 100 years, in little more than 2000 years we should be packed all over the area of the globe, 4 to a square yard. Now we should certainly find some difficulty in providing such numbers with food.

All the results which are important we have before us but it is hard to know what they mean. People put down that the first thing to be done is to check the increase of population; and it is a singular fact that probably in consequence of their having a much keener appreciation of the miseries of the world, women, when they adopt the Malthusian doctrine, adopt it much more strongly than men. But in fact Nature does this; at least it has been in almost every century compelled to destroy population almost as fast as it has grown. By means of famine, war, disease; in 1349, nearly half the population of England was cut off. It has been obliged to limit the number of population to those she has the means of supporting. And the conclusion from this is, there is absolutely no use in saving life per se; if you save it without enabling people to live, without enabling them to increase their means of support you do no good whatever. Is there no use then in saving life? Of course there is, if, as you almost always do, you increase thereby the means at Nature's command for supporting that life; but if not you do positive evil; and if you cause only so much good in one place as evil in another, you do neither good nor harm. This one thing must be enforced. You must not be content with the immediate effects of what you do. Suppose for instance you have the care of a man suffering from gout; he asks you for a bowl of punch, there is nothing he would like so much, and yet nothing that will really do him more harm. You give it to him and think that you have diminished suffering. The doctor comes in and says you have done very wrong. You say you are very sorry, but you 'didn't know.' Just so, and *that* was your error. It is quite true that that kind of error is different in some ways from the deliberate poisoning of a man, but it is much like it in others. To persist in a course which will lead to poisoning a man, is wrong in the same way tho' not in the same degree as poisoning him deliberately. And just so to divert the streams of charity into a direction which causes it to do a little good but a great amount of harm is wrong in the same way tho' not to the same extent as to cause deliberate misery. When you undertake to administer charity, and having the means at hand of ascertaining what kinds of charity do good, and what harm, do not care to investigate the question, but distribute the charity recklessly, you are doing an action of the same kind as the nurse who gives a bowl of punch to a man with gout. Roughly then it may be stated that the whole of history shows us that any attempt to benefit individuals is useless unless you increase the means at Nature's command for supporting life.

Now in what way are these means to be increased? Some people say: 'These means are capital; increase capital and you will thus go the right way; charities have only diverted the means Nature had of supporting life from a channel where they were doing real good'.[11] This is true in one sense but not in another. If by capital you only mean commodities, it seems to me to be an error, the evil consequences of which are without limit. But if it be true that a steam engine in order is more valuable than a steam engine out of order, it may surely be true that in order to increase Nature's means of support it is more important to have men of a high order than of a low order; for the most important productive machine is man, and the most important thing produced is thought. Therefore as a mere consideration of what is the best way to stop consumption and disease, is to open the minds of your fellow men. Promote education at the expense of capital. Educate first; attend to its effects on capital afterwards.

Heads of Lecture III

The wages problem continued. Fluctuations in the supply of capital and labor, in profits and wages, of individual trades. Connexion between various parts of the wages problem.

Lecture III May 9th [1873]

In my last lecture I discussed the question whether a person sometime ago informed of the general changes produced in the arts of production would have been able to anticipate that just at the time of the greatest advancement of these arts, a Royal Commission instituted would have found that man woman and child were systematically sacrificed to the welfare of production, that conduct was systematically carried on, which a moralist, I will not say of a civilized race but even of an average barbarian race, would have regarded as detestable, and was carried on in consequence of the necessity of furthering production; and that all changes proposed to improve the condition of men should be met by the answer 'It is impossible to interfere with production, we can't afford it'. I said that few intelligent men 100 year ago would have anticipated this, but some might; these might have done the little arithmetical sum we did last time, or without accurate statistics, they might have argued that there was a clearly evinced tendency in the human race to multiply itself rather rapidly. And then they would have argued that since population had not increased to such an extent (doubling itself in a century) it must have been checked by some causes, which on investigation they would have found to be war famine pestilence. If they had done this they would have arrived at the conclusion that any increase in the powers of production would not be likely to render man any more what he proudly called himself 'the lord of creation' but rather as he has been justly described 'the servant of machines'.

Take the case of a young prince and a servant attending to his every want, who has just as much food as is necessary to keep him able to look well after his master. So take the case of an expensive machine with a number of men looking after it, whose whole efforts are directed to preserving it in good working order; any accident which would prevent its working well is regarded as calamitous by the masters, and as calamitous to a greater extent than any accident to the men – its servants. For instance, when the question was asked why machinery was not more used in mines, the answer was, that the roof might fall in and injure it, no reference being made to the [equal][12] possibility of the men being injured. Such ways of putting things are brought forward prominently in working men's newspapers. Now, as I said before, the intelligent man of 100 years ago might have anticipated that men would become more and more the servants of machines as machines were more fully developed and the only doubt in his mind would be as to whether men would not refuse to become simply this, whether they would not deliberately have done something to prevent such a state of things. For unless something is *deliberately* done, the laws of nature are such that man is forced to work for bare existence, to work as many hours as he possibly can for wages just enough to keep him alive. This must always be the case unless we *deliberately* oppose these tendencies by which we are surrounded. Unless Nature takes spasmodic action, as in case of war or pestilence, she will be forced to check population by famine hovering on the outskirts of the industrial army. Let us look at the state of things now. It is interesting to compare the number of marriages in the United Kingdom within a certain term with the price of corn at the time. When corn is high the number of marriages is low. At the present time the pressure of insufficient subsistence is felt, not necessarily directly, for the fact we have noted does not imply that those who have not married, and would otherwise have done so, would not have been able to exist if they had married, but simply that they would not have been able to live in that state of comfort to which they had been accustomed. It is this state of comfort to which we have to direct our attention. If we take the history of England, we shall find that the daily wages of an agricultural laborer have always been equivalent to about a peck of wheat; once they have been equivalent to 2; several times rather less. One peck a day amounts to something like 10 or 11 quarters a year (we can't reckon exactly because the number of work days is not certain). This is probably about twice the amount of food necessary to keep up the agricultural population. Thus the agricultural laborer now as formerly has in wages, roughly speaking, about twice as much as he would require to buy food to eat, on the supposition that he would eat merely the simplest form of food. Looking at the general expenditure of the working classes (there are many estimates, this is probably nearly correct) their total wages are £400 million. The amount they spend on wheat butter cheese potatoes (which take [sic] as necessary for the simplest form of living) is about £170 million; on meat about £30 million; on drink £60 million; on tobacco 8 or 10 million; on houses about £36 million; on clothes about £56 million; and on tea sugar and coffee (notice the high expenditure) £20 million. The one important point I want you to notice is that the labouring classes as a body have a good deal more than twice as high wages as would suffice to buy their necessary food.

Now let us take one other statistical enquiry. How far is the pressure of the limitation of land being felt? The income of the whole country may be roughly estimated at £900 million; of this, about £100 million on spirituous liquors, and £100 million on necessary vegetable food (including eggs). This shows us that it would be possible if we chose to give up all but the absolute necessaries of life, to increase population much and at present there is no immediate connection between the increase of population and the want of food.[13] The total expenditure on absolute necessaries is not at present great. Now we come to the question of distribution.

If population be unchecked by any cause, natural or artificial, the wages of labor must fall ultimately, because of the increased difficulty of obtaining food, unless the laborers can obtain a share of the produce of the land some other way. The first thing to be pointed out is that the belief common among the working classes that, but for the oppression of the rich, they could live in absolute luxury, is not true. A very large part of the £500 million of the income of the country left after taking away £400 million for the wages of manual labour is paid as wages to those laborers who do not belong to the so-called working-classes. It may be safely said that, if labor were remunerated in the higher classes according to the same ratio as it is in the lower, with the understanding of course that as a skilled carpenter is paid higher than an agricultural laborer, so should a manager be paid higher than a carpenter, it is certain that the income of the lower classes would be but little raised, perhaps 50 per cent, and the growth of the population would soon take away all the advantage they might gain by this.

The multiplication table is true for capital as for population. At present the capital of England is about £4,000 million – and according to an estimate of Mr. Gladstone, which I have not seen confirmed elsewhere, but which is probably true, the saving of the country varies from £150 million to £300 million. Taking it at £200 million, the capital of the country is increased at about 5 per cent.

Suppose the capital of the world increased at the rate of 5 per cent for 140 years, it would be multiplied in 600 years by a billion. Now this is more startling even than the increase of population. How is it then checked? (Of course it never does increase at this rate.) Capital gets gradually a lower remuneration. (This is arguing on the hypothesis that the growth of capital goes on undisturbed in peace, but war on a grand scale has checked it before and may again.) If no checks arise, capitalists will compete with one another till they force down the rate of interest. Is this necessarily the case? Not unless the world were of limited extent; if capital and population were both multiplied by a billion in 600 years, the same rate of interest might be maintained for capital; as it is capital must obtain a lower rate of interest. The total amount of the diminution of the produce of the world must fall partly on the laborer, the diminution of returns is shared alike by capitalist and laborer. I have been able to give this only very roughly in outline. How far the fall in the rate of interest checks the growth of capital is a very hard question which we cannot discuss here; that it does so to some extent I can only ask you to believe on my dogmatic assertion. Thus we see now that in a long time population will have become larger, but capital will have increased much more than population and the amount of produce due to the individual laborer will be much less, unless indeed there is an improvement in the arts of production, which will of course operate as a counteracting force to the difficulty of getting raw material. Now I want this portion of the work clearly marked off from the next step. We have been inquiring what will happen in the long run if things remain as they are now.

The next question is: what is the present state of the labor market? What causes operate to bring about the inequality of the rate at which labor is paid? And how far is it possible to level up? I have argued that unless we *deliberately* take steps to prevent it, the world will still suffer want; famine is sure to hover round us unless we deliberately take some course to oppose its action. Let us look at the present and see what indications there are that such a course *can* be taken. I have already introduced a number of facts which will be useful to us here.

Thus, a large portion of the population has for wages about twice as much as it needs actually to buy food; it is evident that an increased difficulty in obtaining corn will check the population – and the wages of the labouring class as a whole are much more than are absolutely necessary to support life. Now it is obvious that to obtain our result, in order to diminish the complete slavery of the working classes (by which I mean the necessity of wearisome work) we must if possible raise the wages of all up to the wages of the highest. Then we must not be content with raising wages; for the highest paid laborer is nearly as much under the control of production as the lowest. Those who do not live in a perpetual whirl of work that they may just support themselves, use their wages not really to live, but to gratify their appetites and taste for luxury; ends which unfortunately they see pursued in other classes. And from this point of view we see two grounds of inquiry. First, what is the reason why the lowest paid are paid so badly? Second, why do the highest paid use their wages so badly? There is a definite remedy for each, and a remedy which can be applied by none so well as by the united action of the women of all classes.

Statistics evidence an enormous difference in the rate of wages. Skilled labour gets paid two, three, four times as much as mere agricultural labour; how is it then that men consent to remain agricultural labourers? There is the old doctrine about the cost of production; how that if any commodity is so much in demand that it can be sold at more than a fair remunerative profit for the labour it costs to produce it, the market will soon be overstocked, and its price forced down. But now the difference of the expense of the education of, say a bricklayer and that of an agricultural labourer is very small, the difference in value very great. Suppose a person in the habit of supplying the slave market were asked whether it answered best to train slaves for bricklayers or agricultural laborers (or at least for skilled and unskilled labour; bricklayers would not probably obtain higher wages than unskilled agricultural laborers in the slave countries) he would probably answer that it made little difference in their wages whether he imparted skill to them or not. But that is for this reason, he can't impart moral training; he does not educate because you can't educate one side of a man alone. Otherwise it would obviously be the very best economy for him to educate his slaves to the highest pitch. Now the slave driver would get all the benefit of such a course of action, but when applying the same truth to the education of children, people often forget that the parent is not in the position of the slave driver, and that he in most cases does not reap the benefit of the increased expenditure. Therefore, although the advantage to his children in after life in increased wages would be ten times as much as his present outlay on their education, he won't do it.

This is true mainly of the lower classes; in the higher classes parents do frequently put themselves to very great discomfort to promote the future welfare of their children. Thus the advance of the world depends almost entirely on the extent to which parents will sacrifice themselves for their children; educated classes have always done this; uneducated never. Yet there is one exception to this, at the time of the Royal Commission for enquiry into the state of the mines, the miners almost without exception urged the reduction of the hours of work for the children, although it would sensibly diminish their own income. In all other inquiries about the way in which children were overworked, it was found that the only point the parents considered important was how far it would affect themselves; in some cases they had even pawned their children's future wages at the pawn shop for drink.

When we speak of the pressure of population on the means of subsistence, of course we must refer to that part which has practically no education; where people are able to apprentice their children to say, a bricklayer's trade, they obtain much more than is necessary for their support.

Now as to the rate of remuneration for various trades. When an employment is dangerous or disagreeable it might be thought that higher wages must be offered to induce people to enter upon it; yet in fact, such employments are generally the worst paid. Why? Because such work is done in the roughest possible way by those who have failed in all other employments, and are consequently not worth high wages. Now suppose the world were suddenly to make up its mind to educate the agricultural laborer up to the level of the ordinary artisan. He would not then earn such high wages as the latter (theirs are 'scarcity' wages), but he would earn much more than before. The production of England would be increased 50 per cent and the expenditure necessary to accomplish such a purpose would be comparatively slight. But now comes the question whether society is justified in stepping in between parent and child? We shall want to argue that the great mistake in endeavouring to raise the lower classes has arisen from forgetting the fact that anything which diminishes directly or indirectly the responsibility of the parent over the children does more harm than any amount of good can compensate. But it does not therefore follow that there is any harm in our paying a part of the children's education. The ordinary arguments against such a course are: that it would check production by shortening the hours of the children's labor and take them from productive employments besides what it would cost directly for their education. And some add that in consequence of this, our country would be undersold etc. Now this is sheer nonsense and arises from a mere confusion of ideas. We can't discuss it now. I must ask you to believe me.

The state of things we see at present is that remuneration for labor amongst the manual working classes depends almost entirely upon an accident, on whether these people in their childhood had slight sacrifices made for them, and not on the cost of production. It depends on efficiency of work and that again on one small point, on the amount of education that the man received as a child. Look at the positive advantages of education; compare the so-called educated man with an ordinary working man. Take the case for instance of an educated man of 20 sent out to superintend some works. Probably at first he would know less of his business than many of the more intelligent working men, and might even have to be entirely guided by one. But in the course of about two years he would be completely master of the situation; education would have made his intellect versatile and ready to adopt new ideas, and above all convinced him of the impolicy of dishonesty. Now what are men paid well for? A sound technical education? No not so much; that may easily be acquired, but for trustworthiness, pliability of intellect, rapidity in managing things, and power of managing men. Now all these qualities come by education. If this were given to working men, we should find that the amount of produce of the same kind due to the work of the world would be probably doubled; wages would be nearly doubled, and, if we chose, we might have leisure. This is what we must strive for. Education in childhood will make the laborer an efficient man (it is simply an investment like paying 10 pounds for a machine which will bring in £10 per annum) the country can afford to pay for such an education and be sure it will be repaid in the next generation.

Next, the laboring classes should have their attention drawn to two things: First, the responsibility they take when they marry at all – thus preventing imprudent marriages; Second, the responsibility as regards their children and the necessity of sacrificing themselves for them. So shall we have put aside all evils but two; we shall have put aside the fear of the growth of population and the possibility of the welfare of the little children being sacrificed to production, so that each generation consumes as it were the capital of the next.

But (1) we shall not have destroyed the tendency of men to spend their days in drink. There is a clear connection between this and long hours of work. I have been much impressed by the harshness with which some people treat the drunkenness of the lower classes. I should much like to take such people for, say 15 hours hard mountaineering for three consecutive days, and then tell them to refresh themselves with some intellectual food. It is absolutely impossible as all who have tried it will tell you, even when the brain has been brought into good training for work, to do any brain work when the body is thoroughly tired. If working men have high wages, it means they can obtain luxuries, but there is one and only one which they can enjoy and that is, sitting in a public house, resting and smoking. No attempt to raise the condition of the working classes will be of any avail, unless we can stop the system of manual labour being carried on to such an extent. This may check production in some slight measure but we can have no real reforms till we have this one; unless we have this, working men will go on working till they are tired of that and then drinking till that wearies in its turn and then back to work. If we do this and educate the children to think of a few things when they grow up they will have leisure and power to think of more.

And (2) why should not all be gentlemen? But if so who will do all the disagreeable and the menial work? Why, we all have to do it sometimes, and neither mind it nor are any the worse for it. Being a gentleman incapacitates no one for work, [but this need not be];[14] in the nature of the case there is no reason why everyone should not be a gentleman. And the best investment of the present capital of the country is to educate the next generation and make them all gentlemen.

Heads of Lecture IV.

Trades Union; their origin, present purpose and organisation: the extent of their control over the supply of labour. 'Free trade in labor'; its good and evil effects. Co-operative associations. Summing up of the circumstances of the 'labour market'.

[Lecture IV] May 16th [1873]

In the last lecture we discussed the circumstances which occasion the very great differences in the remuneration of various employments, and we came to the conclusion that the proposition 'if things are left to themselves they will fall into their proper place' could not apply here, as in this position of society there is so little connexion felt between the interests of parent and child that even the little sacrifice required to afford a better education to the latter, will not of itself be made. From this point of view the doctrine that we must let things drift would not hold.

We also came to the conclusion that if we take some pains about arranging the supply of men there is no immediate ground to fear a press of over-population and no reason in the nature of the case why we should not have all this world as full as it is, and yet everybody a gentleman. We found that every attempt to remedy the ills of society by merely diminishing wealth was like trying to increase your wine by pouring water into the bottle, the more you pour in the more will flow away. Unless care is taken there will always be a class of people so miserable that their lives will depress the rest of the world; and the more you prolong these miserable lives in one place, the more you cause to die elsewhere.

We came to the conclusion that there was no reason why we should not all ultimately be gentlemen. *Ultimately*, but not at once, to educate is a long weary task.

And more, what is a gentleman? A gentleman is a man with an agile cultivated mind, but besides that he is self-reliant, impatient of being a burden on society. But further, he is willing to bear and to forbear to do and to suffer for the welfare of those around him. But this many people are willing to do who are not gentlemen. Yes, they have the *will*; but they have not the instinct to feel that what they are doing is jarring on society.

We have now come to the end of what may be called the first half of the question – what is the end to be attained and what is the best way of attaining that end?

The remaining half divides itself into three portions.

1. What have the laborers done to raise themselves
2. What society can do for them (this divides itself into three heads)
   (1) What society can do by legislation
   (2) What it can do by means of private charities; (and this brings us to the third head namely)
3. What *we* as individuals can do.

Thornton has a chapter on Trades Unions. Brentano has made the mistake of talking with great severity of that chapter.[15] What Thornton has said is not inconsistent with history. The value of Brentano's book is that he shows that nature has been the same throughout the last 1,000 years and how the same problems have been constantly recurring applied to different circumstances.

First he takes the growth of the Frith guilds, and shows how men removed (owing to the rise of certain free towns) from boorishness and robber laws, developed an organisation of their own, being thrown together with similar interests and objects they got to work together and developed that particular feeling, that enthusiasm which made the greatness of the early Greek republics. And as they got more power so they got to look more after their own interests. This common wail goes through the whole of history. Free and noble men working for a noble end till they have got cursed with power. Miserable has been the end of all these corporations, they have accumulated wealth and power till at last by a natural apathy they have fallen aside and some more active society has taken their place. After the Frith guilds come the great merchant guilds and after them the craft guilds. This is the important point with regard to craft guilds. They were originally associations of working men oppressed by the petty tyranny of the corporations of their town. They organised themselves; gradually they won and obtained for themselves in most cases complete command of the city; and then they did just exactly what other guilds had done before them, they made a number of oppressive laws and hampered the progress of society. The craft guilds however were not overthrown by any other organisation but rather fell to pieces through the introduction of wholesale manufacture and this was inconsistent with the existence of craft guilds. The reason of the rapid growth of the manufacturing town of Manchester was chiefly owing to its freedom from any societies of that kind. Now this system of manufactures on a large scale had this disadvantage, that it continually threw out of occupation a large number of workmen. Under the old guilds each workmen knew pretty well what sort of life he had before him; but when manufactures on a large scale came in, this fell away. It was no longer customary to hire men by the year. The masters employed them in a casual manner, as they wanted them. It was customary to keep about a third more workmen on the rolls than were actually required so that when there was a press of work they might be ready at hand, and when there wasn't, why then they could starve.

That was the evil against which the workmen combined. Trades Unions were originally associations for petitioning Parliament to enforce their Trades Laws. On this I must not say much. The regulations they made were not so absurd. These societies went through a large amount of severe work [and] to a great extent gained their aim. Gradually they grew into Trades Unions. (As regards the outrages imputed to them) every crime that is told of against the Trades Unions was rife among the workmen then and on a much larger scale before Trades Unions were heard of than since.

I now take the modern Trades Unions.

I don't idealize at all, I draw simply from life; I only reject all Trades Unions which have not aimed at the highest type. Most of the virtues that are required for political life, and unfortunately many of the vices, are to be found in the Trades Unions.

They are organisations of a subtle character with which there is little in history to compare.

The Trades Unions have a separate branch in every district, with its own rules. But the centre is in London.[16] The secretary is paid the wages of a first-class workman. If any branch has been extravagant it has to collect a special fund. These funds belong to the society at large. Any branch can if it please appeal against the central division[17] and in these cases, the case is printed and a copy is sent to every member throughout the kingdom, the votes are then taken. The secretary is elected every year, and though if he gives satisfaction he is pretty sure to be re-elected, [though][18] the members thus have it in their power to choose some one else.

Altogether the centralisation and localisation seems to me to be carried to almost its utmost extent.

As regards the attainment of information it is certainly carried further than in any other society. If the government wanted any precise information with regard to the wages in any particular trade it would be difficult to get at but by means of the union and organisation, the most accurate information with regard to the wages of every single family, how long it has been out of work, what sickness it has been through etc. can be accurately obtained. That is roughly the organisation.

As regards their rules – their plan is generally that benefit objects should be combined with trade objects.

This plan has been attacked, but it is not found to work badly, and further, a trade society proper is an unmitigated evil; for when they have collected a sufficient sum they strike. But when the two objects are combined this evil is prevented. For instance:

The amalgamated engineers have an income of £50,000 and almost all this is spent in supporting people out of work, *not* on strike, and in the sick fund.

As regards strikes, some people imagine that it is just the object of the Trades Unions to organise strikes – but not one of the better unions have organised a strike in any important case.

When a strike occurs, it is managed in this way. A branch writes up to London and says it would like to strike: but it is never allowed till the whole case has been thoroughly investigated. The case is submitted to impartial judges; officials are sent to the branch from London, to see first that there is fair ground for striking, and secondly that there is a chance of success.

The objection to piece-work has much that is bad in it, but it is encouraged by most Trades Unions. They say that if piecework is allowed, every workman has to make a separate arrangement with his employer and is entirely at his mercy and if the workmen are to be left like this entirely alone the union may as well be abolished.

Again, much has been written against the rule forbidding workmen to take more than a fixed amount of wages, but here again they say they must have some rule. Again some people have said that one of the objects of Trades Unions is to equalise the wages of labour. But the fact is that tradesmen haven't at all made up their minds upon this point, whether it would be advisable to equalize them or not; anyhow they are perfectly aware that it would be absurd to attempt to do so now. It is enough for them if in each place there is a minimum rate of wages. Through their acquaintance with the state of trade in all places, the Unions are able to do a great deal of useful work that was originally done by the masters: such as equalizing the supply of labour in different places with the demand for it.

But in one direction they are compelled to make a regulation immensely injurious to society, i.e. the limitations of apprentices. An obstacle is put in the way of education by this rule. But it is necessary, because it is the interest of the masters to have an unlimited supply of labour so as to be able always to supply the places of men on strike. Further there is at present an unlimited supply of unskilled labour and the skilled labourers say: We labour that we may live, here are a number of men who will compete with us and prevent us obtaining a sufficient remuneration to enable us to live comfortably and work not unduly; we *must* exclude interlopers.

I will give you some cases.

Carpenters and bricklayers wages are higher than, so far as I can see, it is for the benefit of society that they should be. (This trade requires so little skill that without their laws) it would be impossible to exclude competition. Hence most of the most absurd rules are to be found in these trades. You have one method however of destroying those rules and that is by cutting off the supply of unskilled labour. One direction in which Trades Unions have turned their attention is co-operation. Co-operation has the advantage of obtaining for the labourers the wages of superintendence which the masters now obtain, merely because here each man looks after his neighbour. It does good in many ways. It enables the workmen to bear and forbear; but it is not likely that they will succeed to any great extent.

It is sometimes said that they take away the profits of retail dealers. I mustn't go into this now; but it is perhaps worth while to say that the idea that a co-operative store[19] which is not on a larger scale than the ordinary shop, saves the expenses of middlemen is a mistake: they have no better means than others of furnishing their stores. The only thing to be said is that, a large co-operative store can buy on better terms than a small shop. Also if the store is a bona fide store, the expenses of obtaining a connection are spared. When amateurs let it be seen that there is no attempt at dishonesty or adulteration, they save themselves the expense of obtaining a guarantee of honesty. For working men these stores enlarge their field of view and bring them into connection with a large number of new facts. But for the upper classes it is a mistake; it is something like an amateur gardening – it is probable that they might do something better with their time.

Some of the unions have formed the brilliant idea of starting co-operative [stores][20] expecting to lose by it: but expecting to obtain better knowledge than they do now of the state of trade and the current rate of profits in different branches as the masters are not in the habit of revealing the circumstances of trade. Now if the workmen could know when the masters were making large profits they would be able to threaten a strike and always win: as it is they sometimes lose, and lose also their prestige. It is not the striking that is the final end of the Union but to *prevent* strikes. If the knowledge of the Trades Unions extended so far that they never struck without winning the results would be that they would scarcely ever strike.

Now looking at Trades Unions as they are we find rules, almost all of which confer direct benefit on the persons concerned. The rules against machinery are almost obsolete; but it is a very evil state of things that workmen should have this rule against apprentices, and do other people an injury incomparably greater than the good they do themselves.

You have to tell the workmen that a rule which diminishes the happiness of the world is a bad rule. And then, you get the question – 'Am I my brother's keeper?' And you give the answer 'Yes you are'.

And how are we to give that answer and advance that doctrine? Stand up and preach it? No, we must show them that we believe it ourselves. When we go to war we commit barbarities on a wholesale scale which put far out of sight those of Trades Unions; and at such times one hears a gloating over the miseries of others stronger than those of workmen over 'the enemy' as they call Capital.

'Ah but' you say 'they belong to another country.' 'How do *you* know' says the labourer, 'that geography is the only mode of classification. There may be more fellow feeling between the labourers of France and the labourers of England than between English laborers and Capitalists'. I don't say that this answer is sufficient, I hold that is *not*. But as I said I am devoting myself now to the workmen's side, and there is much in it to be thought over before we condemn it recklessly. But we must see whether the principle we tell workmen to act upon is the principle we act on ourselves. Now let us see what that requires from us. A person with 10,000 pounds a year might possibly live on £1,000 and give to 90 persons an income of £10 [sic] a year. Would this give to 90 persons more happiness than the £9,000 would give to himself – and if so ought he to do it? Probably not; because he could make a better use of it by keeping it himself, because an educated man could make better use of £9,000, than 90 uneducated ones. Every educated man has had invested in himself such a large amount of the capital of the world, that it would be a great mistake if every rich man became poor in the present state of things.

The question then that we are now brought up to is – What are the limits between which we are compelled to act up to the principle that we are our brother's keeper. xxx [sic] When we have done that we may go about the country to preach with effect, that a regulation which hampers the capitalists and causes the working classes on the whole to suffer, is wrong; that in particular a regulation which cuts at the root of the advance of education and the welfare of the rest of society is wrong. Until we can preach this we can't reorganize society and we are not in a position to preach it until we have learnt to act up to it ourselves.

Heads of Lecture V

Economic legislation, factory acts; education acts; poor laws. Charitable societies – how to select those whose benefits are liable to the least drawbacks.

Lecture V May 23rd [1873]

I will go over at greater length some of the work already gone over; partly in answer to some questions asked me.

It is true that the effect of education on the wages of unskilled labour is not in general direct, but education makes unskilled labour scarce and so raises its wages; what is scarce must be more highly paid.

Now there is an unlimited supply of it; that is why it is so badly paid; if we could educate the mass of the community, unskilled labour, mere manual labour, would be so deficient that to get people to perform it you would have to pay them highly.

This however is looking far forward and supposes us to have educated unskilled labour from off the face of the earth. The total produce of the earth would then be much greater than it is; unskilled labour would have to be very highly paid; the whole world would be benefited and no one would suffer. But it is also to be borne in mind that merely manual labour is capable of being almost entirely superseded.

Carrying corn out of a ship is a thing that you would think must be done by men; but the other day I was watching a machine that was doing the work more efficiently than hundreds of men. No manual labour was required but such as directed the machine; and perhaps one or two men with spades. And when manual labour becomes dear, machine work becomes cheap.

Now in connection with Trades Unions I would say one thing about domestic servants. Long before the present complaint about the difficulty of obtaining good servants set in, Mill foresaw what things would come to pass from the tendency setting in to prefer personal freedom.

(Trades Unions) A member of a Trades Union has a definite aim put before him; he is taught to subordinate his own wishes to that aim. It is absolutely proved that no organization for exterminating humbug is so efficient as a Trades Union. In this way it does some good. But the great benefit of a Trades Union is that it gives the people a political education, and trains them in a habit of subordinating their own personal will to the good of the state. A Trades Union is equal to a Greek republic for imparting a political education to the people.[21]

Great benefit is also gained from co-operative societies. They give education in administration, which Trades Unions do not sufficiently give. Moreover there is an immense amount of labour saved by them; the extra amount of labour and thought which the co-operators give to their store is not an addition to their work; but is just a training to them (I think what I said about this in a previous lecture has been rather misunderstood, I have been accused of informing ladies as to the cheapest method of buying their goods, I should not venture on such impertinence). What I meant to say was that Co-operative Stores are capable of conferring boundless benefits on the human race, but the movement has suffered much from the abuse of the word Co-operation.

A Co-operative Store proper managed by working men *for* working men has all the advantages of a joint stock company[22] on a small scale. But what is *called* a Co-operative association is no more co-operative than it is philanthropic or anything else; it is merely a well-managed shop. When you deal with a co-operative store you have nothing whatever to do with co-operation. There are co-operative stores that are really managed by the people who deal with them; but when the so-called co-operative stores are mere shops managed by gentlemen, all that can be said is, it is a pity such people can't find something better to do with their time.

But these arguments do not invalidate the position that co-operative stores proper are capable of conferring immense benefit. The working men managing the store themselves *do* take up the profits of one middle man. The work educates and amuses them, they save the wages the manager of the shop would otherwise have had (and lead up in turn to better things). They ought in every way to be encouraged. It is because I am so anxious for co-operation proper that I want to distinguish it and a mere shop which has nothing co-operative about it. However the chief subject of the present lecture is to see how we can forward movements for raising the condition of the working classes.

You will recollect that I said that the position of the working classes a little while ago was settled for them by custom; deliberate action was not so imperiously demanded. Hitherto there has been in general some limited check on population (from custom etc. when there was only a limited number of situations or openings for a young man, when there was only a limited number of cottages where he could settle). Even people without any deliberate education could see the effects of marrying too early. In some small countries like Switzerland for instance this fact is so clearly brought home to the people that it is not allowed that the younger ones marry too early.

But now it is different; the wide world is open to everybody and now, unless deliberate steps are taken we shall, in spite of improvements, find that man is gradually being subordinated to production.

The chief lesson that Political Economy has to teach us, is that the arguments from history that one meets with are mere nonsense (because they are taken from a time entirely different from our own). The more we study history, the more we shall feel convinced that it is not fair to say that because the world *has* gone on without some distinct forecasting of the future that therefore it may go on so now.

This opinion is particularly pressed on me by the awful abominations in the factory districts at the beginning of the century. These were partly remedied by the Factory acts. The labour of women and of all persons under 18 is now limited to 10 hours a day. Young children are not allowed to work at all, and children under 13 only half time. When these regulations were first proposed people were almost unanimous in opposing them and said the country was going to be ruined. Sir Robert Peel, when the bill was thrown out for the last time, made a great speech and talked the wildest nonsense. Most men of influence voted with him; but had his opinion ultimately prevailed we should be incomparably worse off than we are now.

If we could only get people to analyse the causes that govern the wealth of the world they would be convinced that the doctrine that 'if wages rise in all trades we shall be undersold' is utter nonsense. This absurdity is proved as distinctly as it can be in any book on Political Economy.

If manufacturers had got to see the effects of the Factory Acts proper they would raise no opposition to their being extended almost without limit; indeed many of them now would like to see the education clauses extended.

But again half timers are extremely intelligent; the general education they obtain in the factory makes them lively; but as soon as their half time is up they forget all they have learnt. If the half time were extended to 18 (so that between the ages of 13 and 18 they could get three hours a day of schooling), they would have carried on their education to a time when they would value it; they could then get help from the working men's colleges etc. and so the country would be ultimately thoroughly educated. This would be sinking capital, but England can well afford it; she would do it for railways etc. (They say it is a poor field for investment, but it is the finest instrument of production in the world.) Granted that production would at first fall off – still we can afford it; and if we take the extreme view it would pay as a nation over and over again. This is the last reference I shall make to Political Economy. The main purport of these lectures is not to urge Economic studies, but rather to defend the position which philanthropists are adopting. I shall pass over the poor laws almost entirely. A history of them can be found in Knight's history and in Prof. Fawcett's 'Pauperism'.[23] I want to come to the main proposition which is this that if a philanthropist gives himself intelligently to the work of raising the working classes the conclusions that he will come to will be the same as those arrived at by Political Economy. I will give the main outline of the rules Miss Hill drew up after working some time among the poor of London.[24]

1. It is best to enforce strictly all such rules as payment of rent; and far better to give work than money or goods.
2. It is most helpful of all to strengthen by sympathy and counsel, the energetic effort which shall bear fruit in time to come.
3. It is essential to remember that each man has his own view of his life and must be free to fulfil it; that in many ways he is a far better judge of it than we, as he has lived through, and felt, what we have only seen, our work is rather to bring him to the point of considering, and to the spirit of judging rightly, than to consider and judge for him.

   [These rules are given rising I presume in their order of importance, at least it seems so to me.][25]
4. The poor of London, as of all large towns, need the development of every power that can open to them '*noble sources of joy*'.

This last sentence seems to me to be the sum of it all. Let us look then at the ways of relieving the poor.

Roughly speaking they may be divided into:

1. Those in which the machinery of organization is prominent.

2. Those in which individual action is prominent.

Organization alone has the effect of being obliged to adopt one of two courses; either that adopted before the Poor Laws (which was swallowing up the wealth of the country without benefiting it), or we can take the other course, we can refuse outdoor relief in almost every case and can give relief in such a manner as to make people consider whether it would not be better to starve outright. Or we can take an intermediate course which avoids some of the evils and retains the others: we can have a number of paid agents whose business it is to detect dishonesty; these persons have to ask all sorts of disagreeable questions and in fact to take for granted that everyone is an impostor and they must obtain by habit a blunted mode of dealing with distress, and it comes almost to this, that no one shall starve unless he is very shy. But there is something incomparably more than this to be done. The relieving of distress is not to be left undone, but there is something altogether different.

There are I believe in the world few things with greater capability of poetry in it than the multiplication table. There is one fact which is at the basis of all true poetry; that if you can get mental and moral capital to *grow* at some rate per annum there is no limit to the advance that may be made; if you can give it the vital force which will make the multiplication table applicable to it, it becomes a little seed that will grow up to a tree of boundless size. If you can get work done that will make the poor help themselves you will have done boundless good.

If you give away 10 millions, that relieves distress, there is so much distress relieved, but if you start a method that makes distress diminish one per cent a year, you have done more ultimately than by giving away the 10 millions. But organization cannot do this, for this you must have personal contact. What is it that makes a man a man? It is his having desires. And what is a miserable pauper? A person who doesn't care for anything. Mental capital makes people care for things, if you can give this you needn't fear for the world's future.

Now let us examine Miss Hill's rules taking them backwards, let us see first what noble sources of joy are. The first that she comes across is the joy of cleanliness; teach them that. Then there is the joy of independence; the power of feeling shame, and the capability of feeling the pleasure of being able to stand up and feel that one is doing one's work. Caring for one's property and one's children. Rejoicing as their children grow in everything that they would have them grow in – everything else will come.

In order to give them these sources of joy, she says, we must bring him [sic] to judge rightly, not bring him into our own groove. We must not patronise the working classes, say to them, 'just jump into the groove and glide along'. We must regard a man as intelligent capital and try to make him productive. The ordinary way of shifting men about is as if a gardener should try to make trees grow by pulling them out by his own strength instead of digging and watering them and then letting them grow in their own way.

Like this rule is the preceding one 'we must strengthen by counsel etc.' and as to *giving* each work, that is an evil that should not be done if it can be avoided but it is less evil than giving alms.

And if these things could be done let us see what would happen. In what sense would the working classes be improved? All their special weaknesses would have fallen away. All the polish due to training through successive generations would not come at once. But what Miss Hill's work has shown is that every thing else that can be done to make people ladies and gentlemen can be done; but it can be done only with untiring work. And organization is needed to prevent individual workers from being overworked and to prevent the same cases from being relieved two or three times over. I should strongly advise you to read Miss Hill's article in the Macmillan's Magazine. Also this organized work can detect imposture. But we *must* kindle new sources of joy. We must make people feel pained to be a drag on society. We must teach them to love their children – to care about what is most important for their children.

We must teach them to love Beauty for its own sake. Of all the works of charity probably the greatest that has been done lately is the opening of the Bethnal Green Museum. This work is incomparably higher than relieving mere physical distress. Let people only take this method of working. But in order to *act* you must *think* first. There is room for relieving physical distress; there is unlimited work to be done in other ways. Now supposing that God had wanted to make a set of people just to do this work. He would, we might imagine, have chosen some that had been educated from their earliest youth; with soft sympathetic hearts, with money (but this is unimportant). And now what is this but an exact description of the hundreds of thousands of ladies who are tatting their tatting and twirling their thumbs. I ask you: what class of people could be more wanted in the world, for whom is there greater need than a number of lady workers doing work like Miss Hill's.

I am aware that there is this paradox 'I ought to do what is wrong'.

Sometimes (such is our social education) it is not thought unreasonable that a person should prevent others from doing important work.

But we must endeavour to act on the supposition that there is more to be done in the world than just taking care of each other.

[Heads of Lecture VI]

The influence of private individuals; the pursuit of wealth; the true meaning of wealth. The harmony between true Political Economy and Ethics; luxury, its direct effects and indirect effects. Rightful luxury and wrongful luxury. Conclusion.

Lecture VI May 30th [1873]

In my last lecture I treated the question of the influence of education on the wages of those even who ultimately would have to do work where their education would be but of little assistance. I touched also upon the history of the Factory Acts. I showed how the non-fulfilment of the prophecies of the ruin they would cause should encourage us to set aside the objections which are now raised to compulsory education on the same grounds. We considered also the Poor Laws; the difficulty of administering them; and the way in which organized individual work is able to supplement what may be called organized mechanical work. [On this last head I have since been challenged with affording a strong argument in favour of sisterhoods, which it is said do thus combine the advantages of individual and organized work. I had not meant to touch on this point, but as the question has been raised, I must give it as my opinion that so far from so doing, they rather combine the disadvantages of each, and do not attain the advantages of either to a full extent. As things are now any sisterhood which should refuse to join a general organization for the administration of charity, would do much harm. If we look at the Charity Organization Society in London, a Society which is doing splendid work, we shall see that any such organization must cover a very large area, must have an immense number of sources of information and must have direct access to the governing bodies of every charitable society within the limits of which it works; and as a necessary portion of any such organization there must be a certain number of individuals who act the part rather of detectives than of any other officer. As a rule charities administered by private individuals or by sisterhoods (though as they do not usually do much in the way of alms-giving, the latter do not do so much harm) have been proved by universal experience to have been generally badly administered. Then the special work of private individuals depends on their having a great amount of freedom, and not proceeding rigidly by any method; of course such rules as any organization lays down must be adopted as far as they go, but beyond that, the more individual freedom there is, the better. It has been found too, that a person who is not wholly cut off from home sympathies herself, has more power to perform what is after all one of the highest parts of charity, to kindle the domestic sympathies among the poorer classes; it has been found that those who have lived for any length of time within the chilling walls of private societies have lost this vigour. I hold too that the voice of history speaks unwaveringly in one direction, viz. that sisterhoods have always had a tendency to accumulate round them a kind of sacred red tape – and even in those sisterhoods where there are no vows demanded, no direct interference from above, the individual character becomes dwarfed, and they have a tendency to develop a partiality for vows and to subject themselves to the dominion of some individual or society.[26] And this evil, intense in itself, is in most cases aggravated by the fact that the persons who obtain the command over such sisterhoods are not the persons who are best fitted to rule the world. In the distant future, there may be a great, an important, even a leading part to be played by sisterhoods, but as they are at present organized, they do not have the advantages of individual action, scarcely any of those of organized action and have a tendency to sap the foundations of the energy of the moral character of the individual.][27]

To return to our subject. I then spoke of the work which had to be done, and of the qualities wanted for doing it; a high education, a power of sympathy, ready yet restrained; leisure; and a certain restlessness which should render inactivity an evil; all these being the distinctive qualities of women in civilised society. I said that if a person were engaged in creating on paper a set of people who should do the work needed to be done in the world, he would give them all the qualities belonging to ladies now, and very few besides. Yet with all this, the large majority of women remain content (or not content as the case may be) to do nothing of this work lamenting they cannot do something more. Some few indeed stand forwards and breaking through conventionalities despising difficulties and suffering, do a great work; against these the accusation of quixotism is often raised, and too often justly, for many of the efforts initiated could do but little good and are based on no foundation of quiet investigation.

In my present lecture I will try to answer the question: is luxury then altogether wrong? Is there no limit to the amount of self-sacrifice required? It is right first to try what grounds may be laid down for separating some portions of our expenditure from others for marking off the one part as harmless, the other not. It seems to me that almost all the difficulty that has arisen on this point is due to a forgetfulness of the fact that a highly cultivated person is in every sense a portion of the wealth of the country. Let us analyse the forms expenditure may take.

I. The ordinary expenditure of every day life; this is spent in obtaining a certain amount of the comforts of every day life. Though casuistical questions are often raised on this point – as for instance whether a person is justified in wearing expensive clothes when she could perform her work just as well in every way whilst wearing common clothes – such questions do not seem to me to be at present of any very great importance. For while it is perfectly clear that any person who contributes to the expensiveness of the prevailing fashion, does an immense injury to society, there does not seem to be at present any advantage in urging people to be eccentric.

II. There is that expenditure which has for its end, directly or indirectly, *culture*. There is an immense difference between such modes of expenditure as keeping an unnecessarily expensive carriage, and having an expensive box at the opera. I don't wish to raise the question whether all operas tend to produce wealth, in so far as cultivated people are wealth, but assuming only that they might be made one of the best ways of promoting education, I hold that to obtain command of a box is one of the ways of subsidizing the professor of fine Arts. And if it be true that there are less expensive seats at the opera open to the common people, and also that the training of good artistes at these operas renders it possible to get better music elsewhere, then this expenditure (getting tickets for good concerts etc.) is something quite different to that on the commodities of production which gives no art education whatever. Expenditure thus of the kind spent in obtaining an art education, such as travelling etc. tends to increase culture, and is in this way productive expenditure. It increases capital – capital being taken in its broad sense as *stored up sources of enjoyment*. And thus in essence for all practical purposes, expenditure of this kind is not in itself wrongful, and subject to limitations, afterwards to be considered, should not be grudged.

III. There is another kind of expenditure of material wealth, that is, the obtaining of means of display. If this is a source of joy to the individual, it implies that he has very low sources of joy: and in any case it creates the pains of envy in others. Therefore all display is vicious, in the fullest sense of the word. All expenditure is wrong which does not give us either direct gratification or tend to cultivate us. Some expenditure is very near the bordering line, such as dressing elegantly: but of this more after.

IV. Let us pass on to the expenditure of *time*. I hold that wrongful luxury in so far as it involves expenditure of money is not so often passed over as that which involves expenditure of time. To begin with: if people will live nearly up to their income and even a little beyond it, they are obliged to spend a large portion of their time in trying to make two ends meet; in that case they are living wrongly, and time, that most valuable wealth, most real capital, is squandered in trying to make things fit in. If, in order to live up to a certain standard of display, this waste of time is necessary, then a lower standard ought to be aimed at. What I said of the first two kinds of expenditure is practically answered here. If in order even to educate ourselves or others, e.g. by taking a box at an opera, or to obtain, what is more distinctly a luxury, a larger house for instance, a great amount of time must be spent in trying to make both ends meet, such expenditure is wrong, for it consumes the most valuable thing in the world – time. If to keep up our expenditure, we have to work so as to cramp our growth, our energies, we are here again destroying time.

To return to the subject of dress. What is said of the shameful waste of money on dress might almost be omitted, for it is nothing to the waste of time. And this not for the attainment of beauty of an aesthetic end; then it would be culture; but if it is devoted to being in the vanguard of the fashion, it is luxury of the very worst kind. These then are the results which follow from the simple principle that time is one of the most important things in the world and that culture is as much real wealth as a carpet or anything of that kind.

Of course there are a great many casuistical questions which will still arise and always disturb people; which cannot be answered by any fixed rule, and will give difficulty even when the individual attempts to solve them for the individual. E.g. expenditure on recreation when we are hard at work is right, but how far? Which of us for instance would be justified in keeping a riding horse? I do not mean to say that there is any simple rule which will help much to solve such questions as these, but I think if we recollect – that any form of expenditure which is necessary for our doing high work is not to be regretted, but that we should be extremely jealous of spending money in this way if it is not necessary, and that if there is any doubt in our mind as to this, it is better usually not to do it – we can generally solve these questions in detail, and it is really only with regard to such questions that difficulties usually arise. The whole drift of these lectures has been rather to insist on the necessity of having general principles, rather than on the possibility of general rules. These general principles must be applied by individuals in a way which cannot be formulated.

With this ends the subject matter of what I have to say. I want now only to go back and consider what has been the aim of these lectures. First, it was not to insist on the urgent necessity of everyone's studying political economy. It was this: to show how the study of political economy has led me, as a study of other subjects has led others, to be impressed with the necessity of acting, with the special circumstances which render it impossible for us to look around us and yet be willing to drift. I wanted to make it clear what must happen if we do drift, to show that if we do so, we shall always have an immense number of people very near starvation's limit. It is a notorious truth that those countries which are richest have also the greatest amount of poverty; the reason of this is obvious – where competition is free, where the movement of every individual is completely unshackled, there wealth is accumulated rapidly, and there also by the same causes, misery, crime and all that is bad is accumulated too.

Well looking back we see that this free circulation of labor and capital, this breaking up of quasi-family, that is, of local life, is the birth of one short century, and that people who are governed by modes of action which have descended from a time when this was not so, have drifted along, not adapting their action to the changed circumstances, and have produced the astonishing result that whilst the powers of production have increased immensely, man has yet been left so completely a slave to production that habits of action which have compelled people to grow up utterly destitute of mental and moral wealth have been insisted on as necessary. I want also to look a little further back to the older civilizations. We shall find that the history of the world is roughly a history of the subordination of custom to competition – of the imparting to man the freedom of individual action, of the sweeping away of the net-work of custom which hindered his action and the leaving him free to make such contracts as he would. You will find little in history which is not connected with this change, depending chiefly on the change in the ethical point of view (on which I must not now touch) and proceeding almost regularly through the Eastern civilization to the Greek and Roman, checked then by the inundation of Teutonic customs, and expanding again until the present time.[28] 'Well,' people are in the habit of saying, 'what has been will be.' Nothing seems to me more utterly false. Greece and Rome have been great and failed; why? Simply because they were utterly void of moral enthusiasm – because they were pagan, and grossly pagan, because on the one hand they practised immorality of the most horrible description – because on the other they had an utter recklessness of human life – because in the whole of their nature there was nothing of that enthusiasm which was the foundation of the position of the man who was the 'Friend of publicans and sinners' who was the greatest anti-dilettante that ever lived.[29]

It is almost impossible to over-estimate the advantages modern civilization has derived from the intellectual vigour of those nations. Our acquaintance with them opened up to us a new life, and overthrew that despotism of mental sluggishness which ruled Europe before the Reformation. But we must also remember that the consciousness of what we owe to them in this respect has made men subordinate their judgements to the ancient Greeks and Romans on points on which they could be no judges. The spirit of dilettantism which has pervaded the world is, I conceive, to be traced to this source more than to any other i.e. to the almost exclusive study of classical history. Much as we have to learn from them, we must remember that their world was not our world and all their fundamental social axioms we must absolutely deny, or put aside the name of the followers of Christ. Slavery, the absolute utilization of some men for the luxury of others had in every single direction grown into Greek and Roman life. Aristotle said: 'Slavery is natural. Nature intended some men should be slaves' and the modern world has said that a proletarian class is necessary and natural. This they say in spite of their professing to be followers of a person who maintained with the most unflinching audacity the doctrine that a proletariat was not necessary. And until we separate culture from emotion, and intellectual and social culture from ethical, until we adore our Greek teachers, but separate ourselves from them, we shall never wholly escape from Paganism.

'A proletariat' says the dilettante, 'is a necessity of nature.' So it is if we drift; suppose we say: 'The most profitable investment of capital is in the production of culture, a form of wealth as real as windmills or factories; the world can afford it, and so far as we are concerned we will set to work to bring it about, and induce others to do the same'; then a proletariat would be a thing of the past. There is no reason why, because unskilled work has to be done, we should have unskilled workmen to do it. There is no reason why much of it should be done at all, no reason why we should not have an incomparably greater surplus to devote to the purposes of production. There is no reason for all this if we can do one thing and that is this; if we can do as Miss Hill says and open up to the people noble sources of joy. I forgot in recapitulating what I said in my last lecture to mention one thing; and it is this – I have been said to allow scarcely any advantage to be gained by soothing pain or giving pleasure by the ordinary work of charity. I did not mean this, but only that we were likely in all such attempts to do harm in indirect ways, and that all the good we do can be seen, the relief of suffering is measured when we have been told what is done, but by the opening of faculties of noble sources of joy we open up a new spring of life, the effects of which have no limit. Is there anything in the conceptions of the wildest dreams more wonderful than some facts which are shown us by the multiplication table? As for instance the fact that a sum of money increasing at 5 per cent for 14 years will be increased by a number with more than a hundred figures. This same multiplication table is the foundation of most of the startling statements made. For instance, if we send a child to school, we do good; but if we induce his father to send him we do much more good; we have opened up to the latter new sources of joy, have given him new tendencies to work for an end. In this way we do a good the end of which we cannot see. The changes in the world due to it are incomparable. A proletariat is not necessary if we do this, and although it is perfectly true that any individual who takes as his bases of action the hope of revolutionising society is not likely to do the world much good (except perhaps by adding to its hilarity), although we must not expect our individual efforts to do much, yet everything that has yet been done in the world has been done by people who make efforts, not knowing whether they will be successful or not. If each soldier led against a fortress were to say: 'I can't take that myself' and so were to fall away, the fortress would not be taken; but if each says: 'If we all go on together the fortress will be taken at last', it will fall. So it is with us: you may say: (and I have noticed much more of this diffidence, restricting their action for good, amongst women than men) 'Am I sure I shall do any [good] at last?' Of course you are not; if you were you would be very likely to fail; but you are an army that is sure to conquer at last. There is then work which must be done: but how? Not as in an army, according to rigid prescriptions laid down. In the battle of life, the strongest force of all is individuality, and anything which crushes that out does more harm than good.

What work then is there to be done?

1. Direct work such as Miss Hill's (account of this in Macmillan's Magazine, July/69, Sept./72).[30]

2. Hospital work.

3. Work more or less like Miss Hill's, capable of being grafted on to it, and in which the only rule is: 'take that which seems the most important and do it.'

4. Then without any work of that kind, there is an immense amount to be done by developing the powers of those around you. This may be done either by formal instruction, or by those informal modes of making people interested in what will raise them, of which penny readings are a type. Such works are eminently fitted to be done by women and can be done more or less by all women.

5. Before all there is the attaining of a knowledge of what difficulties there are to be overcome and of how to overcome them; this can seldom be done without study, and can always be done most rapidly by its help.

It seems to me that much may be gained by seeing what should be the ends of study. People often drift about, not knowing what subjects to take up.

These ends are:

1. To give reasoning power; for which of accessible subjects, arithmetic is incomparably the best; also mathematics and sciences, including of course political economy.

2. To give artistic training: to cultivate the more delicate powers of the human mind. For this, literature and art training are the most important: but here I must explain that the study of literature is not what is sometimes meant, the attainment of the vocabularies (this is as near an approximation to the deadening of the faculties as anything) but the getting to know the way in which people have

thought and felt.

3. Education through personal influence, through getting to know individual people and those who are best worth knowing can generally only be got at through their books; such as Lucretius and Goethe.

Any work that is genuine on any one of these sides and particularly one which does not neglect any, will give you an opinion worth having and power to enforce it. And as in all things there is the most urgent need for the guidance of action, this will always be after all the most important thing.

When that is said, all has been said that can be said as regards the question, how are we to change things so that a proletariat need no longer be? We must increase the wealth of the world, and each one must decide for himself how. We have one general broad rule, the foundation of all; that living as we do in the world, supported by its wealth, consuming its wealth, we must also increase that wealth; and whatever we do must establish clearly its claim to be one of the means of increasing the noble sources of joy.

Notes and References

1. At the time the American spelling (e.g., 'labor') was often preferred in radical and republican circles, as a sign of admiration for the democratic United States (cf. Biagini, 1992, pp. 60–83): both the republican weekly newspaper, *The National Reformer*, and the *Agricultural Laborers' Chronicle* adopted it consistently; *Reynolds's Newspaper* and *The Bee-Hive* more occasionally. It is likely that Alfred and Mary adopted it for a similar purpose: and it is interesting that Mary Paley used also the ordinary British spelling, further reinforcing the impression that, when she chose the American one, she did it for effect.
2. The list of recommended books is similar to the one given by Alfred Marshall in his lecture outlines at the end of the first lesson (see below, p. 133). A more complete list has been inserted just after it (see below, p. 134).
   The books on this first list are:
   W. Thornton, *On Labour. Its Wrongful Claims and Rightful Dues. Its Actual Present and Possible Future*, 2nd ed., London, Macmillan and Co., 1870;
   J. M. Ludlow and Lloyd Jones, *Progress of the Working Class 1832–1867*, London, A. Strahan, 1867;
   T. Brassey, *Work and Wages Practically Illustrated*, London, Bell and Daldy, 1872;
   W. E. Hearn, *Plutology; or The Theory of the Efforts to Satisfy Human Wants*, London, Macmillan and Co., 1864;
   J. Macdonell, *A Survey of Political Economy*, Edinburgh, Edmonston and Douglas, 1871;

J. S. Mill, *Principles of Political Economy, with some of their Applications to Social Philosophy*, 7th ed., London, Longmans, Green, Reader and Dyer, 1871 (or, People's Edition, London, New York, etc., Longmans, Green and Co., 1873);
H. Fawcett, *Pauperism: its Causes and Remedies*, London and New York, Macmillan and Co., 1871;
L. Brentano, *Zur Geschichte der Englischen Gewerkvereine*, Leipzig, Verlag von Duncker und Humblot, 1871 [English translation 'On the history and development of gilds, and the origin of trade-unions', in *English Gilds*, ed. by J. T. Smith, London, Trübner and Co., 1870];
Royal Commission of Inquiry on Trades Unions 1867–69, *Eleventh and Final Report*, 1869;
J. E. Cairnes, *The Character and Logical Method of Political Economy*, London, Longman, Brown, Green, Longmans and Roberts, 1857 [2nd ed., Dublin, W. McGee, 1869].

3. The same word is used by Marshall in his 1885 inaugural lecture (Marshall, 1925, p. 156).
4. See below, p. 189.
5. By a mixed class, Marshall meant a class of mixed ability and preparation. Men were not present at the lectures.
6. On this, cf. also Marshall (1961), vol. I, II.i.4 and the Royal Commission on the Aged Poor, Q. 10,399, in Marshall (1926).
7. Cf. Marshall's polemics against lavish expenditure in Marshall (1925), p. 310.
8. The poet referred to is Antipatros, quoted from Marx (see Marshall's notes of this lecture, below, p. 135). This quotation was repeated in 1883 in the first of the three 'Lectures on progress and poverty' (Marshall, 1969, p. 185), and in Marshall (1919), p. 790, note. In both cases the poet's name was changed to Antiparos.
9. Here Marshall was referring – in the first place – to the great inquiries of the 1810s–1840s. These included: *Select Committee on State of Children Employed in Manufactories of the United Kingdom*, Minutes of Evidence, *Parliamentary Papers* (*P.P.*), 1816, II; *Royal Commission on the Employment of Children in Factories*: First Report, Minutes of Evidence, *P.P.*, 1833, XX; Second Report, Minutes of Evidence, *P.P.*, 1833, XXI; Third Report, Minutes of Evidence, *P.P.*, 1834, XIX; *Royal Commission on Children's Employment in Mines and Manufactories*, First Report (Mines and Collieries), *P.P.*, 1842, XV; Second Report (Manufactures), *P.P.*, 1843, XIII. These commissions prepared the ground for the mine and factory laws of 1842–7, which eliminated most of the worst abuses, especially as far as children and women were concerned (cf. Fraser, 1994, pp. 11–30). However, despite the rather comprehensive character of this legislation, child work had survived in a few cases, such as brickmaking, which is discussed below, cf. 'The future of the working classes', note 7.
10. Senior's famous 'last hour' was discussed in his *Letters on the Factory Act, as it affects the cotton manufacture*, 1837.
11. Marginal note by Marshall: 'Something omitted here. A. M.'.
12. 'Equal' is crossed through and the following marginal note added by

Marshall: 'This is overstated. Men get to know when the roof is unsafe and can move out of danger more rapidly than the machine can. A. M.'.

13. The word 'food' was added by Marshall, replacing 'world' given in Mary Paley's notes.
14. Square brackets added to the text, probably by Marshall.
15. Thornton (1870), book II, chapter IV; Brentano (1871) criticized Thornton (cf. in particular note 353).
16. Marshall was here describing the 'amalgamated' model of trade union: cf. chapter 7 of Briggs, 1990. The most detailed study is still Webb S. and Webb B., 1920, pp. 180–298; however, see Musson, 1972, for a full bibliography.
17. Presumably the word 'decision' is intended here.
18. 'Though' is deleted, probably by Alfred Marshall.
19. He was basically describing the 'Rochdale' model of co-operation: cf. Holyoake, 1907. For more general studies see Holyoake, 1887; and Cole, 1944; a recent reassessment has been tried in Yeo, 1988.
20. Word crossed through and replaced by 'producing societies' in Marshall's handwriting. He added the marginal note: 'I have not heard that much has come of this. A. M.'.
21. Cf. Whitaker (1975), vol. II, p. 351 and p. 364.
22. 'Joint stock company' is followed by a question mark in parenthesis. For Marshall's model of co-operative store see above, footnote 19.
23. For references, see above, note 2 and below, lecture outlines, note 3. For a recent discussion of the Poor Laws and an extensive bibliography see Rose, 1986.
24. Hill (1869). This passage, with the omission of the second part of point 1., is quoted at the end of chapter V of the first book of Marshall A. and Marshall M. P. (1879).
25. The square brackets are given in the original.
26. Similar considerations on sisterhoods are in Marshall's notes of his conversation with an Irish Priest during his voyage to America in 1875 (*Marshall Papers*).
27. The square brackets are given in the original.
28. These passages show the influence of Hegel's *Lectures on the Philosophy of History*, well documented in Groenewegen (1990). For Marshall's later distinction between 'competition' and 'freedom', cf. Marshall (1961), vol. I, pp. 9–10.
29. In the last part of this lecture, Marshall is probably under the influence of Seeley (1866) and Renan (1864). The concept of Christ as an anti-dilettante is taken from Renan 1864 (cf. chapter XIV). In a similar derogatory sense J. S. Mill, in his 1838 article *Bentham*, called Hume 'the prince of *dilettanti*' in a passage later omitted in *Dissertations and Discussions*. 'Enthusiasm' is the title of chapter XIV of Seeley (1866).
30. Hill (1869, 1872).

Bibliography

Biagini E. F. (1992), *Liberty, Retrenchment and Reform. Popular Liberalism in the Age of Gladstone 1860–1880*, Cambridge: Cambridge University Press.

Brentano L. (1871), *Zur Geschichte der Englischen Gewerkvereine*, Leipzig: Duncker und Humblot.

Briggs A. (1990), *Victorian People*, Harmondsworth (Middlesex): Penguin Books.

Cole G. D. H. (1944), *A Century of Co-operation*, Manchester: Co-operative Union.

Fraser D. (1994), *The Evolution of the British Welfare State*, London: MacMillan.

Groenewegen P. D. (1990), 'Marshall and Hegel', *Économie Appliquée*, vol. 43, pp. 63–84.

Hill O. (1869), 'Organized work among the poor: suggestions founded on four years' management of a London court', *Macmillan's Magazine*, vol. 20, pp. 119–26.

Hill O. (1872), 'The work of volunteers in the organization of charity', *Macmillan's Magazine*, vol. 26, pp. 441–9.

Holyoake G. J. (1887), *A Century of Co-operation in England*, Manchester: Central Co-operative Board.

Holyoake G. J. (1907), *Self-Help by the People: The History of the Rochdale Pioneers*, London: Swan Sonnenschein.

Marshall A. (1919), *Industry and Trade*, London: Macmillan.

Marshall A. (1925), *Memorials of Alfred Marshall*, ed. by A. C. Pigou, London: Macmillan.

Marshall A. (1926), *Official Papers by Alfred Marshall*, ed. by J. M. Keynes, London: Macmillan.

Marshall A., (1961) [1890], *Principles of Economics*, ed. by C. W. Guillebaud, London: Macmillan, ninth (variorum) edition in two volumes.

Marshall A. (1969) [1883], 'Lectures on progress and poverty', ed. by G. J. Stigler, *Journal of Law and Economics*, vol. 12.

Marshall A. and Marshall M. P. (1879), *Economics of Industry*, London: Macmillan.

Musson A. E. (1972), *British Trade Unions 1800–1875*, London: Macmillan.

Renan E. (1864), *The Life of Jesus*, London: Trübner & Co.

Rose M. E. (1986), *The Relief of Poverty 1834–1914*, London: Macmillan.

Seeley J. R. (1866), *Ecce Homo. A Survey of the Life and Work of Jesus Christ*, 5th ed., London: Macmillan.

Thornton W. T. (1870) [1868], *On Labour. Its Wrongful Claims and Rightful Dues. Its Actual Present and Possible Future*, 2nd edn, London, Macmillan.

Webb S. and Webb B. (1920), *The History of Trade Unionism*, London: Longmans, Green & Co.

Whitaker J. K. (ed.) (1975), *The Early Economic Writings of Alfred Marshall (1867–1890)*, London: Macmillan.

Yeo S. (ed.) (1988), *New Views of Co-operation*, London, Routledge.

5. Alfred Marshall's lecture outlines

[Lecture] I

What method should you take of solving a complicated problem? Answer don't do it. Look at history. No progress of Greeks. Progress of moderns due to breaking up.

What breaking up means – treating only those things which have a likeness comparing them and making laws. Example ladies dress an art: but you split it up: say certain colors look well together, certain colours look well in certain lights: you make good science of color separately.[1] If you choose you put things together and talk of color separately: and then say such stuffs in such colors shew better at night than others. Just as it would be absurd to blame dressmaker for talking of colors and right to blame her for acting only with reference to colors so it would be to blame economists in parallel cases.

Functions of Political Economy in some cases almost directly constructive, mainly critical. This in ordinary sense of Political Economy but there is a strict sense in which it is purely abstract. If so and so [...].

Disadvantages of short course. Impossible to meet many objections. Necessarily didactic. Those who are dissatisfied must work further by reading or otherwise. In particular those points are slightly treated which, though not always obvious to the 'laboring' classes, are not likely to be overlooked by those who live in the society of employers and who are directly interested in low prices. Of course in addressing an audience of working men the converse mode of action would be the right one.

Most errors due to people using words loosely at first: then propositions get stereotyped and used in wrong senses. E.g. Capital. Confusion between it and money – idea that same money can be used three times.

A person cannot spend lavishly in the sense of spending more than he has: and this much he must spend.

No reading *required*: but
Books recommended[2]

I Thornton 2nd ed. omit Book II Ch III. IV.
II Ludlow and Jones.
III Brassey.
IVHearn? Macdonell?
V Fawcett, Pauperism? Economic position of English Labourer?
IV [sic] Brentano
V [sic]. Cairnes

Ask questions: not undertake to answer them: but can often choose illustrations.

Books[3]

Class A. Time very limited: no intention of pursuing the subject. Thornton, Fawcett's 'Pauperism' and ? [sic] Ludlow and Jones.

Class B. Considerable interest in the practical questions raised: but no desire to study the theory further than is absolutely necessary.
Thornton, Fawcett's 'Pauperism', Ludlow and Jones, Brassey 'Work and Wages'. Brentano or Blue Books. ? [sic] Knight's 'Knowledge is Power'. Thornton on 'Over-population? [sic]' Plener's 'Factory Acts'. 'Contrasts'?
Histories in general. Kebbel's 'Agricultural Labour'. Levi on Wages, or Baxter on Income and Taxation.

Class C. Those who desire to study Political Economy at length, but are not preparing for any examination or likely to attend any lectures. – the same as B only that they should begin to read Hearn's Plutology, or ? [sic] Macdonell's 'Survey of Political Economy', or for those who are accustomed to severe reading, Mill.

Class D. Those preparing for Examinations or going to attend lectures, the same as C: but they should fall into two classes:
i Those who rather court severe reading Brentano (or, if they do not read German, Thornton), Mill, Ludlow, Brassey if convenient.
ii Those not accustomed to severe reading Knight's 'Knowledge is Power'? [sic] Hearn, Thornton, Fawcett's 'Pauperism'.

[Lecture] II

Review: need to point out abstractness of one side of Political Economy – of Political Economy in its narrower acceptation. I want to claim whenever it may be convenient to reason without interruption from sentiment: but these lectures are specially intended to consider the bearing of economical theory on practice and therefore we must devote special attention to consideration of aims etc.

E.g. proposition about lavish expenditure – that you cannot increase your expenditure, unless by increasing first your property, by producing more – is absolutely true: but it is only one of the many considerations to be taken account of when considering what luxury is right and what not. To that we shall come later. Much of what we have to say meanwhile will help us in answering it.

The effect of mechanical improvements.

A Greek poet sang when the cornmill was first driven by water:

'Spare your wearied limbs ye maidens that grind the corn, the unwearied labor of the water nymphs will drive your wheels: while the water foams as it dances in its endless course, sleep the sleep of the blessed; sleep and thank the Gods.'

(K. Marx Kapital 398)[4]

We have found a more powerful servant to toil for us. There is scarcely an important work which She will not do. She carries us and ours by sea and land: she enables one person to do as much work as from 20 to 1000 could in many departments of manufacture – spinning – weaving – working iron. She helps us in our carpenters work etc. Division of labor and specialization of tools contribute. Had then a man a hundred years ago been told this he might have said – 'Oh blessed times – each one may live as a prince – no more struggling for bare existence – no more uncultivated rude men among you – no more need to say in order to exist we must work even to such an extent as scarcely to live. Hard work may remain to be done, but hard work is craved as a change by all: it will be needful to work only for pleasure, recreation and culture will be the business of life'.

Now look at what it is.

I do not want to deny that we have progressed and in particular are progressing.

Read old histories to read of old miseries physical and mental: an artisan has many bodily and mental luxuries that a king has not. Contrast the disturbances of 100 or even 50 years ago with the Lancashire famine; yes, and with the South Wales strike.

I am aware that the popular belief that the working classes spend more upon drink in proportion to their total consumption than before is false. I know that the consumption of tea, sugar, currants, etc. is rapidly increasing; that of spirits and beer per head almost stationary while it is very much less than it was some time ago (in 1750 it was twice as much per head as now).

Nor do I mean to say that to any considerable extent misery has been inflicted gratuitously. I do not accuse for instance employers of being specially hard.

Note the petition from pottery masters in 1862 for regulation.[5]

But I do mean that owing to apathy – apathy of men and apathy of women – the tendency of the new movement has been to sacrifice man to production. And that this tendency has been counteracted partially in consequence of people's arousing themselves from their apathy.

By the phrase sacrificing man to production I mean something definite.

There are cases without number of women and children working hours from 12 to 16, 18, 20. Children working in relays with one set of beds for two sets of children, the beds getting never cold: almost every manufacture had diseases proper to itself. Some trades had deformation of the limbs; many of the spine; many wore out in a short hurried diseased race a feeble life that flickered out in consumption.

And what was the excuse for all this: one – ever the same – one recurring moan, give us this extra hour or we perish; it is but this last hour that enables to work. Could this be? Men stopped not to think, blinded, and deaf looking only onward to one end, not hard-hearted they yet had little time to feel: they could only act. And women – where were they? they could feel: yes and they were willing to do any amount of work for a little sick child that came under their notice and yet they did nothing: women were nowhere: why? because they were ignorant: they were cast aside. This is the great lament, all other rights are nothing as compared with this – the right to have your opinion respected when you utter it and this right can come only through duties. Do your duties, make yourselves striving to think and to act and your rights will take care of themselves. Unless women's real life is strong even their art and culture must be weak. Strong art comes only from a strong life.

But is it quite right to say that people were sacrificed? A diseased body is but a trifle if the spirit be well: but how about education: hear the pottery masters. Hear the answers of the children:

'The Devil was a good man, I do not know where he lived. Jesus Christ was a bad man'. Numbers did not know who Jesus Christ was: one of those who went regularly to Church had the idea that he was in some ways a good man. Many did not know where England was, or that London was a town. Nay even their powers of reading were destroyed by their being kept in dark rooms at low work, those who were quite young and whose eyes were not yet at all weakened being crowded 6 or 8 together round one rush light.

Immorality of Fathers and Mothers.

They, many of them (individuals not bodies) thought only of the wages of their children: some had pawned their children's wages in advance.

Yet the miners as a body were strong for 10 hours work for children, even though told it would diminish their wages; and on the whole the later we look the more alive are the working classes to their duties to their children.

Knowledge then is what we want first.

And first we must show that there is a need for something over and above saving life. These facts often misapplied but they have an important bearing.

They are:

Laws of Growth of Population.

Doubles in some cases in 15 years.

Doubles in America in 25.

Increases in England at present moment at rate corresponding to doubling in 60.

If it is doubled once in 100 years then allowing four to the square yard and rafts all over the sea the earth would be full in a little over 5000 years from time of existence of first pair, or a little over 2000 years from now allowing 100,000,000 for present inhabitants of the world.

In 3000 years at rate of doubling once in 15 years it would have multiplied more than (or in 5000 years if we doubled once in 25 years)

1,000,000,000,000,000,000,000,000,000,000,000,000,000,000,000,000,000,000,000,000 (NB 60 cyphers) times.

In	2000 years if we double once in	15 years
	5000	25
	12000	60

there would be from time of existence of first pair a column of human beings standing on base equal to area of the earth, allowing four to square yard and average height three feet: – how many miles high?

40,000,000,000,000,000,000,000,000,000,000,000,000,000.

What is the conclusion: simply that Nature not having been able to support as many killed them off: by famine disease and war. See Malthus.

Hence if we do anything which does not tend to increase Nature's power of supporting people – if it diminishes it in other directions as fast as it increases this power in the particular place we have in view – what good is done!

None. We give her only more lives to destroy. Do we do no good then by saving lives: yes great good of various kinds when we save life in some ways: but a person who says 'I have saved lives, I have done my duty' is as wrong as would be a person who said I have soothed the agonies of X worn with the gout, I have sent him to sleep with a [?]bowl of punch.

– but I did not know better.

– then that was your great sin that you did not know better.

The means of supporting labor: Some of you may fancy that I mean the only thing to do is to increase capital: if by Capital you mean valuable men you are right: if you mean valuable things you could not be more wrong.

But now let us turn to the means of support of labor and see on what the growth of these means is dependent: we shall find that directly or indirectly the first second and third causes are the culture of the laborers: the only other causes that remain being the parsimony and the efficiency of the upper classes.

[Lecture] III

Resumé of last lecture

If then population is not checked the produce due to each laborer's work must fall off. Will he probably get a smaller share of the produce? The paradox of the multiplication table applies to Capital. There is reason to believe that the Capital of England is 4000 millions, that its yearly increase is 200 million or 5%. At this rate it would be doubled in a little more than 14 years, would be multiplied by a thousand in about 140, by a million in about 28, by a billion in less than 600. How will it be prevented from doing this? By the increasing share it has to give to labor. On this a word now: more hereafter.

What we see then is that ultimately the rate of wages will be the lowest which are [sic] in the then state of civilisation consistent with keeping up the world population at its stationary value; and the lowest interest which is consistent with even keeping up capital. Though owing to the gradual growth of the arts of production this may be pushed off almost sine limite.

But is there any reason for fear at present?: only on the supposition that the return to a laborer's work when supplied with a given amount of capital will fall off. But is this true?[6]

[We find that a fall in the price of corn stimulates marriages, hence some must be near starvation limit: on the other hand we find consumption of working class roughly

	Price
Bread Flour Butter	
Cheese Potatoes	120[7]
Meat	30
Firing	24
Drink	60
Tobacco	8
House rent	36
Clothing	56
Sugar Tea Coffee	20
Etc.	etc.
	400

Less than half on things which need grow rapidly dearer.

We find food for 5 persons at a quarter of corn each cost about

£13 or about 5s per week: while many laborers have more than 5 times as much. Average wages have been in general [a][8] peck a day, i.e. a little over 10 quarters a year.]

This depends on the education of the laborer: wages in different trades: interest of parent in education of child; How far dependent on education of parent: interest of community in education: reasonableness of State aids to education. (The arguments for various kinds of education are of different strengths e.g. for religious, aesthetic and other education of grown men it is weaker than for the same for children: but in general it is strong for all kinds of education that do not distinctly remunerate the 'possessor'.)

The 'natural' and 'artificial' differences in wages. Wages in building trades similar to rents: in agricultural trade the law of equality of profits does not hold, if we count rent among profits: and that is what by their artificial regulation the building trades manage to do.

International differences in wages. Fallacy that they cause 'one nation to undersell another'.

Low wages cause a country to lose its capital: corollary send labor after it.

To sum up influence of education on well being:

i. Increases direct efficiency

ii. Increases indirect efficiency by making the mind pliable and elastic, and by developing trustworthiness.

[Enterprise, pliability, information, trustworthiness cause highly paid labor to be highly paid.][9]

iii. It counteracts that random growth of population which is so injurious to population by strengthening the family tie.

Conclusions: to educate at cost of state will 'pay' though it would not pay a slave dealer to give very high education: for intellectual without moral education is nothing worth and that the slave dealer cannot give; and though the parent yet cannot be induced to give it: but *the* thing to be remembered is that we must not weaken the sense of family obligation.

From this we conclude that the more a man has the more should be given to him: that there is no use in attempting to raise the physical conditions of the laborer without raising the mental: that from whatever angle we look at it the wages question demands a raising of his mental position and strengthening of his moral character, an increasing of his feeling of responsibility in every way and in particular as a father of a family.

Why should you not make every man a gentleman? Every woman a lady?

This peculiarly a woman's question.

I.[10] An account sometimes given of which it is difficult to speak temperately viz. 'it is a merciful dispensation that will, we trust, always prevent the cultivation of the lower classes. Some persons must be doomed to toil to debasing occupations: to give them culture would be only to make them miserable: to strain against this is to fly in the face of Providence: do not enquire into the cause; accept with gratitude the beneficial arrangement and pass on'.

Yes: it is an arrangement of Providence and so is the cholera, yet we may try to avoid it: and who is the man, or woman, for I have heard something of this sort often from the mouths of women, who dares to say thank God that I am comfortable and more or less cultivated and that others are debarred from the higher forms of existence in order that I may thrive in the full plenitude of my might? The position is not a comfortable one: but that would not matter if it were true. Is it true?

Some time ago it was thought that if a man could write he would be unable to wield the sword: yet our soldiers are as brave as ever: now it is thought that education would unfit a man from working in the mines: of course it will if he is more educated than many who are not working in the mines or doing similar things. But it is *only* on account of the social stigma incurred by this work that a cultivated man would be less likely than an uncultivated to do it if he could find nothing else to do. An explorer without servants is not unfitted for roughing it by his culture.

Again then – Why not make every man a gentleman.

[Lecture] IV

Resumé of last lecture.

We have shown that unless we arouse ourselves we shall always live amid misery: that there is no reason why everyone should not be a gentleman in education: that it would be a good investment of national Capital to make him so: i.e. that the condition in which everyone is a gentleman is one to be aimed at: not one that can be produced instantaneously.

We have now to enquire what are the main points which render this more than all previous times one in which deliberate action is required; and in the present lecture the position of working men relatively to this and allied questions: Lectures V and VI.

(i)[11] Servitude of man to machinery: Machinery never tired therefore man ought never to be tired: opposition to short hours work – relays

Trades Unions: their origin:

Effects of change at end of eighteenth and beginning of 19th centuries:

Brief sketch of gilds: first efforts of unionists:

Number of Unionists about 700,000 (Macdonell).[12]

Trades Unions not the authors of the strike movement. The worst strikes occurred in Belgium when there were no Unions. (Macdonell).

Of course a board has no conscience. An unscrupulous board or Union can do very wicked things without pain – almost as bad as those which a country does when it goes needlessly to war.

Aims of Unions.

i. how roughly to enable labor to be sold with a reserve: and this partly by helping masters who are willing to give good wages:

The laborers in a trade must be able
a to work together
b to limit their number and otherwise check supply of labor
c to obtain knowledge
Under head **a** we find
organisation in general
in particular amalgamation of trade and benefit funds
objection to piece work (partly)
minimum of wages

war against overtime partly
under head **b**
limitation of apprentices
objection to piece work (partly)
refusal to allow a man to do the work of two trades

Trades Unions
Extent of their control over the supply of labor.

Centralisation combined with localisation. Each branch manages its funds as it pleases but must submit its accounts to the Executive. If the Executive considers it has been wasteful it may make it levy a special contribution to refund the money. If 2/3 of members of a branch are dissatisfied with the verdict of the Executive they can appeal to the whole society: the case on each side is printed and circulated to each member and then a poll of the whole taken.

The Secretary is the only officer of the Executive whose whole time is devoted to the work. He is paid among Amalgamated Carpenters £2.10.0 per week:[13] there are with them six members of the Council.

The reason why trade societies which are not benefit societies also have failed seems to be not so much the limited power exercised over the members as the rashness and recklessness with which they run into a strike when they have accumulated funds and no use to make of them.

Beesly in Fortnightly March/67[14]

Trades Unions.

Analogous to the plea that a man who has not served his apprenticeship may be inefficient is the plea of 'the Society of Scotch Advocates which declares that no one can be called to the Bar who has been during the previous year in remunerative employment'. Macdonell

Cooperation.

Enables workmen to appropriate wages of superintendence, diminishes total work of superintendence to be done, acquaints workmen with circumstances of trade, so diminishes bickering, and above all things gives a new interest.

So it is with cooperative stores. The advantages of them mainly (i)

educational (ii) dispensing with necessity of guaranteeing honesty by means of reputation: a connexion a hard thing to get, and when got obtains high profits.

In general if a person is well occupied it is a mistake to have anything to do with managing a cooperative store: such work is however good for those who have no taste for any other occupation of more importance open to them.

Break up of old life complete: no more possible to let things drift; to try to do things our own forefathers did and even a little better. This well enough in some states of society but now we must look about us, think and act deliberately.

Summing up.

Unless we educate the lowest class so that none remain who are incapable of making good use of leisure we shall not be able to stop these prejudicial rules of Unions: but if we do there is no economical obstacle to the attainment of Utopias – the Utopias of Communists, i.e. of men whose wishes were divine: but whose knowledge of Political Economy worse than human.

Meanwhile we must preach to the Unionists: to every preachment they will answer 'Am I my brother's keeper?'. 'Yes': we must teach them: but how? by precept while our example is what it is.

i. perverted patriotism, indifference to well being of other nations in peace and to their sufferings in war.[15]

ii. neglect of our social duties.

Study welfare of society – as well as how to be polite: true politeness the offspring of kindliness, true aestheticism the offspring of strong feeling.

Our duty that of not demanding of our near relations that they should do things for us which prevent their working in the world.

[Lecture] V

Treating in detail of some points misunderstood.

Modes in which education benefits unskilled labor: no value in things *per se*: no reason in the nature of the case why any kind of labor should be badly paid: but unskilled labor cannot be scarce in general: make it scarce what remains will be comparatively highly paid: but the fact is that there is no occupation for which education does not make a man more fit, if only by improving his moral tone, giving him self reliance, trustworthiness, capabilities of shame. Domestic Servants.

Educate and efficiency will increase so that though even manual labor is much more highly paid, skilled labor need not have wages insufficient for culture.

The result will be that but little manual work will be done at all: machines will do most and that most laborers who do mere unskilled work will do skilled work also.

Education due to trades unions: to act with a deliberate purpose, to sacrifice individual interests for a common object: to bind yourself by treaties and adhere to them and generally to manage a state organisation.

Cooperation: educates the administrative as Trades Unionism does the political faculties. Saves enormous waste and when practicable is highly beneficial.

Cooperative stores proper have all these advantages but to a much smaller extent.

Practical men jeer at them unduly mistaking their true functions and seeing only that for the purposes of the well to do classes the ordinary stores are if well managed but good shops and if cooperative stores proper waste time. To deal with a cooperative store may save money: just as it does to buy books from a London bookseller who keeps a small stock, and goes in for small profits and quick returns, allowing 25% discount.

Admit what the practical men say: but still preach the great future of cooperation.

Repeat why we dare not drift.

Factory Acts. How they promote education.

1819, 1833, 1847 are the great dates.

In last ordered that

No children employed under 8: Those under thirteen 6½ hours per day (?)

Women and persons under 18 not more than 10 hours per day.

Prophecies of manufacturers, all false.

What ought to be done.

Poor laws: Fawcett's Pauperism. Sketch of history

iniquities under Workhouse test in 34

viz. Poor law is a necessary evil: what is wanted is systematized individual effort. Charitable societies could combine both advantages, have combined both evils.

[Here insert papers on *Charity*][16]

Charity

Organisation: its proper sphere and failure out of its sphere.

'Wherever suffering is to be treated in the lump, wherever persons afflicted with the same or similar distress can be relieved by a regulated treatment; where sick persons are to be collected together in a common hospital ... where blind or deaf or idiots are to be gathered together for an education adapted to their peculiar requirements, there organisation has its proper place, and whatever individual kindness can do is merely in subordination or in addition to the main business in hand which the organized machinery directs or controls. ... But when the association or institution attempts the more general work of charity – tries to fill the place too often left vacant by private benevolence ... it meets with the same difficulties which render the parochial system of relief so incomplete and unsatisfactory .... Imposture is more prominent, more forward often more plausible than real and meritorious penury; and its rules must be framed to defeat and discourage imposture on pain of doing more harm than good. But it is scarcely practicable to frame a code of tests and regulations to exclude impostors which shall not tend to disgust and dishearten innocent and undeserved poverty. And even if a large discretion were allowed to the officers of the charity, these officers themselves, as the inevitable result of their position and fruit of their experience, lean toward the very same error or defect which is characteristic of the rules which that experience forces on their superiors. They find themselves in constant collision with vicious and shameless imposture; they find much imposture and vice involved in cases of real distress; and they acquire insensibly and in their own despite, and while remaining most kind in heart and act, a suspicious hard and vigilant manner, a sharpness of tone which repels the best sort of applicants; whose sensitive pride revolts at questions, tests and precautions which devised against imposture seem to presuppose imposture in every application. Thus except in the first mentioned appropriate sphere of associate charity, the relief dispensed through a machinery of this kind unaided by voluntary charity awakens no gratitude and causes almost as much degradation and demoralisation as pauperism itself carries with it: indeed it is hard to be grateful to a corporation. Where good is to be done to individual men, it should come from the freewill of fellow men; the machinery, if machinery there be, should be in the background, the voluntary benefactor should come into personal contact with his suffering brother, whereas in all endeavours to do good through mechanical organisation it is the machinery alone which is seen by the poor: the givers ... remain invisible and unknown.'

Individual Action.

ii [sic] its weak points when unaided

No power of knowing what others have done.

Difficulty of confining attention to one limited area, unless there be a certainty that the most urgent cases just outside it will not be totally neglected while less urgent cases inside are attended to.

Difficulty of asking the point-blank questions implying distrust which a paid agent working by rule and dispensing others money can do with less pain to himself and with really less insult to the applicant than the amateur who has some reason for suspecting the particular case.

Miss Hill's rules.

Macmillan's Magazine July 1869[17]

'It is best strictly to enforce fulfilment of all such duties as payment of rent &c.

It is far better to give work than either money or goods.

It is most helpful of all to strengthen by sympathy and counsel the energetic effort which shall bear fruit in time to come.

It is essential to remember that each man has his own view of his life, and must be free to fulfil it; that in many ways he is a far better judge of it than we, as he has lived through and felt what we have only seen. Our work is rather to bring him to the point of considering, and to the spirit of judging rightly, than to consider or judge for him.

The poor of London (as of all large towns) need the development of every power that[18] can open to them noble sources of joy.'[19]

NB. Miss Hill's second article in MacMillan's for September 1872.[20]

[Charity[21]

Typical instances of good institutions.
Charity Organisation Society: supplemented by Miss Hill.
Provident Knowledge Society
South London Working Men's[22] College
Kindergarten
Bethnal Green Museum.
Cheap concerts at Albert Hall.]

Joy:

Each new joy is a new stimulus to work; a new cause for avoiding vice; a new means of living.

To add to the welfare of mankind is something: but, if the multiplication table is true, to bring into existence causes that tend perpetually to increase welfare is incomparably more important.

The poetry of the multiplication table (really of course Taylor's theorem is meant).

In so far as poetry is a gospel, it is telling us how of little things come great, if only there be the spirit of growth in them, no clashing or discord, no seeds of death:

And in so far as poetry illuminates it is by giving a new vivifying principle.

A highly educated, mentally, morally, aesthetically cultured staff of strong emotion joy imparting beings [sic] exists in the ladies of modern civilisation.

They are by the nature of the case the priestesses of the highest culture – the priestesses of joy. And they are not willing to stagnate: they desire something higher than to be ornamental, clothed in ornamental fancy work of their own manufacture; but they drift: It must be conceded that they often are as it were bound to do wrong, to humour one person's whims when they might be doing great work: Still they must not, dare not drift:

Next lecture.

[Lecture] VI

Brief Resumé of last lecture.

i. Answered at length the question how education raised indirectly the wages of that small minority of agricultural, menial and other unskilled laborers whose work would not be directly rendered more efficient by education.

ii. Pointed out that cooperative stores might be cheaper than shops, probably would be: but that the small benefits which they might confer must not be exaggerated for fear of causing the reaction which denied the unlimited benefit which may ultimately accrue from cooperative productive associations.

iii. Factory Acts

iv. Poor laws and charity. Will give general principles but the question of mode is best deferred; till we come to the question – What then are we to do.

Reread Miss Hill's rules.

General rules may be summed up in one – give tendencies. Happiness in the sense of physical and other direct enjoyments ought *not* to be despised: but only the tendency is the great point to be attended to.

The poetry of the multiplication table.

The vivifying power of joy.

The special province of ladies: they are adapted for work:

The army of ladies: individual and organised work. In answer to a question – I say– Sisterhoods supply in some cases the only available means: but they have not the elasticity, or the individuality, often not even the freshness that the work of those living at home has. A vow is an unnecessary adjunct of a sisterhood: where this and still more where any such practice as that of systematic confession has been introduced history seems to tell us that a flaccidity of tone – to say the least of it – has come over the moral and intellectual energies and has prevented their doing well the highest portion of their work – which is to open noble sources of joy.

Many of the advantages of a sisterhood may be attained by work in a hospital.

We conclude then that the rule is that charitable societies which relieve pain and impart joy are good – provided they do not tend to crush the sources of joy: while those whose net result is much to foster these sources of joy are very good. Charity Organization

Society: Provident Knowledge Society, Penny readings etc., as well as Miss Hill's work. But to how great an extent must our self denial be carried? Luxury fosters energy in so far as it opens new sources of enjoyment even when not noble: we will analyse. Insert papers on *Luxury*.[23]

Luxury

Expenditure may be of the following kinds.

a. In necessaries and such comforts as are expected by our friends so that their absence would cause a feeling of discomfort to them: these we ought to have on the supposition

(i) that we can do so without hampering ourselves or to any considerable extent preventing our obtaining those things which, as we shall presently see, are of first importance

and (ii) that the standard of comfort so demanded by our friends is not unduly high. In connexion with **a** many casuistical questions may be asked. No general rules can be laid down. Each person must solve the questions, as they arise for himself. It is not worthwhile to concentrate attention on them: they will easily find a practical solution if only attention has been concentrated on the questions arising under the other heads. This may be called expenditure to avoid pain for us and our friends.

b. In such enjoyments as tend to raise our own position as regards knowledge and taste: and that either directly or indirectly as by affording us recreation in the strict sense of the word – a raising up from an overworn and depressed state of the mental system: it being of course assumed that the overwork to which this depression is due is the result of nobly directed efforts. Having expensive instruction in music, attending really good concerts (not merely fashionable ones) and similar places of amusement – especially when there are at such places cheap gallery tickets for the lower classes: indeed one very good form of expenditure is that of subsidizing good concerts for them and there are few ways of doing this better than by taking expensive tickets at such entertainments – travelling and giving such social entertainments as are needful without undue expense to keep us continually in contact with our fellow creatures; (for some) horse exercise, the purchase of works of fine art proper, and of such ordinary commodities as more specially expensive on account of the art and taste displayed in them: all such may be defended on these grounds, subject to limits similar to those laid down for group **a**: but as they are supposed to add to the store of moral wealth of the community, of ourselves and friends directly and of others indirectly, the limits within which they are right are much wider than those for group **a**. They may be called means of procuring for us noble enjoyment, or as Bentham would say, 'pure and productive enjoyment': enjoyment that increases our powers of enjoyment: having a power of assimilation such as colloids have in a living body: nourishing and being nourished: having the power of splitting up by differentiation into new and more complicated forms of life and uniting by integration with their living associates; joy mingling with joy; so that what was joyful becomes more joyous and intervening movements are absorbed into the general life around them.

These then are less likely than **a** to degenerate into **c**: yet even with them there is a danger.

c. Means of display – of flaunting before our fellow creatures the fact that we have the power of enjoying ourselves: hard lifeless; life destroying masses in the social body: the product of moral degradation, the source of moral and physical woe.

d. In reckless alms-giving: of this enough has been said.

e. In chastened, earnestly careful ministration of material help.

f. Expenditure in some commercial undertaking.

g. Expenditure of time: in doing our daily work by which we earn our daily bread.

h. Expenditure of time: in cultivating ourselves.

i. Expenditure of time in teaching and training our relatives or others with whom we may be brought into contact.

k. Expenditure of time in the ministration of the poor: and that (i) in relieving distress and (ii) connected with it, but often made subordinate to it instead of being the sole aim and end of it – the creation of noble sources of joy.

l. Expenditure of time in making two ends meet and in doing other work that if our expenditure were more moderated would not be needful. This is one of the greatest evils of life: and attention should be concentrated on it: and the proper limits of **a** and **b** are exceeded if **l** is needful: or if in any other way they cause considerable diminution to **h**, **i**, **k**.

Thus **c** is altogether wicked: of **g** little need be said, **a** should be kept as low as can be done consistently with the terms given: while, subject to limit above named and to such considerations connected with our duty to our families and with guarding against illness and as are connected with **f**, **b** may be large.

Sluggishness is in itself an evil: the enjoyments of civilisation tend to push it aside to create energy which may be turned to noble ends even though the enjoyments that have called it into being may not be directly productive of nobility.

Well then one's own enjoyment and that of one's own immediate friends counts for something: there is in the long run little fear of its not counting for enough.

But the great end is to become useful fixed capital for producing joy and more than that noble sources of joy: and expenditure of money or time on a large scale to produce any other result is in general and subject to modification in exceptional cases (e.g. when one must give way to the whims and fancies of elderly relations) a wasteful consumption – is wrongful luxury. But when not large in amount it is allowable luxury and even lavish expenditure that has the effect of making us more valuable capital is emphatically rightful.[24]

General aim of lectures

Not to insist on study of Political Economy

But to give reasons which a study of Political Economy had forced upon me why we must not drift.

Two pictures

i. we drift. Evils of old state of things perpetuated and in some way aggravated. Rome and Greece fell: we must not tamely speculate why: they fell because they where pagan, grossly pagan: the fresh youthful vigor of Greek intellectual and aesthetic life, the manly strength of Roman purpose: but they were utterly devoid as a nation of moral enthusiasm. In the full pride of their glory their morality was systematically filthy: their atrocities were fiendish. Much is to be learnt from them: much has been learnt: but that pagan spirit of dilettantism which it is my main object to combat has probably been [due] more to the *exclusive* study by men of our [?]guiding [?]forming intellects than to any other cause. We have to learn from them how to think, but not how to live. Slavery is an ordinance of nature said the Greeks: the Proletariat are an institution of nature say the dilettanti. They are not an institution of nature said the great overthrower of dilettantism – the friend of publicans and sinners: they are not an institution of nature says the Political Economist and the student of human character who has learnt how these evils may be done away. They are not an institution of nature says the student of

Science: for there is another possible state of things.

ii. education universal: little common place work done; that so managed as not to degrade; for each man is to be treated as a man: to grow as a man, therefore to educate his children as a man.

How this is to be effected: the work of women – what must they do?

The one rule is that they must not consume unproductively, or so as not to add to the stores of wealth: they must be impatient of mere existence, discontented with it.

They must work as Miss Hill works or as teachers in schools, or in private – but not in general contented with a few hours wastefully spent over their near relations: for they have to kindle noble sources of joy and when they have done this the joy will be present. The point about home teaching is that it is wasteful in *some* directions:
or organising in some way or other,
or teaching art, giving penny readings &c.

But in order to do this they must think. One of their first duties is to become valuable pieces of fixed capital. And how:

in the main 3 modes

i. to increase their reasoning powers; for this mathematics and science generally including political economy;

ii. to develop their taste – art and literature;

iii. to get to know men – history and literature – the immense importance of this last; the soul killing substitution for it of the learning an immense number of vocabularies.

Let us then each choose our own lives: let us remember only that if we squander the 'talents committed to our charge' ruin awaits the world: that we must work productively: let us each decide what to us seems the most important and let us do that. Let us not lose individuality: but whatever we do let us work to foster 'noble sources of joy'.

Notes and References

1. Marshall uses both spellings of the word 'colour'.
2. For this list, see above, lecture notes, note 2. The only new title given here is H. Fawcett, *The Economic Position of the British Labourer*, Cambridge and London, Macmillan and Co., 1865.
3. The following list of books is written on two unnumbered pages which it has been thought preferable to insert after the preceding list as complementing it. The books which do not appear in the other lists are:

Ch. Knight, *Knowledge is Power; a view of the productive forces of modern society and the results of labor, capital and skill*, London, J. Murray, 1855, (2nd ed., 1859);
E. von Plener, German title, [*The English Factory Legislation from 1802 till the present time*, trans. from German by F. L. Weinmann with an introduction by A. J. Mundella, London, Chapman and Hall, 1873];
W. T. Thornton, *Overpopulation and its Remedy; or, an inquiry into the extent and causes of the distress prevailing among the labouring classes of the British Islands, and into the means of remedying it*, London, Longman, Brown, Green and Longmans, 1846;
T. E. Kebbel, *The Agricultural Labourer: a short summary of his position*, London, Chapman and Hall, 1870;
L. Levi, *Wages and Earnings of the Working Classes, with some facts illustrative of their economic condition, drawn from authentic and official sources*, in a report to Michael T. Bass, London, J. Murray, 1867;
R. D. Baxter, *National Income. The United Kingdom*, London, Macmillan and Co., 1868;
R. D. Baxter, *The Taxation of the United Kingdom*, London, Macmillan and Co., 1869.

4. See above, lecture notes, note 8.
5. Cf. below, 'The future of the working classes', note 7
6. An extra page of notes was inserted here by Marshall. The notes follow in this text in square brackets.
7. There is a discrepancy between Marshall's figure here and the figure of 170 recorded by Mary Paley.
8. Word crossed through.
9. The square brackets are given in the original.
10. This is not followed by any other number.
11. This is not followed by any other number.
12. Marshall probably understated the strength of the trade unions at the time: according to Lovell (1977, p. 16) in 1874 the total number of trade unionists was actually 'one million or more'.
13. This is a reference to the old coinage and is the equivalent of £2.50p.
14. Beesly (1867).
15. It would seem that in foreign affairs Marshall shared one of the main concerns of contemporary Gladstonian liberalism: Gladstone himself was to lead famous campaigns against Disraeli's alleged adoption of this 'perverted patriotism' in 1876–80. Cf. Shannon, 1963 and 1985, pp. 88–103; and Matthew, 1986, pp.xxiii–xcvii.
16. The square brackets are given in the original. The following five pages of the manuscript have the word *Charity* as a running head. The page numbers continue the chapter sequence.
17. Hill (1869).
18. 'Which' in Hill's article.
19. See above, lecture notes, note 24.
20. Hill (1872). The pages with the running head *Charity* here end.
21. The following text inside square brackets is written on a separate, unnumbered page, whose location in the manuscript is between the fifth and

the sixth lecture. It seems appropriate to insert it here. Cf. p. 150.
22. The first four words of this line are crossed through.
23. The following seven pages of the manuscript have the word *Luxury* as a running head. The page numbers are continuous.
24. Here is the end of the pages with the running-head *Luxury*.

Bibliography

Beesly E. S. (1867), 'The amalgamated society of carpenters', *Fortnightly Review*, n. s., vol. 1, pp. 319–34.

Hill O. (1869), 'Organized work among the poor: suggestions founded on four years' management of a London court', *Macmillan's Magazine*, vol. 20, pp. 219–26.

Hill O. (1872), 'The work of volunteers in the organization of charity', *Macmillan's Magazine*, vol. 26, pp. 441–49.

Lovell J. (1977) *British Trade Unions 1875–1933*, London: Macmillan.

Matthew H. C. G. (1986), 'Introduction' to *The Gladstone Diaries, vol.IX (January 1875–December 1880)*, Oxford: Clarendon Press, pp.xxiii–xcvii.

Shannon R. T. (1963), *Gladstone and the Bulgarian Agitation 1876*, London: Thomas Nelson.

Shannon R. T. (1985), 'Midlothian: 100 Years After', in P. J. Jagger (ed.), *Gladstone, Politics and Religion*, London: Macmillan, pp. 88–103.

6. The future of the working classes[1]

Mr Mill has given in his *Autobiography* a more detailed account than we had hitherto possessed of that aid that he derived from his wife in most of the best work he has done. This information has great value at a time at which, partly by the voice of Mr Mill himself, we are being awakened to the importance of the question whether the quick insight of woman may not be trained so as to give material assistance to man in ordering public as well as private affairs. He says – 'In all that concerns the applications of philosophy to the exigencies of human societies I was her pupil, alike in boldness of speculation and cautiousness of practical judgment.'[2] All the instances that he gives of this tend to show how our progress would be accelerated if we would unwrap the swaddling clothes in which artificial customs have enfolded woman's mind and would give her free scope womanfully to discharge her duties to the world. But one instance strikingly illustrates that intimate connection, to which all history testifies, between the free play of the full and strong pulse of woman's thought and the amelioration of the working classes.

'The chapter of the *Political Economy* (he says) which has had a greater influence on opinion than all the rest, that on the "Probable Future of the Labouring Classes", is entirely due to her: in the first draft of the book that chapter did not exist. She pointed out the need of such a chapter and the extreme imperfection of the book without it: she was the cause of my writing it; and the more general part of the chapter – the statement and discussion of the two opposite theories respecting the proper condition of the labouring classes – was wholly an exposition of her thoughts, often in words taken from her own lips.'

Other women may have spoken much as she spoke; but, for one reason or another, their words have been almost as though they had not been. Let us be grateful that on this topic one woman has spoken not in vain.

The course of inquiry which I propose for to-night will never lie far apart from that pursued by Mr and Mrs Mill, but will seldom exactly coincide with it. I propose to sketch in rough outline a portion of the ground that must be worked over if we would rightly examine whether the amelioration of the working classes has limits beyond which it cannot pass; whether it be true that the resources of the world will not suffice for giving to more than a small portion of its inhabitants an education in youth and an occupation in after-life, similar to those which we are now wont to consider proper to gentlemen.

There are large numbers of unselfish men and women who are eager to hope, but who find themselves impelled to doubt. From time to time there reaches them some startling but well-authenticated account of working men, who have misspent their increased wages, who have shown little concern for anything higher than the pleasures of eating and drinking, or possibly those amusements which constitute the miserable creature who is called the sporting man.[3] From time to time they meet with some instance in which servants have made use of such improvements as have already taken place in their position only to adopt a tone of captious frivolity and of almost ostentatious indifference to the interests of those whom they have undertaken to serve. Thus minds unwilling to doubt are harassed by doubts such as these: whether a large amount of hard, nay, of coarse manual work will not always have to be done much as it is done now; whether a very high degree of cultivation would not render those who have to perform this work unfit for it, and, since they cannot escape from it, unhappy in performing it; whether an attempt to extend beyond certain boundaries the mental cultivation of such workers must not be almost certain to fail, and would not, if successful, be almost a calamity; whether what we see and hear is not an indication that these dread boundaries are narrow and not far off.

The question for us to-night is, Can this doubt be resolved? The question is not whether all men will ultimately be equal – that they certainly will not – but whether progress may not go on steadily if slowly, till the official distinction between working man and gentleman has passed away; till, by occupation at least, every man is a gentleman. I hold that it may, and that it will.[4]

Let us first make clear to ourselves what it is that is really implied by the distinction established in usage between the occupation of a gentleman and that of a working man. This usage cannot be defended etymologically, but words better for the purpose are not forthcoming. The distinction is well established, but singularly difficult of definition; and some of those accounts of it which may most readily suggest themselves must be, in explicit terms, set aside if we would free from confusion the inquiry what are the special circumstances of the working classes on the removal of which their progress depends.

Who are the working classes? Of course they are not all who work; for every man, however wealthy he may be, if he be in health and a true man, does work, and work hard. They are not all who live by selling the work of their hands, for our noblest sculptors do that. They are not all who for payment serve and obey, for officers in the army serve for payment, and must implicitly obey. They are not all who for payment perform disagreeable duties, for the surgeon is paid to perform duties most disagreeable. They are not even all those who work hard for a low pay, for hard is the work and low is the pay of the highly cultured governess. Who then are they?

It is not true that when we say a man belongs to the working classes we are thinking of the effect that his work produces on him rather than of the effect that he produces on his work? If a man's daily task tends to give culture and refinement to his character, do we not, however coarse the individual man may happen to be, say that his occupation is that of a gentleman? If a man's daily task tends to keep his character rude and coarse, do we not, however truly refined the individual man may happen to be, say that he belongs to the working classes?

It is needful to examine more closely the characteristics of those occupations which directly promote culture and refinement of character. They demand powers and activities of mind of various kinds. They demand the faculty of maintaining social intercourse with a large number of persons; they demand, in appearance at least, the kindly habit of promptly anticipating the feelings of others on minor points, of ready watchfulness to avoid each trivial word or deed that may pain or annoy. These qualities are required for success, and they are therefore prepared in youth by a careful and a long continued education. Throughout life they are fostered and improved by exercise and by contact with persons who have similar qualities and require them of their associates. A man's sympathies thus become broad because he knows much of life, and is adapted for taking interest in what he knows. He has a wide range of pleasures; each intellectual energy, each artistic perception, each fellow-feeling with men far off and near, gives him a new capacity of enjoyment, removes from him more and more the desire for coarse delights. Wealth is not indispensable; but it frequently gives its aid. It has been said that there is in the breast of every man some portion of the spirit of a flunkey. Possibly: but we do not respect a man half as much as we are wont to suppose we do, simply on account of what he *has*. We are thinking of what he *is* far more than we are aware. The qualities which win entrance into a lucrative career or success in any career are in general, to some extent, admirable. Wealth, in general, implies a liberal education in youth, and throughout life broad interests and refined associations; and it is to these effects on character that the chief attractiveness of wealth is due. Were it true that the homage paid to a wealthy man is in general direct worship of wealth, the prospects of the world would be darker than they are, and the topic to be discussed to-night would require a different treatment.

It is not, however, sufficient to remark that the occupations which we are wont to call the occupations of gentlemen elevate the character and educate the faculties, directly and indirectly, by training and by association, in hours of business and in hours of leisure. We must also remark that such occupations exclude almost entirely those lowering influences which will force themselves upon our notice when we come to examine the lot of the working classes.

We must pause to notice the intermediate class – a class whose occupations bring with them some influences that do elevate and refine, and some influences that do not. The sculptor, the products of whose chisel add to his country's fame, who lives amid material and intellectual luxuries, is distinctly a gentleman by profession. Proceeding downwards along the scale of art, we come to the highly skilled, highly paid artisan, who adorns our public buildings with their exquisite carvings; but there is another long space to be traversed before we arrive at the ordinary mason, who, with much exertion of muscle, and with but little energy of thought, rounds off a block, or makes it square, in obedience to explicit directions. At what point, then, in the scale do we first meet the working man? It is an important and a hopeful fact that we cannot say where – that the chain is absolutely continuous and unbroken. There is a tendency to regard somewhat slightingly the distinction between skilled and unskilled labour. But the fact remains that artisans whose manual labour is not heavy, who are paid chiefly for their skill and the work of their brains, are as conscious of the superiority of their lot over that of their poorer brethren as is the highest nobleman of the land. And they are right; for their lot does just offer them the opportunity of being gentlemen in spirit and in truth; and, to the great honour of the age be it said, many of them are steadily becoming gentlemen.

They are steadily striving upwards; steadily aiming at a higher and more liberal preparation in youth; steadily learning to value time and leisure for themselves, learning to care more for this than for mere increase of wages and material comforts; steadily developing independence and a manly respect for themselves, and, therefore, a courteous respect for others; they are steadily accepting the private and public duties of a citizen; steadily increasing their grasp of the truth that they are men, and not producing machines. They are steadily becoming gentlemen. Steadily: we hope to be able ere long to say 'steadily and rapidly'; but even now the picture is not altogether a gloomy one.

But let us turn our eyes on that darker scene which the lot of unskilled labour presents. Let us look at those vast masses of men who, after long hours of hard and unintellectual toil, are wont to return to their narrow homes with bodies exhausted and with minds dull and sluggish. That men do habitually sustain hard corporeal work for eight, ten or twelve hours a day, is a fact so familiar to us that we scarcely realize the extent to which it governs the moral and mental history of the world; we scarcely realize how subtle, all-pervading and powerful may be the effect of the work of man's body in dwarfing the growth of the man.

Some of us, perhaps, scarcely know what is meant by violent and sustained physical exertion. Others have perhaps had occasional experience of it on walking tours. We are then enlivened by fresh air and by novelty of scene, and a light book or newspaper is never more grateful to us than then. But have we ever, when thoroughly fatigued, attempted really hard study? I remember once in the Alps, after three days of exceptionally severe climbing, resolving to take a day's rest and to read a book on Philosophy. I was in good training. I was not conscious of any but physical weariness; but when the first occasion for hard thought arrived, my mind absolutely refused to move. I was immensely angry with it, but my anger was in vain. A horse when harnessed to a load too great for his strength will sometimes plant his feet firmly in the ground, and back. That is just what my mind did, and I was defeated. I have found that in like cases others are in like manner defeated, though their minds be well broken in to study, even though they be students by profession. And physiologists tell us that it must be so; that by severe bodily exertion the blood is for a time impoverished; that so the brain is not nourished, and that when the brain is not vigorous the mind cannot think.[5]

It is, then, a wonderful thing that the leisure hours of a wearied labourer are not always seized eagerly for self-improvement? It is often a toil to him to read; how, then, can he be incited by the pleasures of study to contend against fatigue? The man born deaf knows not the pleasure of music; but he lives among those who know it, and he believes in it. But the poor labourer may live and die without ever realizing what a joy there is in knowledge, or what delight in art; he may never have conceived how glorious a thing it is to be able to think and to feel about things and with many men.[6] Still he may not be wholly unblessed. He may pass a tranquil and restful evening in a healthy and a happy home, and so may win some of the best happiness that is granted to man. He may, but alas! if he be uneducated, he is not likely to have a very healthy home.

[7]There is another terrible fact about exhausting work. It is that physical fatigue in its extremest forms causes physical unrest and physical cravings that hound a man on to his undoing. There is overwhelming evidence that in all those occupations in which men are tempted to consume in a day's work almost more strength than the vital forces of the body suffice to repair, and in which work is therefore systematically irregular, the pleasures of home cannot compete with the coarse pleasures of the public-house. A man may seek in the public-house, as in a club, the pleasures of social intercourse, which will well supplement the pleasures of home, and will raise, not lower him. He may: but if his toil has been fierce, and so his brain is dulled, he is apt to seek there only the coarser pleasures – drink, ignoble jests, and noise. We have all heard what rude manners have been formed by the rough work of the miners; but even among them the rougher the work of the body, the lower the condition of the mind. Iron miners, for instance, are a superior race to colliers. And if it be true that men such as these do value high wages mainly as affording them an opportunity of using their bodies as furnaces for the conversion of alcohol into fumes, is it not a somewhat pitiful amusement merely to abuse them? it is not more profitable to raise the inquiry – must these things be?

There are some things which we have decided must *not* be. A Parliamentary Commission reports in 1866[8] of the training which the world had given to men such as these, and by which it had formed them. It tells us how lads and maidens, not eight years old, toiled in the brickfields under monstrous loads from five o'clock in the morning till eight o'clock at night; their faces haggard, their limbs misshaped by their work, their bodies clothed with mud, and their minds saturated with filth. Yes; but there is a thing worse than even such filth: that is despair. We are told that 'the worst feature of all is that the brickmakers despair of themselves'; and the words of one of them are quoted – 'You might as well try to raise and improve the devil as a brickie, sir.' These things are not to be; but things nearly as bad are now (1873); and these things have formed the men whose words and deeds are quoted, when it is argued that the working classes cannot rise.

Thus awful, then, is the picture of unduly sustained work that is heavy. But can light work, however long sustained, bring no curse? Let us look at one more picture – our sad old picture of the needle-woman:

Work, work, work,
From weary chime to chime;
Work, work, work,
As prisoners work for crime.
Band and gusset and seam,
Seam and gusset and band,
Till the heart is sick and the brain benumbed
As well as the weary hand.

Work, work, work,
In the dull December light,
And work, work, work
When the weather is warm and bright;
While underneath the eaves
The brooding swallows cling,
As if to show me their sunny backs,
And twit me with the spring.

Oh! but to breathe the breath
Of the cowslip and primrose sweet –
With the sky above my head,
And the grass beneath my feet!
For only one short hour
To feel as I used to feel
Before I knew the woes of want
And the walk that costs a meal!

Oh! but for one short hour,
A respite, however brief!
No blessed leisure for love or hope,
But only time for grief!
A little weeping would ease my heart,
But in their briny bed
My tears must stop, for every drop
Hinders needle and thread.

'The heart is sick and the brain benumbed. No blessed leisure for love or hope, but only time for grief.' Surely we see here how work may depress, and keep low 'the working classes.' Man ought to work in order to live: his life, physical, moral, and mental, should be strengthened and made full by his work. But what if his inner life be almost crushed by his work? Is there not then suggested a terrible truth by the term working man, when applied to the unskilled labourer – a man whose occupation tends in a greater or less degree to make him live for little save for that work that is a burden to bear?

The ancients argued that Nature had ordained slavery: that without slaves the world could not progress; no one would have time for culture; no one could discharge the duties of a citizen. We have outgrown this belief; we have got to see how slavery dries up the sap of moral life in every state, at whose roots it is laid. But our thoughts are from youth upwards dominated by a Pagan belief not very different from the old one – the belief that it is an ordinance of Nature that multitudes of men must toil a weary toil, which may give to others the means of refinement and luxury, but which can afford to themselves scarce any opportunity of mental growth. May not the world outgrow this belief, as it has outgrown the other? It may, and it will.

We shall find it easier to see how exaggerated have been the difficulties which lie in the way of the removal of those circumstances which are distinctive of the lot of the working classes in the narrower sense of the term, if we allow ourselves a little license. Let us venture to picture to ourselves the state of a country from which such circumstances have been excluded. We shall have made much progress on our way, when we have seen that such a country would contain within it no seeds of the ruin of its material[9] or moral prosperity; that it would be vigorous and full of healthy life.

The picture to be drawn will resemble in many respects those which have been shown to us by some socialists,[10] who attributed to every man an unlimited capacity for those self-forgetting virtues that they found in their own breasts; who recklessly suggested means which were always insufficient and not seldom pernicious – recklessly, because their minds were untrained, and their souls absorbed in the consciousness of the grandeur of their ends. Their memories are therefore scorned by all but a very few men:[11] but among those very few is included perhaps every single man who has ever studied patiently the wild deep poetry of their faiths. The schemes of the socialists involved a subversion of existing arrangements, according to which the work of every man is chosen by himself and the remuneration he obtains for it is decided by free competition; and their schemes have failed.

But such a subversion is not required for the country which we are to picture to ourselves. All that is required is that no one in it should have any occupation which tends to make him anything else than a gentleman.

We have seen that manual and disagreeable work is now performed for payment at competition prices by gentlemen. It is true that their work involves mental training, and that the associations by which they are surrounded are refined; but, since the brain cannot always be in full action, it is clear that, provided these associations be retained, we need not exclude from our new society even manual and disagreeable work that does not give direct training to the mental faculties. A moderate amount of such work is not inconsistent with refinement. Such work has to be done by every lady who takes part in the duties of a hospital. She sees that it is necessary, and she does not shrink from it; for, if she did, she would not be a lady. It is true that such work is not now willingly undertaken for payment by an educated man, because in general he can obtain higher pay for doing work in which the training of his mental faculties can be turned to account; and because, as his associates would be uneducated, he would incur incidental discomforts and would lose social position. But, by the very definition of the circumstances of our supposed country, such deterrent motives would not exist in it. An educated man, who took a share of such little unskilled labour as required to be done in such a country,[12] would find that such labour was highly paid, because without high pay no one would undertake it: and as his associates would be as refined as himself and in the same position, he would have no social discomfort to undergo. We all require for the purposes of health an hour or two daily of bodily exercise, during which the mind is at rest, and, in general, a few hours more of such work would not interfere materially with our true life.

We know then pretty clearly what are the conditions under which our fancied country is to start; and we may formulate them as follows. It is to have a fair share of wealth, and not an abnormally large population. Everyone is to have in youth an education which is thorough while it lasts, and which lasts long. No one is to do in the day so much manual work as will leave him little time or little aptitude for intellectual and artistic enjoyment in the evening. Since there will be nothing tending to render the individual coarse and unrefined, there will be nothing tending to render society coarse and unrefined. Exceptional morbid growths must exist in every society; but otherwise every man will be surrounded from birth upwards by almost all the influences which we have seen to be at present characteristic of the occupations of gentlemen; everyone who is not a gentleman will have himself alone to blame for it. This, then, is the condition in which our fancied country is to be when we first consider it. We have to inquire whether this condition can be maintained. Let us examine such obstacles to its maintenance as may be supposed to exist.

First, it may be argued that a great diminution of the hours of manual labour below their present amount would prevent the industry of the country from meeting its requirements, so that the wealth of the country could not be sustained. This objection is an instance of the difficulty with which we perceive things that are familiar. We all know that the progress of science and invention has multiplied enormously the efficiency of labour within the last century. We all know that even in agriculture the returns to labour have much increased; and most of us have heard that, if farmers had that little knowledge which is even now obtainable, the whole of the produce consumed in a country as thickly populated as England is, might be grown in it with less proportionate expenditure of labour than that now required. In most other branches of production the increase in the efficiency of labour has been almost past computation. Take a cotton factory for example. We must allow for the expense of making and driving the machinery; but when this is provided, a man working it will spin more than three thousand times as rapidly as he could by hand. With numbers such as this before us, can we believe that the resources of the world would fail if the hours of our daily labour were halved, and yet believe that our simple ancestors obtained an adequate subsistence? Should we not be driven to the conclusion that the accounts we have received of men who lived and flourished before the invention of the steam engine are myths? But, further, the only labour excluded from our new society is that which is so conducted as to stunt the mental growth, preventing people from rising out of old narrow grooves of thought and feeling, from obtaining increased knowledge, higher tastes, and more comprehensive interests. Now it is to such stunting almost alone that indolence is due. Remove it, and work rightly applied, the vigorous exercise of faculties would be the main aim of every man. The total work done per head of the population would be greater than now. Less of it would be devoted directly to the increase of material wealth, but far more would be indirectly efficient for this end. Knowledge is power; and men would have knowledge. Inventions would increase, and they would be readily applied. All labour would be skilled, and there would be no premium on setting men to tasks that required no skill. The work which man directs the forces of nature to perform for him, would thus be incomparably greater than now. In the competition for employment between man's muscles and the forces of nature, victory would remain with the latter. This competition has been sustained so long, only because the supply of mere muscular force fit only to contend against nature has been so plentiful, and the supply of skill fit to direct nature has been so scarce.[13] Recollect that even with the imperfect machinery we now have one pound of coal will raise a hundred pounds twelve thousand feet high;[14] and that the daily work of a man cannot exceed this even if we work him into the dust, and obtain, in lieu of a man's life, so much pulling and pushing and hewing and hammering. Recollect that with an ordinary tide the water rushing in and out of a reservoir of a square mile in area, even if nine-tenths of its force were wasted through imperfections of machinery, would do as much work in a day as the muscles of one hundred thousand men.

But, secondly, it might[15] be argued that short hours of work might ruin the foreign trade of the country. Such a doctrine might derive support from the language of some of our public men, even in recent times. But it is a fallacy.[16] It contradicts a proposition which no one who had thought on the subject would dream of deliberately denying; one which is as well established and as rigorously proved as any in Euclid. This proposition is, that low wages, if common to all occupations, cannot enable one country to undersell another. A high rate of wages, or[17] short hours of work, if common to all industries, cannot cause a country to be undersold: though, if they were confined to some industries, they might of course cause these particular industries to be undersold.

A danger, however, might be incurred by high wages or[18] short hours of work. If the rate of profits were reduced thereby, capital would be tempted to migrate. But the country we are picturing to ourselves would be specially defended against such a danger. To begin with, its labourers would be highly skilled. And the history of the progress of manufactures in England and throughout the world proves that, if the number of hours' work per day be given, the capitalist can afford to pay almost any rate of wages in order to secure highly skilled labour. But such labour, partly as a cause and partly as a consequence of its skill, has in general not very many hours in its working-day; and for every hour, during which his untiring machinery is lying idle, the capitalist suffers loss. In our society the hours of labour are to be very short, but it does not follow that the hours of work of the machinery would be short too. The obstacles that now exist to the general adoption of the system of working in 'shifts' are due partly to the unenlightened selfishness of workmen, partly to their careless and dishonest maltreatment[19] of machinery, but mainly to the fact that, with the present number of hours' work done by each shift, one shift would have to commence work very early and the other to end work very late. But in our new society none of these obstacles would[20] exist. A man would not in general perform manual work[21] for more than six hours a day. Thus one set would work perhaps from 6 to 9.30 a.m. and from 2 to 4.30 p.m.; the other set from 10 a.m. to 1.30 p.m. and from 5 to 7.30 p.m. In heavy work three sets of men might each work a shift of four hours. For we must not suppose that an educated man would consent for any pay whatever to continue exhausting physical work so far as to cause the stupefaction of his intellect. For his severe work he would be highly paid; and, if necessary, he might add to his income by a few hours of lighter work.

But there is another special reason why capital should not leave our fancied country. All industries might be partly conducted by capitalists with labourers working for hire under them. But in many industries production would be mainly carried on, as Mr and Mrs Mill have prophesied, by 'the association of labourers among themselves on terms of equality, collectively owning the capital with which they carry on their operations, and working under managers elected and removable by themselves.'[22] It will be said that such associations have been tried, and have seldom succeeded. They have not been tried. What have been tried are associations among, comparatively speaking, uneducated men, men who are unable to follow even the financial calculations that are required for an extensive and complicated business. What have to be tried are associations among men as highly educated as are manufacturers now. Such associations could not but succeed; and the capital that belonged to them would run no risk of being separated from them.

Again, it might be objected that it would be impossible to maintain that high standard of education which we have throughout assumed. Some parents, it might be said, would neglect their duty to their children. A class of unskilled labourers might again grow up, competing for hard toil, ready to sacrifice the means of their own culture to increased wages and physical indulgences. This class would marry improvidently: an increased population would press on the means of subsistence, the difficulty of imparting a high education would increase, and society would retrograde until it had arrived at a position similar to that which it now occupies – a position in which man, to a great extent, ignores his duty of anticipating, before he marries, the requirements of the bodily and mental nurture of his children; and thereby compels Nature, with her sorrowful but stern hands, to thin out the young lives before they grow up to misery. This is the danger most to be dreaded. But even this danger is not so great as it appears. An educated man would not only have a high conception of his duty to his children; he would be deeply sensitive to the social degradation which he and they would incur if he failed in it. Society would be keenly alive to the peril to itself of such failure, and would punish it as a form of treason against the State. Education would be unfailingly maintained. Every man, before he married, would prepare for the expense of properly educating his family; since he could not, even if he would, shirk this expense. The population would, therefore, be retained within due limits. Thus every single condition would be fulfilled which was requisite for the continued and progressive prosperity of the country which we have pictured. It would grow in wealth – material and mental. Vigorous mental faculties imply continual activity. Work in its best sense, the healthy energetic exercise of faculties, is the aim of life, is life itself; and in this sense every one would be a worker more completely than now. But men would have ceased to carry on mere physical work to such an extent as to dull their higher energies. In the bad sense, in which work crushes a man's life, it would be regarded as a wrong. The active vigour of the people would continually increase; and in each successive generation it would be more completely true that every man was by occupation a gentleman.

Such a state of society in a country would then, if once attained, be ever maintained. Such a country would have in it the conditions of vitality more fully satisfied than any other country would. It is not, then, a reasonable thing to believe that every movement towards the attainment of such conditions has vitality also? And, if we look around us, do we not find that we are steadily, if slowly, moving towards that attainment? All ranks of society are rising; on the whole they are better and more cultivated than their forefathers were; they are no less eager to do, and they are much more powerful greatly to bear, and greatly to forbear. Read of the ignorant crime that accompanied popular outbreaks even a generation ago, and then look at the orderly meetings by which the people now expresses its will. In the broad backbone of moral strength our people have never been wanting; but now, by the aid of education, their moral strength is gaining new life. Look at the grand conduct of the Lancashire artisans during the cotton famine.[23] In old times of ignorance they would have struggled violently against the inevitable; but now their knowledge restrained them, and they suffered with quiet constancy. Nay, more; the Northern army was destroying the cotton on which their bread depended; yet, firm in their allegiance to the struggle against slavery, they never faltered. Listen to the reply that President Lincoln gave to the address of sympathy that they sent him: 'Under the circumstances, I cannot but regard your decisive utterances upon the question as an instance of sublime Christian heroism which has not been surpassed in any age or country.'[24]

And thus it is. In every age of the world people have delighted in piquant stories, which tell of some local or partial retrogression; but, if we look at the broad facts of history, we find progress. Of the progress of the artisans we have spoken; how all are rising; how some are, in the true sense of the word, becoming gentlemen. Some few of them may, indeed, interpret this to mean little more than becoming, at times, dandyfied perambulating machines, for the display of the cheaper triumphs of the haberdasher and the tailor. But many artisans are becoming artists, who take a proud interest in the glories of their art, are truly citizens, are courteous, gentle, thoughtful, able, and independent men. Even if we take the ruder labourers, we find something to set off against the accounts of their habits of indulging in drink and rough pastimes. Such habits were but a short time ago common among country squires. But country squires had in them the seeds of better things, and when a new age opened to them broader and higher interests, they threw off the old and narrow ones. And our colliers even are doing the same. A series of reports by well-informed, unprejudiced men proves that, on the whole, their faults have diminished and their virtues increased. And the late Parliamentary Commission has shown how a solid foundation of their further improvement has been laid in the improvement of their houses, how they are now learning to take pride in their homes and to love them.

What limits are there then to the rapidity of our progress? How are we let or hindered? History shows that on a basis of mere energy a marvellous edifice can be speedily erected. Two centuries ago England exported raw in exchange for manufactured produce; she had no mechanical skill,[25] and imported foreigners one after another to overcome her engineering difficulties. A century ago the agriculture of the Scotch lowlands seemed as hopelessly bad as any in Europe: now it is a model school for the world. It was mainly from the rough uncultured population of the trading cities of Italy and the Netherlands that there arose that bright glory of art which in the middle ages illuminated all Europe. Why the should not the energy which our working classes have, when once turned in the right direction, lead to a progress as rapid and as brilliant?

Alas! there is one great hindrance. One of the first uses we are making of our increased knowledge is, as it ought to be, to save from disease and want multitudes who, even a few years ago, would have sunk under their influence. As a result, population is increasing rapidly. The truth that every father owes to his children the duty of providing them with a lot in life, happier and better than his own, has not yet been grasped. Men who have been brought up, to use their own phrase, 'anyhow', are contented that their children should be brought up 'anyhow'. Thus there is kept up a constant supply of unskilled labourers, who have nothing but their hands to offer for hire, and who offer these without stint or reserve. Thus competition for food dogs the heels of progress, and perpetually hinders it. The first most difficult step is to get rid of this competition. It is difficult, but it can be made. We shall in vain tell[26] the working man that he must raise his standard while we do not raise ours: he will laugh at us, or glare on us. But let the same measure be meted out to all. Let this one principle of action be adopted by us all – *just as a man who has borrowed money is bound to pay it back with interest, so a man is bound to give to his children an education better and more thorough than he has himself received.* This he is bound to do. We may hope that many will do more than they are bound to do.

And what is society bound to do? It is bound to see that no child grows up in ignorance, able only to be a producing machine, unable to be a man; himself low and limited in his thoughts, his tastes, his feelings, his interests and his aims, to some extent probably low and limited in his virtues, and in every way lowering and limiting his neighbours. It is bound to compel children, and to help them, to take the first step upwards; and it is bound to help them to make, if they will, many steps upwards.[27] If the growth of a man's mind, if his spiritual cultivation be the end of life; and material wealth, houses and horses, carpets and French cookery merely means; what temporary pecuniary loss can we set against the education of the nation? It is abundantly clear that, unless we can compel children into the schools, we cannot enable multitudes of them to escape from a life of ignorance so complete that they cannot fail to be brutish and degraded. It is not denied that a school-board alone can save from this ruin those children whose parents are averse to education;[28] that at least in our towns there are many whom no voluntary system can reach. And yet throughout the length and breadth of the country we are startled by finding that some of those, who are most anxious that the Bible should be taught, are those who are most unwilling that a State, which has with success invested capital in telegraphs, should now venture to invest capital in men; that they are those who are most ready to urge men 'not to rush headlong on' a rate of some pence in the pound.[29] I will only urge that, for consistency, such people should teach an expurgated edition of the Bible. Let every page be cut out in which it is implied that material wealth may be less important than the culture of the man himself, the nurture of his inner life. They will not have heavy work, they will not have many pages left to teach.[30]

But in truth material welfare, as well as spiritual, will be the lot of that country which, by public and private action, devotes its full energies to raising the standard of the culture of the people. The difference between the value of the labour of the educated man and that of the uneducated is, as a rule, many times greater than the difference between the costs of their education. If the difference between the value of the work done by a good breed of horses and a bad one be much greater than the difference between the costs of maintaining them, can there be any doubt that the good breed will drive out the bad one? But no individual reaps the full gains derived from educating a child, from taking a step towards supplanting the race of uneducated labourers by a race of educated labourers. Still, if the State work for this end, the State will gain. If we all work together for this end, we shall all gain together. Then will be removed every let and hindrance to the attainment of that condition which we have pictured – a condition which, if it be hard to be attained, is easy to be maintained – a condition in which every man's energies and activities will be fully developed – a condition in which men will work not less than they do now but more; only, to use a good old phrase, most of their work will be a work of love; it will be a work which, whether conducted for payment or not, will exercise and nurture their faculties. Manual work, carried to such an excess that it leaves little opportunity for the free growth of his higher nature, that alone will be absent; but that *will* be absent. In so far as the working classes are men who have such excessive work to do, in so far will the working classes have been abolished.

Notes and References

1. 'A paper read at a Conversazione of the Cambridge reform Club, 25 November 1873, and printed shortly afterwards for private circulation. It is here reproduced without amendment or alteration of any kind; though it bears marks of the over-sanguine temperament of youth. A few passages in it have been included in more recent writings, which are still in print'. (Manuscript footnote about 1923.)
   [The text of this footnote, whose manuscript has not been found, is reprinted from *Memorials of Alfred Marshall*. The comment inside round brackets is by Pigou.
   In the *Marshall Papers* there is a copy of an off-print with Marshall's annotations. Mary Paley has written on the pale blue cover of the off-print: 'This version seems to be an off-print from *The Eagle* without the magazine's heading and vol. reference – the lay-out is identical'. The footnote of the article (A Conversazione read at the Cambridge 'Reform Club,' Nov. 25.1873) is replaced by Alfred Marshall with 'Read at a Conversazione in

Nov. 1873. Large numbers of it were printed in the following year, and circulated privately'.
In the following footnotes notice will be given of Marshall's comments and corrections, introduced with [A.M.:]. Some differences of the Tofts edition – in its turn a reprint of the article published in the *Cambridge Independent Press* – will also be given [Tofts:].
Both the off-print from *The Eagle* and the Tofts printing bear the writing 'For private circulation only'. Marshall's handwritten introduction on the inside front cover of his copy of the off-print from *The Eagle* runs as follows:]
[A.M.:] ' Read on ... at ... , printed local magazine and then was privately circulated: not publicly because I hoped to get time for a more scientific analysis of issues which I have treated slightly here and in a declamatory style. But much pressed to publish it in its present form and agreed to publish practically unaltered. Too much stress on leisure for adults. This only one of many movements: would in many ways do harm at present: machinery takes off excessive strain. Education of children far more important. Don't regard Utopia as likely to come soon or as likely to come ever unless "self-forgetting virtues" become common. Argue only that not *economically* impracticable. (Note on clergy at end called forth by one or two of the clergy who on night before delivery of lecture had in arguing against schoolboard implored the ratepayers to guard jealously their own pockets. I have not suppressed this because it appears that there yet remain in Cambridge and other towns a few clergy who are not ashamed to endeavour to maintain their power by such means.)'

2 Mill (1981), p. 257.

3. [A. M.:] '... the betting or sporting man'.

4. [A. M.:] the sentences 'The question for us to-night is, Can this doubt be resolved?' and 'I hold that it may, and that it will' are crossed out. 'Parable' is annotated in the margin

5. [A. M.:] the whole paragraph is crossed through, but 'Stet' is annotated in the margin.

6. [A. M.:] sign to start a new paragraph and 'N. B.' in the margin.

7. [A. M.:] sign to attach to the previous paragraph and 'For' added to start the sentence.

8. *Report by the Assistant Commissioner of the Children's Employment Commission relative to brickmaking, employment of children therein, and relative to brickyards in Staffordshire and Shropshire, Parliamentary Papers*, 1866, XXIV.

9. [Tofts:] 'mineral' [sic].

10. [Tofts:] '... by the Socialists, that noble set of untutored enthusiasts, who attributed ...' This difference had been noticed and emphasized by T. H. Marshall, in the 1949 Alfred Marshall Lectures, 'Citizenship and social class', in Marshall T. H. (1950), *Citizenship and Social Class and Other Essays*, Cambridge: Cambridge University Press.

11. [Tofts:] '... but a few men: ...'

12. [A. M.:] 'in such a country' is crossed out.

13. [Tofts:] the sentence from 'competion' to 'scarce' is substituted with 'But what an insane competition this is!'.

14. [A. M.:] '... we now have, we may by burning one pound of coal raise a weight of one hundred pounds ...'
15. [A. M.:] 'may'.
16. [Tofts:] 'But it is a monstrous fallacy – monstrous because it contradicts ...'.
17. [A. M.:] crossed out from 'low wages' to 'wages, or'. The revised text is 'This proposition is, that short hours of work ...'
18. [A. M.:] 'high wages or' is crossed out.
19. [Tofts:] '... to their foolishly dishonest treatment ...'
20. [Tofts:] 'could'.
21. [Tofts:] 'A man would not perform even light manual work ...'
22. Mill (1965), vol. III, book IV, chapter vii, p. 775.
23. Biagini (1992), pp. 69–83
24. Lincoln (1863), in Basler (ed.), p. 64. The context and precise text of the quotation was: 'I know and deeply deplore the sufferings which the workingmen at Manchester and in all Europe are called to endure in this crisis. It has been often studiously represented that the attempt to overthrow this government, which was built upon the foundation of human rights, and to substitute for it one which should rest exclusively on the basis of human slavery, was likely to obtain the favour of Europe. Through the action of our disloyal citizens the workingmen of Europe have been subjected to a severe trial, for the purpose of forcing their sanction to that attempt. Under *these* circumstances, I cannot but regard your decisive utterance upon the question as an instance of sublime Christian heroism which has not been surpassed in any age or *in any* country.' (Italics added to mark the differences from Marshall's quotation.)
25. [Tofts:] 'Two centuries ago English artificers were among the rudest in Europe. We had no mechanical skill ...'
26. [Tofts:] 'There is no use in telling ...'
27. [Tofts:] new sentence inserted here: 'The State has invested capital in telegraphs; it has been a successful investment; and the return will not be less if it invests capital in men.'
28. The Education Act of 1870 – by which a national network of rate-supported schools had begun to be established – left to locally-elected school boards to decide whether education ought to be made compulsory: but this presupposed either secular education or 'non-sectarian' religious instruction – and both proposals were very controversial. Marshall was here criticizing the 'voluntary' party, who opposed compulsory schooling on conscience grounds. On the question see Murphy, 1972; Fraser, 1973, pp. 196–203; Parry, 1986, pp. 295–320; Biagini, 1992, pp. 198–217 and bibliography.
29. [Tofts:] from 'It is not denied' to 'some pence in the pound' the text is substituted with 'And yet, throughout the length and breadth of the country we are startled by finding that some of those who are most anxious that the Bible should be taught are those who are most eager to come forward and say "Be careful what you are doing. Though a school-board alone can save from ruin those children whose parents are adverse to education, who will escape any voluntary system, do not rush headlong on a rate of some pence in the pound".'
30. [A. M.:] 'These remarks were called forth by the arguments against a

schoolboard by one or two of the local clergy at a meeting in the Town Hall in the evening previous to that on which this address was delivered'.

Bibliography

Biagini E. F. (1992), *Liberty, Retrenchment and Reform. Popular Liberalism in the Age of Gladstone, 1860–1880*, Cambridge: Cambridge University Press.

Fraser D. (1973), 'Edward Baines', in P. Hollis (ed.) *Pressure from Without in Early Victorian England*, London: E. Arnold, pp. 183–209.

Lincoln A. (1863), 'To the workingmen of Manchester, England', 19 January 1863, in R. P. Basler (ed.) (1953), *The Collected Works of Abraham Lincoln*, vol. VI, New Brunswick (NJ): Rutgers University Press.

Mill J. S. (1965) [1848], *Principles of Political Economy, with some of their Applications to Social Philosophy*, (1862 edition), in *Collected Works of John Stuart Mill*, ed. by V. W. Bladen and J. M. Robson, Toronto and London: Toronto University Press, vols. 2 and 3.

Mill J. S. (1981) [1873], *Autobiography*, in *Collected Works of John Stuart Mill*, ed. by J. M. Robson and J. Sanger, Toronto and London: University of Toronto Press, Routledge & Kegan Paul, vol. 1.

Murphy J. (ed.) (1972), *The Education Act of 1870. Text and Commentary*, Newton Abbot (Devon): David and Charles.

Parry J. P. (1986), *Democracy & Religion*, Cambridge: Cambridge University Press.

7. The *Bee-Hive* debate

Coal

11 April 1874

The importance of coal to our national progress, and its value to individual comfort and well-being can scarcely be over-estimated. All that relates to these is of importance, both public and private; and that which is published should be reliable. We therefore hold that the mineral statistics of the United Kingdom are of a far higher importance than many more popular subjects. It matters very little to the world whether Oxford or Cambridge boats went ahead one or two lenghts; it does that the yield of coal should meet our requirements, and that the price should be regulated to the mutual advantage of both producers and cosumers.

For many years 'Robert Hunt, F.R.S.' has been Keeper of the Mineral Records at the *Mining Record* Office, Museum of Practical Geology, Jermyn Street, London. We give the address in full to establish the authority of the reports, which reports are backed by the force or rather facility that Government can give, both by legislation and recommendation, to arrive at accuracy, and to sanction results; and while, on the whole, we have no reason to expect any desire, or even to suppose any tendency to misrepresent or to falsify, we are yet desirous of realising the verity of the records themselves, and the impartiality and truth of the inferences to be derived therefrom.

In this spirit we look to the report recently published, ending year 1872, and in many respects we find all that might be expected. With the growth of the nation and trade, we might expect to find the increase of coal yields, both as a cause and as an effect. Thus from 1854 to 1870 the yields have been *gradually* increasing, beginning with, in round numbers, 64 millions of tons, and getting up to 110 millions in 1870. Mr. Hunt says that there is a considerable difficulty in ascertaining *exactly* the yields – but we accept these as being generally and approximately correct. In the same way, the 'estimated value at the place of production' has increased in amount, pro rata, to the yields; and, with slight variations in years, it has only slightly increased per ton from 1854 to 1870. In round numbers, if the cost of coal at the pit's mouth was 4s. per ton in 1854, it was by the same estimate 4s. 5d. in 1870. In 1870 the ordinary rates of both yield and price took a very different scale to the years previous. Thus, while the yields of coal increased about 2 millions of tons a year from 1866 to 1870, the two years of 1871–72 are exceptional. The average yield was 105,426,176 for four years before, and 115,420,672 for 1871–72, or nearly 10 millions of tons yearly in excess of previous yields.

The price, too, not only increased to the amount of the yields, but it increased in ratio from an average of 5s. per ton for the five years, to 6s. 9½d. for the two years 1871–2. These figures are taken as fact from Mr. Hunt's returns, and they should be correct. We think that the averages of 1856 to 1871 are, and so are the yields of 1871–2. But when we come to the estimated value of the place of production we stand dissatisfied, and even staggered, with the figures (as not facts), that Mr. Hunt has placed before us. Thus the yields and values as published are:

	Tons of Coal.	Value.
1871	117,352,028	£35,205,608
1872	123,497,316	46,311,143
Half	240,849,344	81,516,751
Averaging yearly	120,424,672	£40,379,185

Average, 6s. 9½d. per ton.

The yields Mr. Hunt has subsequently verified before the Statistical Society, and we cannot but wish that he had done the same with prices, for we all know by practical experience that not only has the average price of coal been above 6s. 9¼d. per ton, but that coal of any kind whatever was exceptional to be obtained so low as 6s. 9¼d. for the two years 1871–2.

We will take West Yorkshire prices as evidence – and West Yorkshire, as the most central coal field of England, has the most central *and least disturbing influences* of either home or foreign markets that can be instanced. Having returns from various sources before me, I find that the average list prices for 1871 was, for coal at the pit's mouth, 9s. 10d. per ton all round, varying from 11s. 6d. best, to 6s. 6d. slack. But 1872 averaged 13s. 10d., varying from 16s. 6d. 'best,' to 9s. 'slack.' The average of 9s. 10d, and 13s. 10d., will be 11s. 10d. per ton. But the list yields were altered; for, while up to 1871 there were four qualities, from 1871 there were only three obtainable, the thirds were mixed as seconds, and cannot thus and therefore make the average prices, the out-put of coal to be less than 13s. a ton for 1871–2, and *not* 6s. 9¼d., as the yield, divided by the estimated value Mr. Hunt gives in figures, would lead us to suppose. What, then, will be the difference in the amount of estimated value for the two years, if we put it at 12s. per ton – instead of 6s. 9¼d.? In the latter case it is £40,379,085, in the former, £72,254,812, or only £31,875,737 a year, or £63,751,454 during 1871–2.

Mr. Hunt makes the total value of metals and minerals for 1872 to be £70,193,416, and increase of £12,871,523 on 1871, and then he adds, 'that the increase is chiefly due to the additional cost of getting each ton of coal.' Why Mr. Hunt should have referred the cost of minerals wholly to the advance of coals is curious, but as he gives the additional cost of getting coal to be 1s. 6d. per ton, on the evidence of the Royal Commissioner of 1873, we get the gross additional cost to be £9,262,302 for 1872; and deducting this from the increase of value, which he puts at £12,871,523, it leaves only £3,609,221 additional to the whole of the coal and iron capitalists for that year. Now this is an error as certain as that coal only averaged 6s. 9¼d. per ton. Let us, however, keep to the coal question, and we find that the increase is 6,145,288 tons, and £11,105,535 in value in 1872 over 1871; and taking the 1s. 6d. per ton added in cost, £466,896, it will still leave £10,739,739 increase, to coal capital only, for 1872. But, put the average at 12s. per ton, and that upon the yield of 123,497,316 tons, it will come to £74,098,889. Divide the extra cost of getting 1s. 6d. or £9,212,297, and it will leave a net advance of £64,786,592, or £18,475,449 more than Mr. Hunt, the keeper of the mining records, makes it to be. This is an addition to former profits of at least one-fourth of the entire income of the United Kingdom, and tells either for or against the economy of the system under which we are at present yoked, for better and worse.

Our article has extended too far in developing these facts to admit of considering the economy of this system; but we beg our readers to retain the facts, as we propose to go further into them. At present we will merely add that 1873 gave a decided advance in prices over 1872, so that we have the statement of Mr. Tennant, the Chairman of the West Yorkshire Coalowners, 'that, except in March of 1873, the average of the year for coal all round was 15s. 6d., and that is has now (March 31) fallen to barely 11s. 9d.' – See *Leeds Mercury*, April 1.

Why coal should thus rise and fall, and the ratios have been hitherto taught, as the inevitable results of demand and supply, and that these were laws of nature against which politcal economy told us was in vain to kick against. other views are, however, beginning to prevail, and some of the Cambridge teachers of political economy now tell us, that advances may be made regardless of demand, in accordance with their individual or class selfishness; and that in violation of all economy. Believing this, we now simply direct attention to the facts that the published records of the 'estimated value of coal at the place of production' are seriously, and most seriously, wrong for the years 1871–2, and that therefore the public may be seriously misled as to the economy in regulations supposed to rule the laws of supply and demand.

John Holmes

The Laws of Political Economy. What they can teach, and what they cannot teach

18 April 1874

We frequently hear from one party, if not both parties to a controversy, some such phrase as 'The laws of political economy justify our action.' But such phrases are incorrect; the laws of political economy have not this power.

The occasion of my wishing to offer some explanation on this point will be found in the following extract from a letter from Mr. Holmes which appeared in the last number of the *Bee-Hive*. He says, 'Why coal should thus rise and fall, and the ratios (in which it rises and falls) have hitherto been taught as the inevitable result of demand and supply; and these were laws of nature against which political economy told us that it was in vain to kick. Other views are, however, beginning to prevail, and some of the Cambridge teachers of political economy now tell us that advances may be made regardless of demand, in accordance with individual or class selfishness.' I have reason to believe that Mr. Holmes is here referring in part to a conversation that he recently had with me; and I therefore feel responsible for not allowing his account of the doctrine which issue from Cambridge to pass without comment.[1]

Political economy is a science. The term 'law,' when used in relation to a science, differs as much from the term 'law' when used to denote a precept of morality or Government, as the word 'bat,' which is frequent in the account of a cricket match, differs from the word 'bat' which heads a chapter in a book on natural history. A law of science is simply a statement of the consequences which follow from a given set of causes. A science may tell us that a certain course of action will produce a certain event. If it be considered wrong to produce this event, we may hear such phrases as – 'the action is condemned by the science in question,' or 'is contrary to its laws.' But such phrases are always inaccurate, and often mischievous.

First, let us take instances from a physical science. The laws of a science may prove that great risk would be run if twenty persons assembled on a certain balcony to see a fete. No one would deny that it would be wrong to incur a great risk for this purpose. Hence people might easily glide into the use of the phrase, 'The laws of mechanics forbid the letting out of twenty seats on that balcony in its present condition.' This phrase may not be directly mischievous here; but it is inaccurate. Suppose, however, that it is disputed whether the officer of a fire-brigade should have ordered his men to advance along the crazy balcony of a certain burning house in order to rescue its inmates. The laws of mechanics may decide the amount of danger which would have been thus incurred. But when this is known, there remains the question whether he ought to have ordered his men to incur so great a danger. If the real point at issue between the disputants be the answer that is to be given to this question, it would introduce mischievous confusion to contend that 'the laws of mechanics decide what course the officer should have pursued.'

Next, let us take instances from political economy. Let us suppose that some particular mode of conducting strikes is under discussion. Political economy may perhaps prove that if a strike be conducted in this mode, it will cause but little net gain to the class of workmen who strike, that it will arrest against their will the work of vast numbers of work-men of other classes, that it will cause great losses, direct and indirect, to the consumer and the capitalist, and that it will give rise needlessly to habits of distrust and unfriendliness. Everyone would agree in condemning as selfish the deliberate adoption of a plan which was known to lead up to such consequences. Men proposing to enter on it would be likely to be warned that their course was condemned as selfish by political economy, and the inaccuracy in the form of the warning might not do mischief directly. Let us take an instance of another kind. We may suppose that the wages of labourers in a certain district are insufficient to support vigorous life; that if higher wages ruled, the efficiency of labour would, after some years, rise more than in proportion to the rise in wages; but that any single employer who wished to raise the wages of his men would have special difficulties to contend against if he acted alone, so that without a strike the rise cannot be easily effected. It may then be proposed that the labourers should accumulate a fund with which to enable some of them to migrate, and others to sustain a strike. It might perhaps be shown that this course would probably be successful in causing a permanent rise in wages – that the rise would, in the long run, be a benefit to the employers themselves, and to the general public as consumers, while it would diminish the poor rates, and cause no important evils, directly or indirectly, with the exception of the not very important losses at the time of the strike. It is obvious that if, in the interests of themselves and their families, labourers were to adopt a plan which was known to lead up to such consequences, their conduct would not be selfish. It might be said that this was the verdict of political economy, and in this instance also the inaccuracy in the form of the statement would not be directly mischievous. In each of these instances political economy has done nothing more than declare the consequences of a proposed course of action, and submit to our moral judgment the question whether actions which have such consequences are justifiable. The cases thus presented are so clear that our moral judgment is given without hesitation, almost instinctively, and we are scarcely aware that any other judgment than that of political economy has been given.

But many of the case which political economy presents to our moral judgment are not so clear. With regard to these it is absolutely necessary to keep entirely distinct two questions; that which must be decided according to the laws of political economy, viz., what consequences will follow from a proposed[2] course of action, and that which must be decided by our moral judgments, viz., whether an action which produces these consequences is right.

The student of political economy is at liberty, as everyone else is, to express an opinion on this latter question, and to approve or condemn the action under discussion; but his special science can give him no commission to do so. He may happen to have a minute practical acquaintance with some special questions; but, in general, the chief aid which he will have derived from his study, the chief aid which he will be able to lend to others, will consist in his command of two instruments, which are needed for the accertainment of the consequences which will follow from a proposed course of action. These instruments are closely allied in character. The first assists him to discover what are the circumstances which bear upon the question at issue, what are the matters of fact upon which the decision turns, and how these matters must be investigated. The second instrument assists him to reason accurately as to the results which would be produced by a given course of action under given circumstances.

The chief worth of political economy consists in that she possesses highly-organised machinery for these two processes, machinery in the successive improvements of which are stored up the results of the work of many generations of careful and observant thinkers. Just so are the results of the work of many generations of careful and observant thinkers, stored up in the successive improvements that are embodied in the spinning mule. A man might complain that the mule only spins, and does not also weave the yarn into cloth; and might, therefore, refuse to derive any aid from the discoveries of his predecessors. He would then act no more foolishly than one who should complain that political economy will not perform all the stages of the enquiry that he desired to pursue, and should therefore decline all aid from his predecessors in working over these stages to assist him in which political economy is charged, according to that system of division of labour which rules in the world of thought.

To be blamed by such folly need be the fear of no one. Political economy does not fear such blame. But she laments if her disciples claim for her a power which she does not possess – the power of giving direct and complete answers on points involving questions of right and wrong. For thereby two grievous evils will be caused. Firstly, men who have not the patience, the training, the intelligence, and the knowledge required for an accurate treatment of that stage of the inquiry with which political economy can deal, will find it easy to conceal their deficiency from themselves, if not from others. They will be apt to give vague declamation not only in addition to, but also as substitute for an elaborately reasoned investigation of the causes which operate in the case under discussion, and of the consequences which follow from them. And, secondly, the heat of excited feeling is likely to be introduced unnecessarily at an early stage of the inquiry. If the rigidly scientific character of political economy be forgotten, those questions even, which belong strictly to her domain, will not be discussed with scientific calmness and thoroughness.

Although I have chosen to take my illustrations from combinations to raise the price of labour rather than from combinations to raise the price of coal, the reader who has followed me thus far may almost anticipate the mode in which I should treat the positions taken up by Mr. Holmes in the passage quoted above. I hold, not indeed as a new doctrine, but as a doctrine common to all economists as well as to business men, that a combination of sellers, if it can be effected, may for the time raise prices. (I do not, of course, hold that this can be done 'without any reference to the demand.' But Mr. Holmes must have made a slip of the pen when he said this. He cannot have meant to say it.) I think the question how much of the recent rise in the price of coal has been due to a combination tacit or avowed in any portion of the coal trade, is an interesting and important one, though I think it is a harder one than Mr. Holmes seems to consider it to be. But I should not brand as selfish the action which traders may have thus taken in their own interest, until I had fully inquired into the nature of their action, and examined the consequences which were attributable to it. This difficult but necessary preliminary step I should take as an economist. Ultimately, I should probably not hesitate to give my opinion that action which produced consequences such as theirs had done was selfish, or was not selfish, as the case might be. But I should give this opinion merely as deduced from my own belief about morality. I should not give the opinion on the authority of political economy.

Alfred Marshall
Cambridge University

The Teachings of Political Economy 25 April 1874

There is, I believe, little real difference betwixt me and your able correspondent, Professor Marshall, of the University of Cambridge, upon the province and the teachings of political economy. My article upon the coal trade prices was in type before I had the pleasure of conversing with the professor at Halifax, and, therefore, must stand, with all its errors, as published by you on the 6th of April. Perhaps it is of little meaning to the world of what I know or think upon the subject of the laws and teachings of political economy; but it is of what the practical world thinks and holds. The world generally think, or I generally mistaken, that political economy does teach that we *ought* and *ought not* to do such and certain things. Of course it is competent to students and professors to limit their teaching and studies on science in a certain and definite way; but I take that it is common usage for the time being which determines the common meaning of both words, things, and sciences. Dr. Johnson tells us that, in order to avoid confusion and arbitrary application of works [*sic, sc.* words] to meanings, he took the use of the best writers of both the past and present, upon those in his Dictionary, and so he registered the meaning by the use made of words by the bad authorities. Now, I take it that if we did the same of the province of political economy, and of its teaching; (*i.e.* by the rule of writers) we should find a different aspect held to the one laid before us by Professor Marshall. The fact is, in the multiplicity of counsel, one is tempted to ask, what is and who are the political economists? From Andrew Torringing, our first, to Professors Fawcett and Marshall, our last teachers, there is such a diversity of views and teachings on political economy, that 'Dundrearies' may well be pardoned for saying 'no fellar can tell which is t'other.' If political economy, however, is the proper term, it must mean, properly, the economy of the body politic, and to descend closely to definition, we must fix economy to be well-being, welfare or progress. We thus come to its real meaning as the science which indicates and so teaches that course of action which will produce the greatest well-being to the greatest number, and realize this. Let us, as painters sometimes do, reverse the picture in a glass, and the false drawing will then be seen at once. Make the 'politic' to be the few, and economy to be deterioration, and then the fallacy will be felt as well as seen of such a definition.

Assuming then, with writers in common, that the science is to be for the use and development of general good, then I admit that, for the purpose of study, it may be well to separate its relations and phenomenon into various and separated departments. We may thus study the facts and phenomenon of social life as existing. We may register the facts as they arise, and we may place them in a certain order in relation to consequences supposed to precede and to follow certain facts existing. We may thus call such arrangements science, and we may teach the events preceding and succeeding such facts to be *laws*. But our defining will not make them either, nor will our teachings be accepted of men generally unless we go a little further, viz., to show how, in the words of Milton, they can worthily lead us 'to the glory of God, *and the good of man's estate*.' It appears to me that in order to correct the indefinite application of some to the teachings of political economy, the Professors of the Cambridge school are defining too narrowly the bearings of what they teach, both well and worthily. In this they do justice neither to the science nor themselves. Thus limited, political economy becomes merely a branch of statistics, which would ascertain the nature of actions like the mateirals, good, bad and indifferent, for a building, but which leaves out the higher use and the more glorious use of architecture. Now, good materials for a building are good things, involving both art and science; but they would be of very little use if the art and science of arranging them in order for *use* (economy) and in place for *beauty* (science), for the benefit and elevation of humanity, was wanting. So good actions are good things, and the shortest line to make wealth is the most economic doubtless; but, unless we have the consideration of use and application of that wealth taught also – as economic – the science will be of little use – nay, it may become a positive evil. To make men skilful thieves and economic scoundrels is, I submit, not the objects of either art and science. Political economy, in the highest sense, does, therefore, involve the science of morality as well as the science of statistics. I would even go so far as to submit that you can have neither science properly understood or worked separately. In other words, that economics and morals are so inseparably linked that the [*sic, sc.* they] must both go together, and that they will alike flourish, and together fade under the circumstances involving both. Mrs. Somerville's connection of the physical sciences should now have a parallel brought before us of the connection of the social and economic sciences. Sir James Kay

Shuttleworth gave us a glance at it, in his priceless addres before the Social Sciences [congress] at Glasgow in 1860; when he showed that the simple acqusition of skilfully-gained wealth would not, in the end, be economic. To starve a horse down to a bean a day is not economic, for it kills the horse; and to defraud the labourer, or to give a hire inadequate to maintain his strength of body, and his health of morals, must and will necessarily end in a loss. It is not economic to leave the labourer dissatisfied, with a conviction that he has not a fair share of the results of his labour. Nor is it economic to have the *idea* of what is fair, right, or wrong, a question of dispute. (See our strikes and locks-out.) Economy thus becomes a direct factor of and to morality; and had economies been more linked to, instead of being separated from, morals, both sciences would have advanced in a way little suspected. I thus and therefore think that Cambridge will do a great injustice to itself, and an injury to the science of political economy, to teach that morality and economy have any *separate* interest. Right and duty are both *truly* economic; and the highest economy necessitates both being involved and evolved. *Vice versa* follows necessarily, and thus I look upon the immense wealth recently 'screwed' from the public by the coal owners as both *not* economic and purely *selfish*. Evidences of this I purpose to lay before your readers in further consideration of the facts. But let not me blame them wholly. Political economy, as understood, and taught by some of its head writers and highest authorities, justifies them *fully* for all they have done, or would do, to acquire wealth for themselves. As a case in point I instance one from 'Lessons on Political Economy,' where we are told of the benefit to the public when a corn-dealer holds back his stock in famine, in order to sell it at the highest price. The benefit described is, in inducing storing up for scarcity, and economy in the use of the corn. And then the teacher goes on to say, 'It is curious to see how, through the wise and beneficient arrangement of Providence, men thus do the greatest service to the public, when they are thinking of nothing but their own gain. And this happens not only in the case of corn-dealers, but generally. When men are left quite free to employ their capital as each thinks best for his own advantage, he will almost always benefit the public, though he may have not such design in thought.' (Page 39.) Now put coal for corn-dealers, and you have here a case of perfect justification of a coal-ring rig, advancing coal – *irrespective of demand even* – when they have the power. And yet this is political economy, as now taught in national schools – 'published under the direction of the Committee of General Literature and Education, appointed by the Society for Promoting Christian Knowledge. London: 1857.' Archbishop Whately is said to have been the author, and he was no fool, but deemed a good authority in political science. Presto, however, let us see what he says upon the wisdom of Providence, where working men use their liberty and capital for *their* own advantage. In some instances the lessons speak of the 'unmitigated evil' resulting from strikes – of the workers to obatin advances – and those of colliers and ironworkers are given, showing that whereas 3s. 6d. to 4s. a day could be earned by ten hours reasonable labour, 'by combinations the miners had so raised the price of raw materials that the iron master was *obliged* to charge 70s. to 75s. a ton for the iron which *ought* to have been produced for 60s. to 65s. a ton,' which caused the order to go from Lanarkshire to Belgium. Thus trade was lost &c., &c. 'It is very sad that colliers and miners should be so blind to their own interests, and to that of the community, as thus to labour hard to destroy the very foundation of our national advantages – cheap coal and iron – and thus encourage foreign trade, instead of successfully combating it, and, inasmuch as in them lies, destroy and estinguish the very trade which is their mainstay for future employment.' (Page 26.) Put this beside the last, and what was a public blessing in the selfishness of the cornholders becomes a public curse in the colliers. Liberty of capital is commended in one case as providential, and its same use in the other condemned. And both are taught effectually in the same book, and by the same authority, as 'Lessons on Political Economy.' What, then, is to be expected of the uninitiated, if the professors so far differ, but confused ideas, in which the selfish will see justification for his selfishness, and the sufferer will see wrongs in the teachings and science, and will even declaim not 'vaguely' of both? It may be all right for well-to-do professors to preach patience to the hungry and coolness to the injured, and to tell them, as William Hill, F.R.S., Esq., did, at the Leeds Social Science meeting, that the inviolable laws of political economy will certainly, in the long run, strike a perfect balance of injury. But the world is not thus to be dealt with. We must deal with human nature, and call a spade a spade, and deam selfishness as selfishness. And, as these act upon the body politic, so they may wisely be taught, as according to or against the 'principles of political economy.'

John Holmes

The Province of Political Economy 2 May 1874

Mr. Holmes is not content that the proper work of political economy should be to investigate the economic consequences which will follow from a proposed course of action. He is not content that whoever proceeds further to award praise or blame to an action of which the results are determined should do so on the authority of his own moral beliefs, and not on the authority of political economy. He says, with much truth, that 'the world generally thinks that political economy does teach that we ought and ought not to do such and certain things.' But he is mistaken in supposing that this popular opinion finds countenance in the definitions of the science which have been adopted by the leading writers on it.

There have, indeed, been important controversies respecting the limits of political economy. But none of the chief authors of the science have defended, many have spent much pains in protesting against, that account of it which Mr. Holmes quotes as the popular account. They have not, indeed, abstained themselves from the broadest ethical and social problems. Even the title of the book which is commonly called 'Mill's Principles of Political Economy' is 'principles of political economy with some of its applications to social philosophy.' Those writers who have most furthered the science have not in general been those for whom its chief attractions were in the athletic exercise which its reasonings offer to the vigorous intellect, or in the entertainment which its results provide for the curious inquirer. Rather have they been men whose eager interest in the great problems of social life and well-being rendered it intolerable to them that one of the constituent elements of the solution of these problems should needlessly remain in a condition of vague uncertainty. They have seen that those portions of the problems of life to which political economy devotes herself are at once so complex that they cannot be treated well[3] without the aid of a special machinery, and so nearly homogeneous that they can well be treated by such machinery. Such men have set themselves to work to make and to perfect such machinery; but neither by their precept nor by their practice have they given support to the doctrine that the student of economic science should rest content there with. Mill does not stop short of saying that 'a person is not likely to be a good political economist who is nothing else.' But he has certainly not been less strenuous that others in insisting that economic investigations should be clearly *distinguished* from ethical discussions, even when they cannot be *separated* from them.

Mr. Holmes brings forward two charges; one against a particular doctrine of some economists; one against a particular application of economic doctrines. I believe that I agree in the main with him on the broad questions which he thus raises. I cannot discuss them here; but I wish to show that the difficulties connected with them afford no argument for claiming the authority of political economy in favour of any particular decision on a disputed ethical question; but rather the contrary.

First, he argues that 'any coal-ring rig' may be justified by an account which he quotes from a book of 'Lessons on Political Economy' of the benefit which speculators in corn will in general confer on society in a famine. It happens that the words of the particular passage he quotes are guarded, and do not exclude the possibility of exceptional cases, to which the doctrine that is 'almost always' true does not apply. Mr. Holmes might have found in writings of higher authority a less guarded statement, to the effect that a rise in prices which is artificially caused, and which is not required by the circumstances of the market, must *necessarily* be injurious to speculators as a body. The question whether this is so or not is strictly an economic one. I agree with Mr. Holmes that the answer given to it in many works on political economy is not accurate; and I think that if Mr. Holmes succeeds in his attempt to analyse the history of the recent rise in the price of coals, he will have rendered valuable service by supplying an important illustration of the action of a principle which is not thoroughly understood.

The main work of the science of political economy during the seventeenth, the eighteenth and part of the present century was, by a series of victories over popular fallacies, to establish the truth of the proposition that a trader in pursuit of his own interests will be led, in almost every instance, to adopt that course by which he can confer the greatest benefits to the country in which he lives, and to the world at large. Arguments by analogy[4] from this economic proposition have been brought to bear with great effect on questions in other branches of social inquiry, and have powerfully contributed to the extension of the belief in the harmfulness of avoidable restraints on liberty of the individual in any form. But now the time has come for a discussion of the exceptions to the general rule. The present course of events is calling loudly on political economy to devote her energies to a careful investigation of the question – What are the exceptional cases in which the interest of traders, whether they offer for sale commodities or labour, may be in collision with the interests of society as a whole? If she is to pursue this arduous task with the best advantage, she must avoid irrelevant wrangling, and unite for it the efforts of workers of all shades of political opinion, and with all varieties of social bias. She must disclaim jurisdiction in the further question – To what extent may a man sacrifice under given circumstances the interests of society to his own interests without meriting the charge of selfishness? This question ought not be shirked. If Mr. Holmes proves that coalowners have sacrificed the welfare of society to their own interests to an extent which appears to him blameworthy, let him not hesitate to condemn their conduct as selfish.

But while he claims the authority of political economy for some of the premises from which his ultimate conclusion is drawn, let him admit that this conclusion involves one premise which, however true it may be, political economy is not competent to authorize.

Mr. Holmes further complains of a tendency to be found in some circles of society, and of which he seeks an illustration in the 'Lessons' published by the 'Society for Promoting Christian Knowledge'. Some persons will condemn with a reckless confidence and without inquiry all actions by work-men in limitation of trade. Yet such persons are almost invariably among those who are least patient of questions as to the morality of actions in limitation of trade when adopted by the 'better' classes. If, for instance, it be asked whether railway shareholders are right in refusing to make a reduction in fares, by which, at a very trifling nett cost to themselves, they can confer an enormous benefit to the community, such men will answer curtly – 'business is business; in matters of trade everyone must look out for himself.' Those, again, who condemn most fiercely the refusal of a workman to teach many apprentices are those among whom are to be found the most ardent supporters of the doctrine that medical men 'have a right' to exclude women from their profession. I am prepared to go as far as anyone can go in condemning such inequalities in judgment as iniquitous, only it must be remembered that men whose moral judgments are thus perverted by class bias are not to be found exclusively in one grade of society.

But the stronger this class bias, the greater is the need for excluding, as far as possible, its influence from the discussion of the question – What are the consequences of limitations of the number of apprentices in any occupation? I believe that political economy will prove that when such limitations are made by a fixed and inelastic rule, their nett result in the long run must in almost every case be an immense preponderance of evil to society. But there are some exceptional cases in which, if a partial temporary hindrance be not opposed to the influx of fresh hands into the trade, those who are in it may be in danger of suffering a distress, the gross amount of which will not be small in comparison with the loss which such a hindrance would occasion to society. We must then deliberately deal with the question how great the danger must be, in order that the limitation may be morally justifiable. But on this question political economy has no mission to speak with authority. She may do nothing that will impair the efficiency with which she performs her special task.

Hers it is to combine together men of all classes of society, with their various interests and their various opportunities of obtaining information, for the limited but difficult and necessary inquiry: What are the effects of rules which exclude from an occupation those who would enter into it? Let her bring together, for instance, the medical man, who may think that the rules of the Printers' Union prevent him from affording to have printed as many of his scientific researches as he otherwise might, and the printer, who may think that the restrictions of the medical schools prevent him from affording skilled advice for his wife as often as he might. Let political economy bring them together to discuss, and to hear discussed, the widely ramified consequences of preventing men or women from preparing themselves for rendering their service to society in that way in which they would wish to render it. And finally, when they have arrived at general results, let her cause them together to consider how the special circumstances of printing or of medicine may occasion special qualifications or modifications of these results. Such is the nature of the work which, during the past winter, political economy has been performing in many of our northern towns. The Cambridge University Extension Scheme is widening the sphere of its work, and an increased number of towns demand, and will be supplied with, lectures on political economy, among other subjects, during next winter. Political economy will have wider opportunities of aiding each man to judge his own conduct by analysing it, and by putting before him, as Nathan did before David, the likeness between it and other conduct on which he is able to give an unbiassed judgment. In this indirect mode will she contribute to the clearness of men's notions about duty; direct decisions on questions of moral principle she must leave to her sister, the Science of Ethics.

Alfred Marshall
Cambridge University

Notes and References

1. The text printed in the *Bee-Hive* and left unchanged by R. Harrison, 1963, was 'in that'. The correction was made by Marshall himself in the margin of one of his copies of the printed article (*Marshall Papers*).
2. The text printed in the *Bee-Hive* was 'postponed'. The correction was made by Marshall; cf. also Coats A. W., 'Marshall and ethics', in R. McWilliams Tullberg (ed.), *Alfred Marshall in Retrospect*, Aldershot: Elgar, 1990, p. 160 and note 10.
3. The text printed in the *Bee-Hive* was 'at all'. The correction was made by Marshall.
4. The text printed in the *Bee-Hive* was 'analysis'. The correction was made by Marshall.

Name Index